A SEASON OF STONES

A SEASON OF STONES

LIVING IN A PALESTINIAN VILLAGE

HELEN WINTERNITZ

THE ATLANTIC MONTHLY PRESS
NEW YORK

Published simultaneously in Canada
Printed in the United States of America
FIRST EDITION

ISBN 0-87113-514-0
Library of Congress card number 91-27142

Design by Laura Hough

The Atlantic Monthly Press
19 Union Square West
New York, NY 10003

FIRST PRINTING

TO MY FATHER,
DR. WILLIAM WELCH WINTERNITZ
AND
IN MEMORY OF MY MOTHER,
MARY PRYMAK WINTERNITZ

The Green Line

• Battir

• Wadi Fukin

Husan

Valley of the Cow

Betar

Daher al-Matarsiya Mountain

El Khader •

Abu al-Koroun Mountain

• NAHALIN

Nahal
Gevaot

Rosh Zurim

Neve Dani
Kilo Sabatas

Alon
Shvut

Kfar
Etzion

TO Hebron

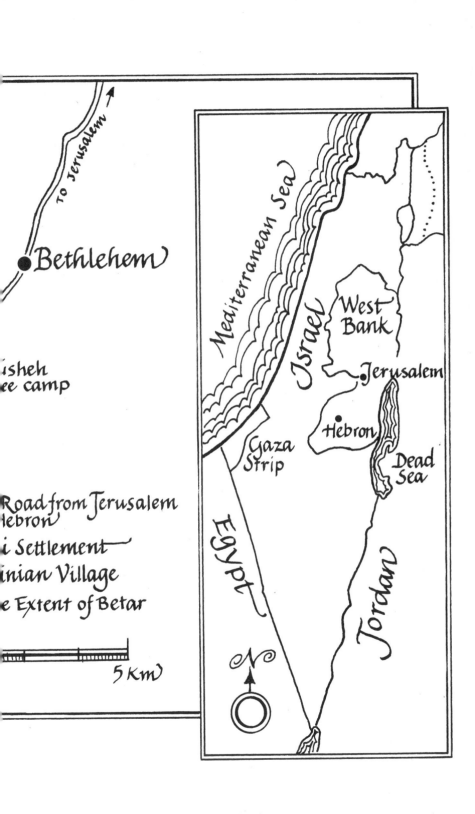

TO Jerusalem

● Bethlehem

Mediterranean Sea

Israel

West
Bank

● Jerusalem

● Hebron

Gaza
Strip

Dead
Sea

Egypt

Jordan

...isheh
...ee camp

...Road from Jerusalem
...Hebron
...i Settlement
...inian Village
...e Extent of Betar

5 Km

N

ACKNOWLEDGMENTS

Tim Phelps believed in this book, from its beginnings to its endings. He also gave me his love.

Others who helped were my stepmother, Madeleine Hill, and my neighbors in Bethlehem—Jamila, Jabra, Leila and Rosa Khaliliya.

I want also to thank my literary agent, Lizzie Grossman, as well as Katharine and Clinton Bamberger, John and Regina Amos, Lucia Annunziata, Dan Williams, Ann Lesch, Carol Spencer, Dr. Richard Johnson and Dr. Oded Abramsky.

At Atlantic Monthly Press, the book prospered in the hands of Ann Godoff, Robbin Schiff, Matthew Kapsner, John Barstow, Bonnie Levy and Abigail Winograd.

In Jerusalem, Bill Lee and Ina Friedman gave me encouragement.

In Bethlehem, the Beit Jala Writers Club provided company. In the United States, Yaddo provided shelter.

I want finally to thank the villagers of Nahalin for tolerating me most of the time.

INTRODUCTION

I happened upon Nahalin in early 1987. Hidden in mountains near Bethlehem on the West Bank, the village seemed almost indifferent to the larger politics of the region. The Palestinians of Nahalin lived quietly. Shepherds took their flocks up the rocky slopes around the village; peasant farmers tended their vegetable plots near the village springs and plowed the terraced strips of land on which their groves of olive and fruit trees grew; women washed the stone floors of their small homes and cooked copious meals for their large families; and children went to school. The villagers could almost pretend to live as their ancestors had, long before the modern-day crisis between Arab and Israeli.

These villagers were ordinary Palestinians—not those who were exiled or who were notorious for hijacking airplanes or who were reduced to the status of refugees. These were Palestinians who had stayed home and avoided much of the endlessly intricate turmoil of the Middle East.

When I first visited the West Bank as a journalist working for a newspaper, the Palestinians had not yet revolted against the Israelis. But everywhere, even in Nahalin, I felt a tension. I wondered about what the Palestinians were thinking, other than what was expressed in brief articles about them or in interviews with their exiled leaders. The stories of the Palestinians of Nahalin—and of the hundreds of other villages on the West Bank—had not been told in any detail. I wanted to find out more about these Palestinians, and the best way to do that was to live with them. Whether it was possible or not, I didn't know; no one had attempted anything like it in recent years.

I was not immediately certain that Nahalin, which I had stumbled upon accidentally, was the best place to try to live. I looked elsewhere. I investigated villages that, built of stone and perched on the shoulders of ancient mountains, looked like the settings of fables. I found others where the villagers were locked in daily conflict with Israeli settlers. I traveled to some villages where the Palestinians were sincere in their invitations to have me live with them. Nahalin was not the most beautiful, the most exciting or the most enlightened village on the West Bank, but I decided finally that it was perhaps the most typical. If I could understand the villagers of Nahalin in their own landscape, I could understand the Palestinians.

When I returned to the West Bank in early 1988 to live, the world's attention was riveted by scenes of young Palestinians hurling stones at Israeli soldiers. The uprising had begun. Violence had become an unavoidable part of the landscape and of the lives of the Palestinians. I went ahead with my idea, even though my potentially difficult plan had now become obviously dangerous.

The villagers of Nahalin, although seemingly removed from much of what happened on the West Bank, were, inevitably, drawn into and surrounded by the crisis. Piece by piece, the Israelis were building their settlements on Nahalin's traditional pasturage and farmland. Their settlements were on the ridges looking down upon the village. In the most elemental way, this scene summed up the Palestinian dilemma. It explained the Palestinian anger that has so traumatized the world.

To live in Nahalin I needed to learn Arabic. I wanted to talk to the oldest villagers, who had never been to school, and the youngest, who had not yet entered school. Many of the other villagers could speak at least some English, because the Palestinians as a people placed great value on learning, but I wanted to talk to everyone.

When I had been in foreign countries before, I had studied the languages. I had learned Amharic in Ethiopia, Swahili while driving overland in eastern Africa, Spanish during the time of the Falklands war in Argentina and Lingala traveling up the Congo River.

But none of these compared to Arabic. I had never encountered any language so rich and simultaneously so daunting. Sometimes I had to back off and just stare at its structure in awe, as one would at a series of mathematical equations explaining the workings of the solar system. Sometimes I was able to grasp enough of the deeper structure of the language to get an idea of how Arabic speakers thought. This was the beginning of seeing beyond the strictures of my own language and logic to a culture unlike any I had experienced.

I spent most of the next three years with the Palestinians, although not all of that time in Nahalin. After much persistence, I found a place to live in the village and I stayed for more than a year, retreating sometimes to the far more cosmopolitan world of Jerusalem.

During that time, almost nothing happened the way I had imagined. Nahalin, although small, was not simple. The villagers were divided by clans, by political factions and by religious sects. Villagers belonged to all three major factions of the Palestine Liberation Organization. Eventually, Muslim fundamentalists gained a foothold in the village. Sufis, mystics who refused to acknowledge the importance of politics on earth, also had their own self-illuminated niche in the village.

At times, the villagers suspected me of spying. But in a region where identity is of paramount concern, I did have one advantage: I could not be classified. My grandparents on one side were Ukrainian Catholic immigrants to the United States. On the other side, my grandfather was an atheistic Jew of Austrian origins who married into English Christian stock. My surname is Jewish but I look like the Catholics of the Ukraine.

At times, the villagers showed me the most munificent hospitality. And at times, they welcomed me as a trustworthy friend. Still, some of them never made up their minds about me.

In the end, Nahalin was dragged into the uprising, and the villagers made a bloody passage into the news. But this account is not first about the uprising. It is not an analysis of the Palestinians. It is not a history of hatreds. It is an amalgamation of stories that chronicle a year in the lives of some of the villagers of Nahalin. It is about village-sized truths that have much larger import.

O N E

Nothing went wrong my first night in the village of Nahalin. Long after the Palestinians fell asleep, I remained awake, lying on a pallet on the flat roof of a simple house, gazing at the sickle moon and relishing my good fortune at having entered the village with such ease. The Palestinians, members of a family named Najajra, were rolled up in blankets beneath the moon, which hung like the slimmest of blades in the chill springtime sky. The moon marked the end of Ramadan, the Muslim month of holy fasting. The Najajras were not strict about observing the regimens of Islam, but they had waited for the end of Ramadan to invite me to stay with them. They didn't want other villagers talking about their having a heathen guest. A foreigner could not stay the night without attracting attention, and none had tried recently.

That the Palestinians had revolted against the Israeli occupiers several months earlier made my plan to live in the village all the more difficult. Knowing these things, I was surprised by the seeming peace around me, the sleeping forms of the people on the roof and the quiet of the village spread below me. A dog barked and another answered. A donkey brayed and silence answered.

In the spring of 1988, Nahalin was not well-known to the outside world. It did not figure large on any map, this village where nothing of tremendous historic note had happened. Home to four thousand Palestinians, Nahalin was enfolded in the valleys of the Judean Mountains on the West Bank southeast of Bethlehem. From afar, it looked like nothing more than a gathering of low buildings capping a hillock, which rose at the junction of three long valleys. The village was still on the periphery of the *intifada,* as the uprising is called in Arabic. In other villages, Palestinians were ambushing Israeli soldiers, but Nahalin remained quiet.

Nahalin tended to lag behind many of the five hundred other villages on the West Bank. It sat on a side road off side roads at the end of a valley, and although it was surrounded by settlements and not far from Bethlehem, neither Israeli settlers nor the Israeli army nor other Palestinians needed to pass through the village. It had been a backwater for a long time.

My fears—that the villagers of Nahalin would turn their backs on me, threaten me or think me a spy from the Israeli camp—had not been borne out, at least not yet. I had misgivings of all sorts, about being able to live in a village completely different from anything I knew and about the suspicions the villagers would have of any outsider, particularly with the constant tensions created by the uprising. I was swept into the Najajra household so swiftly that I hadn't had time to fret. Suddenly I was where I wanted to be, among the villagers of Nahalin.

More precisely, I was on the women's side of the roof, between Ratiba Najajra, a peasant woman whose husband had been crushed to death in a bulldozer accident on an Israeli construction site, and Sena Najajra, a daughter determined to study law despite the odds against her. On the men's side of the roof, I could make out the short body of Fawzi Najajra, the eldest son, who slept near his brothers and a cousin. With his father's death twelve years earlier, Fawzi had taken over as head of the family at the age of

sixteen. He was a serious man to whose word the whole family
listened. Under another pile of blankets was Farouk, a tall and
gentle teenager who kept a menagerie of birds and rabbits in a dirt
cellar under the house. Deeb, a cousin who lived nearby, had placed
his wire-rimmed glasses carefully beside his mattress. He deemed
himself a Marxist, having studied the philosophy in prison after he
was arrested for hurling a homemade gasoline bomb at an Israeli
army jeep. The bomb was a dud, but as it turned out, Deeb had been
precocious in a way. He had carried out his attack years before the
uprising. I didn't ask Deeb whether he had other plans to fight the
Israelis. Questions like that were better kept to a minimum.

The Najajras were among the first villagers I met. I had visited
Nahalin several times before on brief outings, but the invitation
from them was the best chance I had of gaining a foothold in the
village. If I could win their trust, perhaps I could win the confidence
of others, enough so that I could find a place to reside. Somewhere
in the village there had to be room for me.

The Najajra house was poor. Other than the guest porch, a requisite
of Palestinian domestic architecture, the house had two rooms, each
with a bedstead and each with a pair of worn closets in which the
family stored its possessions, its clothes, its blankets—the entirety
of its household stuff. Also in these rooms were neatly piled mattresses, to be spread out every night and then restacked during the
day. In the winter, nine Najajras slept in these rooms. In the long
rainless months of spring and summer and fall, however, space
blossomed because the Palestinians could sleep on the roof.

When I arrived the afternoon before, I was ushered through
the single door. The Palestinians seated me on the least battered of
the chairs that furnished the porch, which was enclosed by windows
on two sides. On the window ledges, plants grew in ranks of tin cans,

some flowering gloriously and distracting the eye from the paint peeling from the walls. The cement floors were spotless, as is usual in Palestinian households both rich and poor.

Half a dozen Najajras sat around me on chairs or on the ledges between the plants, and they expressed delight at my promise that I would come and stay for a while. From the closetlike kitchen adjoining the porch, I heard the noise of a kerosene stove being pumped and hissingly lighted and then the sound of water boiling. A table was plunked down in front of me and on it a large glass of orangeade.

"Drink," I was told. "Drink. You are tired from the trip. Relax. Drink."

"*Beitna beitek,*" I was told. "Our house is your house. Feel at home."

I almost did, if only from the sheer weight of the hospitality being concentrated on me. I almost laughed at myself, too, for the list of fears I was dragging around with me. Palestinians might not be so hard to understand, I thought as I sat with the Najajras, a family I would come to know well as the months passed.

Fawzi impressed me initially as an unassuming man who was walking a path several safe steps away from the mad cliffs of Palestinian politics. He had, after all, taken over responsibility for the family, raising six brothers and sisters. He learned to survive and to keep the family going. He had run a small store in the village, tended the family's parcel of farmland above the village and ordered his siblings to apply themselves at school. When I came to Nahalin, he was married and had two children of his own and a job working with the handicapped. With his tan skin and dark, wavy hair and deep eyes, he looked typically Palestinian. The one thing that struck me about him was a quick candor.

He had quizzed me at the outset about my ideas and told me what he thought. "You should write about Nahalin," he said, "but don't think you can live like a Palestinian. That is too hard. Palestinians won't believe you." I listened but I didn't want to believe him. He spoke in English because my Arabic was rudimentary, even though I was studying it furiously.

Fawzi recently had started a chicken farm with one thousand egg layers in a long shed next to the home. Using the three brothers under his command, he was selling the eggs in neighboring villages and in Bethlehem. Sena tended the chickens. With her thick hair pulled back with a rubber band, she poured feed into tin troughs while she dreamed of escaping the confines of the village. She brooded on her dilemma—her only means of escaping was to go to college, but she was stuck halfway through secondary school. All the West Bank schools had been closed by the Israeli military authorities as part of their effort to quell the uprising. Meanwhile, Ratiba watched over the whole project with a matriarchal omnipresence. She peered from beneath a white scarf that enveloped her head, revealing a sharp profile, and fell to the shoulders of her black *thobe*, the long village dress she always wore. Ratiba missed nothing that went on in the household, as with everything else that occurred under her purview on the surrounding bit of land.

Smoke from a *taboun* house, a mud-walled shed for baking flat village bread, drifted through the air; a eucalyptus tree shaded the bread house; a dozen sheep dozed in a patched-together pen whose fence was made of scraps of tin and wire shored up against the trunks of a couple of olive trees. The Najajras' land also supported a rickety outhouse, a fig tree and a spreading grape arbor. This was the workaday side of the house. Out front near the well an anomalously grand flight of flagstone steps led from a path past a profusion of flowering bushes and bougainvillea to a neat, square vegetable garden.

Off to a side of the compound was the cinder-block infrastructure of another house, which the second eldest brother, Sa'ed, was trying to complete for his wife and growing family. But he had not been able to save enough money from his work laying terrazzo floors. When the uprising began, he stopped taking jobs at Israeli buildings.

Tea from the Najajras' kitchen arrived soon, village-style tea saturated with sugar and spiced with fresh sprigs of mint, served in thick glasses and passed around by Sena. Flies buzzed about the guest porch, attracted by the sugary perfume of the tea and the odor of the chickens that pervaded the house. Sena was exuding frustration; her eyes were blank with unhappiness.

She sat with me outside as evening gathered and the other women of the household jammed into the kitchen to work. Sena disliked cooking, cleaning, sewing, embroidering—all the skills that make for a well-adjusted village woman. We watched the sun drop down the western side of the sky to uneven mountain ridges.

Dinner was served on the top of the well, a deep catchment for water from the winter rains. The Najajras used the wide concrete top as an outdoor room when the weather was agreeable. The meal was a bounty of rice and chicken heaped on a round metal platter. We had no chairs and sat instead on mats and cushions, not from poverty but from preference. The Palestinians were comfortable reclining as they ate, while I struggled to sit cross-legged without revealing an immodest portion of my shins beneath my modestly long skirt.

Each of us tore pieces from wheels of peasant bread, using these to scoop up the food. The Palestinians again managed gracefully. I spilled rice on myself more than once and finally had to wrestle the chicken meat free with both hands in an unavoidable breach of etiquette. Everyone was insisting that I eat a lot, and not just chicken, but rice, too, as well as the fried eggs, mashed eggplant and fried potatoes that the women had prepared in an abundance of side dishes. Despite a series of protests from my hosts, I eventually quit eating, and in the darkness I tried to wipe the grease from my hands onto my legs without, I hoped, anyone noticing.

From the well top, we had a broad night view down over the village lights, a random smattering coming from windows and lamps on posts, and then out across the silent darkness of the valleys. There were other lights, too: the row of Clorox-white lights from the prefabricated trailers of a newly initiated Israeli settlement in the distance toward Jerusalem and the radiating orange lights of an army encampment over to the left. And behind us was the diffuse glow of the lights from kibbutzim and other settlements spread beyond a southern ridgeline. Despite the distances and seeming immutability of the mountains, I could feel the pressure of the spotty circle of Israeli lights.

The ridges around Nahalin once protected the village against the larger world. This was so from the time when people inhabited caves in the mountains to the time when the first stone houses were built and honey was plentiful, and when the events of the day were measured by the passage of the sun from one formerly empty mountaintop to another. Now the ridges were threatening the village from on high.

As we were sitting, drinking more tea, a couple of army jeeps came through the village and headed toward their encampment. In order to make sure that no Palestinians were lurking behind some boulder planning to stone them, the soldiers switched on spotlights and swept the mountainside with cones of brilliance that illuminated each stone, each olive tree, each bump on each rise.

After eating, Farouk, the third son, got up and disappeared into the darkness, for what purpose he did not say. For me, the village by night and likewise by day, although not so dramatically, contained a thousand mysteries. After a while, Farouk returned and all was peaceful. The family was together, Ramadan had passed and everyone's belly was full, even though the Najajras did not feast on the meat of a sheep or goat, as custom would dictate for a family of more wealth. We spent the next hours atop the well drinking yet more tea and talking.

Farouk began a joke. He told me that the village donkeys sang at night. I said if that were true, then the sheep must dance and the roosters must stand on their heads. This fantasy was commented upon by everyone to great amusement. It was agreed that when dawn arrived, of course, the animals returned to their normal habits and never revealed their gambols of the night.

At midnight, the time came to sleep. Sena laid out a pair of pajamas and watched over me as I changed discreetly in one of the two inside rooms. The house had no bathroom, so Sena, handing me a couple of squares of tissue paper, directed me to the outhouse and waited for my return with a basin, a jug of cold water, soap and a towel. She poured the water as I washed my hands and face. We both brushed our teeth outside, using a cup of water between us and spitting onto the rocky soil behind the house.

The roof of the house was reached by climbing an uneven wooden ladder, which I ascended with Sena, who carried a pallet stuffed with wool, a pillow and a blanket for me.

Ratiba, who already was lying on the roof, spoke no English, but Sena could, and well enough so that with some effort we conversed without having to depend upon my fledgling knowledge of the sinuously logical Arabic language. The two of us talked in whispers about school. The academic interruption was a blow to her. The schools, from first grade through university, had been closed for months. The reasoning of the Israeli government was that classes congregated students, who then provoked violence by demonstrating and throwing stones. For their part, the Palestinians claimed that the Israelis provoked the confrontations at the schools and closed them as punishment.

Sena was in the upper echelon of her class. "I don't want to get married and live the rest of my life here," she said. "I don't want to have ten children and scrub the house all day. I want to learn about the world and do something important. I think all the time about becoming a lawyer."

I told Sena I would give her English lessons so that part of her mind could remain engaged. She sighed and rolled over in order to sleep, pulling her blanket over her head. Mosquitoes had replaced the daytime flies, so I pulled my blankets up over everything except my eyes.

T W O

With the dawn, I woke to the sound of a sizable flock of sheep being herded out into the mountains. A hundred sheep, with four hundred hooves, made more noise than the worst alarm clock. The clatter of the sheep inspired the village donkeys, who let out inflated brays that rose in a hoarse chorus and then died into strangulated-sounding huffings, waking the village dogs into energetic spasms of barking. To protect myself from the mosquitoes, I had wrapped myself entirely in a blanket during the night, and the dawn was heating me like a roasting cocoon.

But after loosening my blanket and watching the sunrise blend into the encompassing valley sky, I fell back to sleep. When I opened my eyes again, the Najajras' sheep were bleating in their pen. Ratiba was up and about, baking flat bread and watering her vegetable plot with a hose. She was staking up some bean vines and building little earthen walls around the plants so that the water would soak to their roots. Mountain birds were bathing and fluttering in the spray from the hose.

The rest of the family was long since up, so I breakfasted solitarily on the guest porch. Ratiba served me wordlessly, nodding at my apologies and appreciations while dishing out a hearty breakfast of eggs, fried eggplant and the fresh *taboun* she had baked while I slept. It was the tastiest bread I had ever eaten.

After breakfast, Ratiba prepared a second batch of dough and carried it to the shed by the sheep pen. Inside the *taboun* house was a clay dome over which she had layered smoldering chicken dung and ash. The dome had a top, which she pulled off to drop the circle of dough onto an inner bed of clean stones. The *taboun* cooked in minutes, so that it was crusty outside but elastic inside. Just as Palestinian women had done long before her, Ratiba plucked the scorchingly hot bread from the oven and tossed it in the air until it was cool enough to handle. She gave me a piece and then paused to look out over the village before resuming her tasks.

Down near the middle of Nahalin, on the southwestern edge of the village, where the land fell away into a valley planted in olive trees, lived the last of Nahalin's beekeepers. Sheikh Deeb had inherited from his father bees that had been bred in the village generation after generation from a time further back than anyone could remember. These could be descendants of the bees from which the village took its name, by most accounts, *nahl* being the Arabic word for "bee" and *Nahalin* for "beekeepers."

Sheikh Deeb, the one aging master of the craft left, happened to be Deeb's grandfather. I went to visit the old man, taking a dirt path to a paved lane. It angled through a series of stiff curves, what must have been natural switchbacks on a path shepherds took to higher pasturage.

The village hardly altered the contour of the land. The houses took their colors from the surrounding mountains, from the light shades of stone from which they were built, mostly by the villagers themselves. The newer houses were made of more modern stuff, cinder blocks and concrete, but they blended with the older stone dwellings. They all had the same flat roofs, which looked from on high like series of stepping-stones. Nearer the village center the houses crowded together: one cement wall joined another in a stark jumble from which there was little relief. There were no lawns or meadows. A few of the houses with two stories were graced with narrow balconies, where women could sit and watch the comings and goings on the paths below.

Nahalin's two asphalt lanes formed a lopsided and spidery cross. A network of dirt byways fed into the larger roadways, and each was lined by repetitions of the same inornate rectangular houses. At night, goats, sheep and donkeys were penned beneath many of the houses or in shanties alongside. The village smelled of a mixture of animals and hay.

The roads continued to serve as paths for Nahalin's herds and flocks, which competed for the right-of-way with a scattering of automobiles and several heavy trucks. Sometimes the vehicles took precedence, nosing through the bunched goats and sheep without stopping. Sometimes the animals so filled the road that they forced the drivers to stop until they passed, brushing the sides of the vehicles as their shepherds yelled and wielded sticks to make them trot along faster.

Walking alone, I proceeded resolutely down the roadway. I had donned my least sexy skirt, buttoned myself into a long-sleeved and high-collared shirt, pulled my hair back tightly with a barrette, and looked as demure as I was able. The hill was steep and I descended slowly. I could feel the eyes of people boring into me, bewildered by what they saw.

As I followed the switchbacks, I found myself dodging an occasional car or flock, scuttling off the narrow asphalt strip onto the side of the road, where loose stones sliding under the soles of my shoes made the footing difficult. Stones and dust, goat dung and old walls edged the roadway. The land was hard to tread. Nothing was soft.

Here and there were patches of color—a grape arbor shaped above a courtyard; panes of yellow and green glass fitted into the upper windows of a house, fracturing the monotony of the stone-colored village; some doorways painted with auspicious pastel blues; small gardens of mint, jasmine bushes and roses, delicate plants painstakingly tended to survive in the rough terrain. From the rooftops, long lines of laundry were flapping in breezes that played constantly through the mountains, the laundry testifying to the fertility of the village families and to the hardworking cleanliness of the women. Alongside the roadway ran rivulets of water from another morning of washing floors, stairways and porches.

Inside a doorway, I noticed the long stare of a woman in an ankle-length dress, a couple of children tucked in her skirts. I tried to ignore the look because I wanted to proceed inconspicuously, an impossibility that I pretended was not impossible, given my fair complexion and the fact that my skirt looked like it came from New York rather than Bethlehem.

I also ignored the first dusty plunk, which I recognized was a pebble tossed my way. The second and the third I also disdained to notice. But when the pebbles started coming plunkety-plunk-plunk-plunk, I deliberately turned around and fixed a severe look on a tittering group of boys. I knew they were playing a game that they learned from the intifada—stone the stranger; keep the outsider away from our land and our village—but it was a serious game. I shouted at them, as best as I could, in Arabic, to stop, to get lost, to go home. And, to my surprise, they did.

Down the winding road were more children, plentiful and practically toyless, and I braced myself, my good spirits dampened. But they had heard me scolding the others and politely allowed my passage. A couple of boys were playing horse and rider using a length of knotted rags to represent bridle, reins and saddle. One child held the would-be harness around his chest, and the other ran behind, both prancing in the pretense of galloping. This also was a favorite spot for playing coasting games. Large floor tiles served as toboggans. Balancing on the tiles, children went scooting down the roadway, time after time. One boy had engineered a cart with bits and pieces of wood, wire and wheels, in which he sped recklessly downhill and around the curves toward whatever might be coming uphill.

The village's center was nothing more than the widened intersection of the two main roadways, one of which ran across the mountainside. The other went up toward the Najajras' house or down to the school at the bottom end of the village. Several austere shops opened their metal doors onto this junction, a few selling an almost-identical selection of canned food, such as sardines and non-descript meat, one selling vegetables and another selling falafel. A couple of village institutions also faced the intersection, a kindergarten and the smaller of Nahalin's two mosques, a squat, domed building protected by a formidable wall of stone blocks. At almost any time of day, a group of Muslim elders lingered by the mosque, bearded men clothed in decorous robes and carrying walking staffs. They seemed to do little other than grow their beards and tend to their prayers. Most of them ignored me from the start. A few were Sufis, the mystics of Islam, and they were far friendlier.

A stone's throw from the first mosque was a second, larger one, whose white minaret spired above the village dwellings. Opposite it was Sheikh Deeb's compound.

All the villagers, even brazen boys who pretended to fear nothing, approached the house cautiously because of the considerable stack of beehives next to the arched entrance to the sheikh's storerooms. The hives, made of barrels daubed with mud, gave forth a flurry of honeybees that transformed into a hostile cloud on the approach of anyone other than the sheikh.

Sheikh Deeb did not know his exact age, because in bygone eras villagers did not bother with registering births, but he estimated it at a year or so beyond seventy. His gray robe was patched in many places, and his trimmed beard had turned white. He wore a turban that served to emphasize the prominence of his large ears. During the span of his life, he had seen Nahalin transform from an isolated hamlet to a village touched by the politics of the larger world.

Sheikh Deeb was one of the leading village Sufis, and his mind existed partly in another world, one ruled by Allah and inhabited by spirits. He had made the hajj, the pilgrimage to Mecca—the birthplace of Mohammad, the prophet of Islam. It is a journey that the most dedicated Muslims are obligated to undertake if they have the wherewithal. From Mecca, Sheikh Deeb brought back a string of ninety-nine prayer beads instead of the shorter version used by many Muslims nowadays. He wore the string around his neck, except when he was twisting it through his hands, performing his reflexive recitation of verses from the Koran, mumbling the familiar phrases and fingering the smooth beads. His hands had the texture of leather, and he let the bees land on them.

"They are like friends. If they know you will not hurt them, they will not hurt you," he said.

Deeb, who had come down earlier, translated along with a village woman named Hanan who taught at the kindergarten. The others were with me for two reasons. I needed someone to decipher the sheikh's Arabic, a thick dialect from the past that was completely beyond my comprehension, and I could not breach village propriety by going alone into a room with a man, no matter what his age and no matter what the intent.

The old Sufi's full name was Deeb Abdul Hamid Ahmed. He also had a not-so-respectful village nickname, which was never uttered in his presence, Abu Thinayn, or Father Ears.

He lived a monastic life, except for the television set placed in the corner of his room, which was situated a flight of uneven stone stairs above the bees. The room had a vaulted ceiling classic of the architecture practiced for centuries in the Middle East. Lacking cement, steel rods and wood, masons built intersecting arches of stone, making sturdy structures whose aesthetics were impeccably simple. Following the lines of the arches, four curvaceous triangular vaults met at the top of the ceiling of each room.

Having invited us upstairs to taste some freshly picked mulberries, Sheikh Deeb settled on the sofa and reminisced. When he was a boy, the mountains were calm. The First World War was over, and the British had mandatory power over all of what was then called Palestine and is now divided into the state of Israel and the Palestinian territories. He remembered, too, when Muslims and Jews cooperated rather than clashed. Indeed, his house was the creation of a Jew who had traveled from the southern city of Hebron to Nahalin and other villages when there was work. It was only about fifty years ago that this master builder worked on Sheikh Deeb's house and on others dwellings near the mosque, back in the days when villagers were willing to cooperate with Jews who were willing to work with them.

"His name was Itzhak. We were friends. He used to sleep here with us when he was building other houses. We ate together like one," the sheikh said.

As proof, he had the younger Deeb show me the symbol of coexistence that was Itzhak's imprimatur. Despite his history of rebellion, Deeb obeyed his elder to the letter, as was mandatory in the village culture. Chiseled in a slab of stone above the lintel of the entranceway to the compound was an Islamic sickle moon cupping in wordless embrace the six-pointed Star of David. Deeb later led me to more of Itzhak's symbols, set above the doorways of half a dozen other houses, the rest of them abandoned and given over to age. Nowhere else on the West Bank did I see anything like the symbol of Itzhak. Not only was the mark lost but also the sentiment.

"If Itzhak came now, he could not sleep in my house, the house he himself built. Even if I wanted it, the village would not permit it. Since the wars, the people have changed," the old man said.

The sheikh had not seen his Jewish friend since what he called the first war, fought between Jews and Arabs when the state of Israel was created in 1948. Before then, he remembered with a dash of nostalgia obfuscating massacres each side had carried out against the other, the Jews and Arabs did not struggle over controlling the land of the West Bank.

"They had their land, and we had our land, without any problem."

Several days of Nahalin at a stretch were about all I could manage at first, balancing as I had to between wanting to learn everything about the village immediately and thinking that only patience would enable that. Fawzi had warned me to step lightly at first.

"Don't hurry," he advised. "Many people don't understand you. They are afraid. They don't understand very much about the world."

When I wasn't in the village, I holed up in a spare apartment in East Jerusalem, a booming metropolis compared with the village. The apartment, which I had rented easily enough from a family of Palestinian Christians, was a place where I could type up the notes I was keeping about Nahalin, wear pants and drink beer, flouting in private the traditional moral codes of the village. I also didn't have to worry about boys throwing pebbles. I didn't have to try to explain myself in Arabic. I could relax until I made my next foray onto the West Bank.

The fact that I did not have any permanent place to stay in Nahalin was improving my situation in unexpected ways. I was being hosted by one family or another, passed from house to house, and some of the children began to consider me a friend rather than a target.

Palestinians in general, no matter their income, their religion or their political beliefs, are extraordinarily hospitable. Their custom dictates it. A legend repeatedly told in order to illustrate the depth of Palestinian generosity was the story of Hatim al-Ta'ee. This Hatim was a poor man, as poor as could be except for one possession, a horse that he valued with all his heart. One day guests showed up at Hatim's house, and he had nothing to offer them to eat, not a piece of meat, not an egg, not even a cucumber. Having no alternative, he cut the choicest steaks from his horse's flanks and feasted his visitors.

I never got horse meat, which the Palestinians do not normally eat. But I got plenty of hospitality, so much that I became accustomed to eating the most delectable parts of the chicken breast, the choicest of the rolled grape leaves and the lion's share of the stuffed squash. I made the inevitable mistakes, too. I stated that I was not hungry, a point that was irrelevant to the host's mandate to feed me. I argued, detailing what I had eaten for breakfast or lunch, and still I was fed.

I found it impossible to visit any house in the village, no matter how poor, without being served endless glasses of tea or miniature cups of thick Turkish coffee, without being invited to eat, to eat more, to stay and talk, to stay and spend the night and begin eating again with breakfast. Although few villagers could tolerate the idea of my wanting to live in Nahalin alone, many were militant about providing temporary room and board.

"*Tfaddali.* Welcome. *Faddali. Faddali.*" I heard the phrase more often than my name.

I met more and more of the Najajra family: cousins, uncles, second cousins, grandmothers, daughters-in-law, brothers of daughters-in-law. Everyone I was introduced to had the same last name, Najajra, and I soon lost my way in tangles of relatives. The first names were strange to my ear—Hilmi, Halima, Hani, Raatib, Rula, Ibtisam, Intisar, Hamid, Shawki, Fou'ad—and slipped through my memory. I could not keep straight whether Hilmi was Ibtisam's brother or uncle or cousin or only a distant relative. I had enough trouble trying to remember the names, much less where the person fit in the system of interlocking families. The West Bank villagers had a penchant for marrying their first cousins, making for complexities that became with each new generation only more confusing to the outsider, like the patterns of a pile of Persian carpets.

The place I felt most honestly welcomed was the compound of the original Najajra family. I sat there one afternoon with Ratiba while she made yogurt under the fig tree. She had slung a plastic jerry can in a cradle of sacking from a branch of the tree and was rocking it to sour the sheep milk within. Instead of using a sack of animal hide, as everyone else did, she was using plastic, because it was more sanitary. This was one of Fawzi's ideas.

Other women stopped by to talk and sip tea. I listened to the melange of conversation, ranging from the arthritis that was troubling Ratiba's mother-in-law to predictions about the coming olive crop to whether the tactics of the uprising were working to whether world opinion about the Palestinians was changing to whether the Najajras should expand their chicken farm. It was a mixture of the small-town talk typical of any place and the geopolitics peculiar to this part of the world. Half of the talk was in English for my benefit. I understood about a quarter of the Arabic and let the rest slide into the background.

A dozen sheep were snuffling in the corners of the pen. All at once their heads bobbed to attention at a whistle from Farouk, the third son. They were looking for a fistful of hay. Farouk loved animals. If you peered through the metal-barred door to the cellar beneath the house, you could see a cavelike room and a series of large tin cans with round holes cut in them. Doves poked their heads from these nest cans. When Farouk opened the door, birds surged out. A couple of the doves landed on his shoulders, a trio of orange-plumed chickens gathered at his feet and ducks waddled up the ramp into a concrete-sided pool he had made for them to swim. He then reached under the stairway to the visitors' porch and, like a magician, pulled out a pair of spotted rabbits, which hopped back into their haven as soon as he put them down. Farouk also had a black dog, which came running to him from a patch of shade by the eucalyptus. From then on, I dubbed him Saint Francis in the notes I was keeping about Nahalin.

One evening with Farouk and his cousin Ahmed, I clambered over to a white rock that was a favorite meditation spot for the family. Ahmed was a thin and comedic young man, slightly out of place among his brawnier peers. He was in his twenties, born during the time Jordan occupied the West Bank. Farouk, on the other hand, had known only the Israeli occupation.

The sun was setting red again into the gray of the Judean Mountains. Leaving thoughts of the occupation aside, Farouk talked about what obsessed teenagers anywhere, the opposite sex. We three sat down, and Farouk elucidated how things were in the village. A girl was not allowed to talk with a boy, even on the bus that ran to the secondary school near Bethlehem when the schools were open. If any girl did such a thing and it became known, her father would punish her. Farouk flirted anyway, but he was miserable romantically because the girl he thought he was in love with—from a distance—recently married.

"This system is not right," he said, gesturing with his hand to his heart. "You have two people who have never had a chance to know each other, and then immediately they are living in the same house with each other. What happens when they decide they don't like each other, or they hate each other, but they are living with each other and they have no choice?"

Farouk sensed what he did not know, what he was missing.

I explained to him how free teenagers are with each other in the United States, but I also talked about some of the troubles these freedoms gave rise to, exaggerating the problems in order not to dismay him too deeply in his plight. I told him about the high divorce rate in America.

I went on to talk about some of the things that were lacking in life in the United States—graciousness, time to talk, time to think about the predicaments, miraculous or otherwise, of life. I described a harried day in the existence of a New York commuter. I told the two Palestinians how Americans had no custom of unconditional hospitality for strangers, how difficult it was to be a foreigner in the United States, even though it was the land of so much of what the rural world covets.

We talked about how the Middle East in some ways was more civilized because people were not in a great hurry and could afford to linger with their neighbors over tea or coffee. Ahmed agreed that the Arabs took time over the centuries to develop beauty, as was illustrated by their language. But he said that in the meantime much of the rest of the world leapt ahead.

As we walked back up to the house in the dusk, a bearded man came by on a donkey. He was one of the old-fashioned Muslims known to avoid politics of any kind.

Ahmed became instantly critical. "That man is one of the stupid ones," he burst out. "He only cares about himself and his God. These are the kind of people who allowed the occupation for twenty years."

I offered no opinion, not wanting to be snarled so early in any part of the web of village politics and religion. I wanted to stay out of trouble.

Later that night Sa'ed, the second brother, brought out a double-barreled reed flute, a traditional shepherds' instrument. A tall, bearded man with two piratical gold teeth, Sa'ed did not act as tough as he looked. He was a natural musician. In his hands, the simple flute sounded like a bagpipe. The music inspired the family to put tapes on their small stereo set, their only luxury besides the television set that almost no Palestinian household was without. Several of us sat on the single bed in the room, across from the dilapidated cupboards where all the things of everyday life were stored. Sa'ed's wife sat on the table near the tape machine, and Ratiba leaned against the doorway. Farouk and Ahmed started dancing to the flute, Palestinian dances with high kicks and repetitive stamping, and then Ahmed kept dancing when the music was changed to the whining Egyptian tunes of Uum Kalthoum, and he began mimicking a willowy Nilotic dance. Everyone, including the widow Ratiba—who at first impression I had summed up as a nose, a squint and a gold tooth—was in stitches. The music changed again, this time to American disco, and Ahmed mimed Michael Jackson and the rock star's swagger. He danced, and the drabness of the room melted away with our common laughter.

T H R E E

About two months after I stayed the first night on the Najajra's rooftop, I took a step toward moving into the village. I had been sporadically coming and going without problem, but I wanted to end that, so I packed a bag of clothes and included my toothbrush.

With the light bag and a heavy bottle of water, I left my apartment to find transport at the dirt lot where Palestinian drivers run taxis to points all over the West Bank. The taxi lot was at the edge of no-man's-land—the space between East and West Jerusalem left empty after the 1948 war that bisected the city, separating Arab from Jew. The subsequent 1967 war reunited the city under a victorious Israel. The same war also left Israel in military possession of the entire West Bank, surrendered by a defeated Jordan. This name for the territory came from the fact that it lies on the western side of the Jordan River.

From the lot, the taxis left when they were full. Seven passengers crowded into a long Mercedes, known as a *service,* and paid a fare that was a little more than that for a bus. I found myself seated in the rear corner of a *service* bound for Hebron, planning to get off at the halfway point, at Kilo Sabatash, or Kilometer Seventeen, from which I could walk down a high back road to the village. The distance I had to go was short, less than ten miles to Bethlehem and a couple of miles beyond that to Kilo Sabatash, but the landscape I had to traverse was intricate.

It was a cloudless day in the late spring. The woman wedged next to me, a fat, jolly type, pulled a loaf of sesame bread from her sack and was chewing hunks of it, washed down with swigs from a large plastic bottle of orangeade. To strike up neutral conversation, I remarked to her in Arabic that the weather was hot. This stopped her in midswig.

"If you think it is hot here, you don't have any idea how hot it is in the Negev. The heat there is torture."

She proceeded with a speech about a cousin of hers who was incarcerated in Ansar Three, an Israeli detention camp for Palestinian political prisoners situated in the Negev Desert. I had ruined the woman's appetite, and we continued riding south in silence.

We passed Gilo and the unmarked border of the West Bank. Gilo jutted from a ridge, its phalanxes of multistoried stone apartments a final Israeli outpost before the road reached the West Bank. Inside the settlement, antennae rose from a reclusive structure. It was a headquarters building for the Shin Bet, the Israeli intelligence police, who handled the West Bank from there.

Beyond the border, the Israeli military government issued the blue license plates that labeled the cars of Palestinians residing in the West Bank. Residents of Israel, Jerusalem or the settlements that increasingly speckled the West Bank had yellow plates. The Israelis marked their enemies, but in the process they marked themselves, too. The West Bank was not a safe place for Israelis to drive. After army jeeps, cars driven by Israelis were the prime targets for the *shabab*—literally, "boys," but a term that came to refer to the Palestinian youths constituting the makeshift army of the intifada. Almost seven months had passed since the uprising began and quickly gained a momentum that the Israeli army was unable to break. The Palestinians were unleashing decades of pent-up anger at the occupiers. They were hurling stones, and the Israeli army was shooting back. Scores of Palestinians had been killed, a handful of Israelis had died and countless automobile windows had been smashed.

The West Bank, though, was deceptively pastoral. It opened upon the landscape of the Torah, the Bible and the Koran, a sweep of timeworn stony mountains under a pure blue sky. That day the countryside did not look as if it was suffering a violent rebellion. Terraced groves of olive trees cut into the slopes, their thick trunks gnarled into contortions by the centuries, their patient limbs clothed in silvery green leaves and the buds of yet another season's fruits. The walls of the terraces were built of hand-hewn rock that wound in tier after tier through the countryside like verses of hard poetry. The earth in the olive groves was bare, plowed clean of thistles and other weeds by Palestinian peasants tending their fields with hand tools. The stones, littering these mountains as if a rain once fell that turned from water to mineral, were also cleared from the groves.

An occasional peasant rode his donkey on the shoulder of the main road, his head bowed against the brightness of the vernal light, seemingly oblivious to the traffic of cars and trucks whizzing past, to the facts of modern time. Bethlehem, a collection of dun buildings embellished with steeples and the minaret of a central mosque, lay cradled in distant hills. The horizon was broken by the peculiarly truncated Herodion, a lone mountain whose crest appeared flattened by the ruins of one of King Herod's grand fortresses. Beyond, to the east, the land fell down the drought-wrinkled hills of a desert to the Dead Sea. Hidden in the greener mountains to the west was Nahalin.

Bethlehem itself looked a bit more tattered each time I went through, as if the soul of the town were being torn by the intifada. Travelers were greeted by a roadblock manned by soldiers. They were waving snub-barreled Uzi submachine guns and M-16 combat rifles at the Palestinian cars, ordering them to the side of the road to look for troublemakers among the passengers.

They directed the yellow-plated cars of Israelis through the barricades of red-painted spikes without pause. The *service* came to a stop at the end of a line of Palestinian cars. The other passengers grumbled at the delay but were not perturbed. They were accustomed to being checked by soldiers. When their turn came, they obediently handed a soldier their identification cards, called *hawiyas*, which they had to carry always or risk arrest. I was in a quandary, not wanting to be spotted with a carload of Palestinians and knowing my blond hair made me stand out. I handed over my American passport, fearing that the soldiers would order me from the taxi and question me about my destination. Perhaps they would make me turn back to Jerusalem. It was rare for foreigners to travel by *service*. But the soldier returned my passport and the *hawiyas* without comment and let us proceed.

Beyond the roadblock, the burned contents of several overturned garbage dumpsters were smoldering on the road, the aftermath of an anti-Israeli demonstration. The stores on the main road through town had been shuttered since noon, their metal doors padlocked tightly in keeping with the rules of rebellion the Palestinians imposed upon themselves. By shutting, they were declaring their outrage, even at the cost of their own commerce. The fronts of every store and the walls between were splotched with graffiti. The *shabab* had been working with cans of spray paint, declaring their battle slogans in elaborate Arabic lettering. MAY THE LAND BURN UNDER YOUR FEET, OH ISRAELIS, one wall declaimed. Another announced simply, PALESTINE LIBERATION ORGANIZATION.

Shreds of outlawed Palestinian flags flapped from the electric wires running along the town's smudged side streets. The smudges were patches of carbonized rubber, the remains of tires set ablaze by the *shabab* to send up a protest of fire and smoke and to lure the army into an ambush of stones.

Just south of Bethlehem the road took a bend around a softly rounded hill crowned by a stand of evergreen trees leaning in a wind-blown group, like the inspiration for an Asian painting. When the road straightened out, the sudden mass of the Deheisheh refugee camp appeared. A twenty-foot-high chain link fence reinforced with steel struts divided the road from a hillside crammed with the homes of six thousand Palestinians.

Four decades earlier the United Nations had established Deheisheh with the concept that the camp was to be temporary, providing tents on the boulder-strewn slope for Palestinians fleeing Israel. But the refugees stayed, and the tents were replaced by concrete shelters, which the Palestinians elaborated into a warren of houses and courtyards, leaving hardly a square yard of unused space. The camp's fence stretched three hundred yards along the road, and children clung to it as if it were the side of a cage. The army erected the fence to prevent the angry refugees, who had lost their original homes to the Jewish state, from pelting Israeli vehicles on the road below them.

The road twisted on along the route of a ridgeline path once taken by prophets. At the Kilo Sabatash turnoff, the driver stopped to let me off, as I had asked. My fellow passengers craned their necks to watch as the *service* continued on its way and I started walking down the empty track toward Nahalin.

I guessed the distance to the village to be under two miles. It was a hot afternoon, but there was a good wind blowing in my face. Following the roadway, I crossed a saddle of land beneath an Israeli settlement called Neve Daniel. I saw immediately that a bull-dozer had been at work: a raw thoroughfare headed through a Palestinian vineyard and up toward the settlement, where homes were going up. The houses were being roofed with orange tiles that reverberated against the blueness of the sky. I saw also the mark of the Palestinians' anger, their retaliation—the mangled wire and posts of a Neve Daniel fence. The fence had staked off a new Israeli field of fruit-tree seedlings, which the Palestinians had uprooted and trampled. An intifada skirmish had occurred.

As I went down the dusty track toward Nahalin, I scanned the valleys among which the village rested and saw how time had sculpted their contours, laying bare haunches of white limestone that looked like the bold bones of the earth itself. Down the road, I came upon a pile of rocks bulldozed to the side of the road. I had learned enough about the political topography of the land to deduce what had happened: the rocks, smallish boulders, were the remnants of a roadblock built not by the Israelis but by the Palestinians to impede and aggravate the occupiers. The pile of boulders was crowned by the abandoned shell of a refrigerator that the *shabab* had employed for their roadblock. The structure had then been cleared with a bulldozer by the Israeli army as part of its effort to preserve the landscape's demeanor of normalcy.

Nahalin sat directly at the foot of a particularly hard and lovely valley called Wadi al-Baqara, or the Valley of the Cow, although no cattle grazed in it anymore. Outcrops of rock, some furrowed as if combed by a long-ago giant who wanted to unsnarl and smooth the land, twisted down the sides of the valley. A dozen ravines joined the larger valley, braiding strands of terraced greenery into the rock.

Every patch of earth in the ravines was cultivated by peasant farmers, the *fellahin* as they are called in Arabic. The ravines collected the water that is precious to life during the long dry season following the winter rains. But with the imminent arrival of summer, the air was laced with dust carried by the mountain winds. Thistles already had bloomed purple and turned sere.

Grapes and almonds and olives stepped in groves up the

terraces. Other than the carefully ordered crops, no trees softened the valley. High on the hillsides, boys and old men were shepherding long-haired goats and black-headed sheep. Doves with dusky blue wings flashed the white bands on their tail feathers as they flitted from boulder to boulder.

In the middle distance, the land humped into a round knoll, and beyond that was Ain Feres, which translated as the Spring of the Warrior, a name that derived from a time when mounted soldiers and travelers would camp by the pool. This spring watered Nahalin's best land, a flat expanse where the *fellahin* did not have to struggle with terraces and arduous slopes. Ain Feres fed into a pond and then into channels irrigating fields planted with onions, tomatoes, parsley, squash, eggplant, wheat and barley. This ground was the pride of the village and the wide pedestal of its agriculture.

The knoll was the site of a Christian monastery, whose ruins still ran along its top. It also was the site of archaic caves where people had lived during epochs whose local history was not known. More recently, in the time of the Roman Empire, people inhabited these caves, and they carved squared lines into the rocks to decorate the openings.

From where I was, it was possible to see the grandeur of the village's setting, the complex of mountains that encircled the village, and also see the surrounding trouble. It was possible to see the cow sheds of Rosh Zurim, one of a bloc of settlements pressing down upon the village from the south and making a rough horseshoe of Israeli-held land where Sheikh Deeb's contemporaries once hunted and farmed. Rosh Zurim dominated the crest of a ridge south of the village and facing Neve Daniel. At the far end of the kibbutz, beyond the sheds, was a massive dirt dike that held a pond of liquid manure generated by the dairy cattle, a lake that soundlessly loomed above the fields of the *fellahin* below. From Nahalin, the dike looked like the wall of a sand castle.

The larger Kfar Etzion kibbutz and another settlement formed the rest of the horseshoe. Although only a few kilometers away, they were hidden by ridges.

The Kfar Etzion kibbutz to Nahalin's south was the centerpiece of the group of settlements known as the Gush Etzion bloc. The kibbutz bore the distinction of being the oldest settlement on the West Bank, and it had an unusual history. Unlike most other settlements, Jewish pioneers bought the land for Kfar Etzion before the creation of Israel. During the 1948 war, the kibbutz—which lay in the middle of Palestinian territory—was besieged by Arab fighters. The men of the kibbutz made a final stand to protect their settlement and the road to Jerusalem against Jordan's Arab Legion. Most of those defending the kibbutz, farmers and soldiers alike, died in the battle. Nineteen years later, when Israel won the 1967 war, the kibbutz returned to Jewish hands. The sons and daughters of the first kibbutzniks went back to resettle Kfar Etzion. Rosh Zurim, its satellite kibbutz, was resettled two years later. Within three years, the religious community of Alon Shvut also sprang up beside the kibbutzim. The core of these settlements was land that had been bought before the war. But soon after the war, the Israeli military government began confiscating Palestinian territory, and enlarging its toehold on the West Bank.

From then on, the Israelis took much land, settling to the north and south, to the east and west. Another twenty years later Israel controlled about half of the West Bank's land, just as it controlled about half of Nahalin's land. About two thousand settlers lived in the settlements to Nahalin's immediate south.

To the west of the village, closer and more obvious to the eye, was Nahal Gevaot, an army encampment that occupied the nearer peak of Abu al-Koroun, the tallest mountain around, whose hulking twin summits defined the view to the village's southwest. The Arabic name of the mountain means Father of the Horns, because the peaks resemble blunt horns. The actual encampment was not visible from the high back road. A forest of pines, demarcated by militarily straight borders, notched a solid green wedge into the otherwise bald-looking mountain. The pines hid the rectangular barracks of the Israeli soldiers. Over the years, the pines had come to symbolize Israeli control, whereas the olive trees planted before the Jews returned in numbers to the region of King David's historical kingdom were the emblem of the Palestinians.

Looking from Nahalin toward the northwest, my eyes came to rest on the most puzzling settlement of all, the one named Betar. It was the farthest away, a few kilometers from the village, and looked like a whitish spot on a far ridge. It was small, a grouping of a dozen or so prefabricated trailers on a tract of land staked out by stout fences reinforced by rolls of barbed wire and surveiled by an armed sentry, the seed of a settlement determined to take root among the Palestinian villages. As with all new settlements, Betar had plans to grow, although I did not know precisely what they were. I had heard rumors that it was meant to be a settlement of religiously Orthodox Israelis. Completing the panorama to the north, at the top of the Valley of the Cow, was another Palestinian village, Husan.

When I looked at the landscape, I saw war written in the placement of every settlement and resistance written in the low profiles of the villages. War of the purest kind, for the land. I looked at the land, the villages tucked away in the folds of the mountains, the cascading terraces, the settlements commanding the heights, and I saw blood. If time could run backward, war could be avoided. But of course time was running forward with an awful determination, squeezing Palestinians and Israelis closer and closer in unwelcome embrace.

The two peoples wanted the same piece of stony and yet addictively seductive ground, a geographically insignificant territory of immense human significance. The Palestinians believed devoutly that the land was theirs, just as it was the land of their ancestors. They wanted this land of the West Bank as well as the patch of Gaza Strip to meld into their own state unencumbered by Israeli strictures or the laws of any other occupier. The Israelis wanted the same land as a buffer to protect their tiny state against the surrounding Arab nations. Many also believed, as devoutly as did the Palestinians, that the land was rightfully theirs. By regaining it, by settling it and fighting to control it, they thought they were enacting a biblical promise, for it is written in the book of Genesis that their God pledged this land to the descendants of their forefather Abraham, who passed on the entitlement to the Jews. They also believed that the land, which was under the hegemony of King David two thousand years before, was still Jewish land.

I kept walking. A car pulled up from behind. The driver was a Nahalini, a Palestinian from Nahalin, and he wanted to know who I was, what a foreign woman was doing marching toward Nahalin. I told him I was a writer and wanted to stay in the village. He was astounded and wanted to know the whereabouts of my car. How was it that a foreigner did not have her own car to drive?

The foreigners who do report from the West Bank seldom tarry, usually driving back to their homes in Jerusalem after doing their day's work. He had never heard of a journalist who wanted to stay, one without a car, one who walked instead of riding. I declined his offer to give me a lift since I was near my destination, having almost reached the rock-cutting factory at the top of the village.

The factory was nothing more than a cavernous tin shed employing a handful of men, but it was Nahalin's only industry. When I got that far, I was confused as to which tangential road went to the Najajras' home a few hundred yards below. I started down a track alongside the shed. A man with a white beard, his head wrapped in a *kefiyeh*, an Arab headcloth, started yelling and telling me that the road went nowhere. His name was Abu Nimar and he owned the factory. I stopped, and when I told him I was from the United States, he summoned another fellow. The point was not to give me directions but to pontificate. The conversation, which was as friendly as it was intense, shifted quickly from how angry the villagers were about the Neve Daniel road through the vineyard to the subject of the United States.

"If the United States stops, the problems will stop. Israel will stop. It is your country who decides our life. The United States, if she wants to make Israel change, she can make Israel change. If not, we lose our land. *Shou bidna nsawi.* What can we do?" the workman asked, mixing English with Arabic.

He gestured expansively at the mountains and the settlements, trying to make his point by physical vehemence if not by sheer personal conviction. I had understood the point beforehand, as did the policy makers in Washington who were providing more than three billion dollars annually in aid to keep Israel functioning as an ally in the Middle East. What I was learning, though, was how deeply this information was lodged in the Palestinians' collective mind.

No enmity on account of American political policy was directed toward me, though. On the contrary, the two men wanted to use me as a messenger, as someone who would listen to their plaints and carry that information out from the mountains.

I made it down to the Najajras without further ado. But that evening, as I sat with some of the family, I became enmeshed in a debate about my living in Nahalin. The talk focused on impediments to my idea of renting a vacant room or an empty house. For one thing, my presence might attract the attention of the Shin Bet and bring suspicions down upon whomever let me rent. The Israeli intelligence police, as much as the Nahalinis, must already have been wondering why a foreigner was spending so much time in this unremarkable village. On the other hand, my presence might deter the Shin Bet, because the Israelis would not want to cause any trouble in front of a foreign writer, especially an American, given Israel's close ties with the United States.

I complicated the discussion by insisting that I wanted an abode to myself, a heretical idea in a village where most women married as teenagers and nobody lived apart. This in all likelihood was the biggest single difficulty; women did not live alone in this society unless they were prostitutes.

Fawzi was there, listening to the arguments and counterarguments before saying anything. Then he raised the possibility of a problem that had not crossed my mind, that of collaborators. Some Palestinians did cooperate with the occupiers, providing information to the Shin Bet in order to get money, or receive permission to travel or simply stay out of prison. But I had not imagined that collaborators would cause me problems. Fawzi predicted they would go to the Shin Bet and tell lies about me, which would rebound through the village via other collaborators and force me out.

I persisted, mentioning a vacant house, the only one I knew about. Fawzi was doubtful. "The owner will be afraid that someone will cause him trouble—a collaborator or the *mukhabarat*," he concluded succinctly, using the Arabic word for the secret police, the Shin Bet.

Fawzi said he would try to talk with the owner. But he expanded on the reasons for his doubt. The owner of the tiny, empty place was a religious elder with the strictest of mentalities. "He won't like renting to a woman or to a Christian," he said.

His response led to an offer that he must have considered beforehand. "You must come and live with me and my family," he announced.

I refused on the grounds we had already discussed. My presence might cause him problems.

"It doesn't matter," he replied.

"Why?" I asked.

"I expect I will be taken to prison anyway."

"Why?"

Fawzi answered obliquely and at length. "Because I do things differently, because I have ideas. The Israelis do not want Palestinians with ideas. They want the villages to stay always the same, always following tradition, always herding their goats, always surviving and always ignoring the occupation. They want people whose minds are occupied. People have learned to adjust their minds to the situation just to survive. The occupation is a real thing. The Israelis have a real army, and they are building real settlements. But there is another occupation that is real, too, and that one is in the minds of the people. They think they have no power of their own. It is only the *shabab*, with their stones, who are changing the occupation. The old people are learning from the young ones. It is the opposite of the past."

The more I watched Fawzi and listened to him, the more I saw. Fawzi was always looking for new ideas to bring back to the village. Rather than goatherding like his ancestors, he was introducing into the village thoroughbred Romanian sheep, which produce more offspring and more meat. He not only made certain his sheep were innoculated against brucellosis, but he also wanted all the village livestock innoculated as well, even if that meant chauffeuring a government veterinarian to the village from Bethlehem. I had seen him do that a few weeks earlier, taking the veterinarian from flock to herd to flock.

The next suggestion, far from meeting my wish that I live among average villagers, was that I stay with Deeb Najajra and his brothers and sister. They lived in a house by themselves because their mother and then their father, in a deed abhorrent to Palestinian custom, had abandoned them. Deeb had recently finished building the house. It had two rooms with a hallway between that served as a kitchen.

Since first meeting Deeb, I had learned more about him. Before he attacked the Israeli jeep, he had been a diligent student of English at Bethlehem University. But he also had been manufacturing bombs by filling a bathtub with an explosive mixture and bottling the substance. With his arrest, his study became the politics of national liberation and revolution. His cellmates and teachers were political prisoners, their minds set against the Israeli occupation. Deeb read economics. He listened to the theories of his jailed peers. During eleven months of solitary confinement, he had nothing to do but read. He perused scores of political books, until he could no longer differentiate between what he was reading and what he was living. When he reentered the world outside the prison, his views had changed. He emerged toughened and wiry, jobless and morose.

The room where he slept in the winter months, which also served as a sitting room, was decorated with two posters, one of Che Guevara and another of a dramatized scene of a silhouetted soldier fatally wounded and toppling backward with his gun flung in the air. The second poster was titled in large black letters WHY?

One day I stood with Deeb on a knoll overlooking Ain Feres, the fields of vegetables watered by the spring and the ridges beyond. He complained about the lack of trees, not for aesthetic but for political reasons. Deeb was imagining what the mountains would look like if they were covered with jungle foliage, the same thick greenery that Guevara and other Latin guerrillas used for cover.

"Everything would be different if we had more trees here. We would have enough protection from the army to make a revolution," he said.

Deeb saw even his fellow villagers through his Marxist philosophy. Abu Nimar and his rock factory was to Deeb in Nahalin the exemplar of "our petite bourgeoisie."

Now Deeb was offering me shelter. But I did not want to live with one of the village's political heavyweights. So Deeb's offer wouldn't do. It was important to me that I cultivate the impression of being indifferent to Palestinian politics, if that was possible, of not being associated with whatever faction he claimed.

I did spend time at Deeb's, though, because it was a place where young men—by my guess, members of Nahalin's *shabab*—came and went. They would talk among themselves for hours. Farouk sometimes dropped by, too. One evening he started joking again about the donkeys singing at night. My Arabic was getting better, and I could keep up with some of the conversation. One of the other young men added that the people cry at night, tears that nobody ever sees in the hard light of day.

Another of the Palestinians, a young Muslim sheikh, abruptly broke into Hebrew from Arabic. I asked him what he had said, and he laughed without answering. Later Deeb told me that I had failed a test of whether I knew Hebrew. If I had understood, I could have been pegged as a spy. As it was, the night ended ordinarily, with everyone drinking too much coffee and heading off to sleep well after midnight.

I slept mostly with one family of Najajras or another in the neighborhood called Sobiha at the top of the village. I slept on rooftops, on cots in crowded rooms, in double beds with one or two other women. I stayed with a family whose young children cried at night and then woke everybody with their laughter at dawn. Frequently, though, I returned to the original Najajras. There was plenty of room on the roof, and the family seemed to trust me. With the Najajras, looking out over most of the village, I didn't have to worry about what was coming my way. I slept next to Sena and gave her lessons in English in the morning. I tried to speak in Arabic with Ratiba, although she was not one to talk much in any case. On the village roadways, small boys still took potshots at me with pebbles, but I was able to shut them up with increasing fluency.

One morning just after spring had turned to summer, I left Nahalin with my little suitcase, riding away on the village bus. It was a bus that had withstood decades of service and was driven by Abu Sayal, a Nahalini who once chauffeured officers in Jordan. He was wearing a spotless white *kefiyeh*, folded up on both sides of his head so that he could better see, and glasses with black rims. He looked like a Palestinian in command of a magnificent yacht or a deluxe limousine, so dignified was his bearing and confident his handling of the aging bus. Next to his seat were a worn wooden money box, a plastic trash can and a broom. Pasted on the windshield were decorative flower and palm-tree decals. I handed Abu Sayal the fare to Bethlehem, a shekel worth about fifty cents, but he refused to take it.

"You are a guest of the village. You must not pay me," he said and brooked no arguments.

My problem was that I did not want to be a guest. Moving into Nahalin was turning out to be harder and trickier than I had guessed. I was ready to settle for a cubbyhole of a room at almost any rent just so that I could retire at will and bolt my door against the Palestinians' militant hospitality. That desire, which seemed so natural to me, was puzzling them the most. Why did I want to be alone?

Fawzi was one of the few who understood why I desired privacy—that I needed time to think, to observe and to scribble notes. I could only wait anxiously to see whether he could find me a place, a room of my own with perhaps a window that looked out over the mountains and a kerosene cooker on which to boil a pot of tea.

As the bus rolled out the main roadway, a murmuring arose among the passengers. I looked up to see a large banner hanging from one of the electric lines. It was a flag in the Palestinian colors— white, red, green and black—the flag outlawed by the Israelis. The sight of the flag was not what shocked me; rather, it was the fact that Nahalin had taken a stand or, more accurately, the village *shabab* had acted. For months neighboring villages had been flying the prohibited flag from the tall minarets of their mosques while Nahalin watched from the sidelines of the uprising.

No one on the bus remarked openly about the flag. To do so might be dangerous if the wrong person overheard, if a collaborator happened to be listening. But the significance of the flag was undeniable. Nahalin had made a gesture and would probably have to face the army as a result. Standard army procedure was to force Palestinians, whomever might be around at the time, to climb minarets or poles and tear down the flags. Newspapers had reported a dozen incidents of Palestinians falling or being electrocuted during flag-demolishing undertakings. The army regarded these hand-stitched banners with gravity, for they symbolized the Palestinian demand for a state and control of the land, power that could threaten Israel itself. For the Palestinians, the sight of the flag sent an illicit and unspoken thrill through the bus that June morning. I could see peoples' eyes widen.

The village bus made two runs every morning into Bethlehem, taking the road that climbed up a precipitous side of the Valley of the Cow to Husan, a village distinguished by a stately rose-colored mosque, then twisted past a turnoff to a village called Battir and then down to the village of El Khader, which possessed a fair stretch of flat, fertile farmland and an anomalous archway built by early Christians and dedicated to Saint George and the dragon. On its early trip, the bus transported workers to the main road, where they could pick up another ride to Jerusalem or to one of the Israeli settlements.

During the Israeli occupation, the Palestinians on the West Bank had grown ever more dependent upon Israeli pay. They worked as construction laborers, stone cutters, street cleaners, waiters, garbagemen, janitors, gas pumpers, plasterers or gardeners. People called these ill-paying jobs black work, and Palestinians did most of it.

Abu Sayal made a second trip at eight o'clock for the women taking the fruits and vegetables of the season into the Bethlehem market, their produce stashed in plastic baskets and cardboard boxes that they carried on their heads to the bus and then heaved up the stairs into its narrow aisleway.

The bus made a halting journey to Bethlehem, pulling over to the side of the main road near the Deheisheh refugee camp to let faster traffic pass. I stared at the fence as I had when I first laid eyes on it, incredulous that six thousand people lived in the jumble of concrete homes behind it. What amazed me more was that the camp's *shabab* were able to get an occasional stone over or through the fence and hit the window of a yellow-plated Israeli car. At the base of the fence, recently added rolls of barbed wire lay coiled like a bright warning in the roadside dust.

At Bethlehem, Abu Sayal parked in front of the town's defunct El Amal Cinema—in English, the Hope Cinema. Dominating a central crossroads, it served as a general meeting place. The cinema was originally a grand structure with columns and glass doors and rounded windows. But now holes pocked the windows; Xeroxed political notices were pasted to the columns; wood and metal sheets patched the broken doors. Its limestone steps went unswept. People sat on them, some eating shish kebab from a grill on the sidewalk opposite. Taxis loitered with their engines running.

The women dragged their boxes and baskets of dried apricots and fresh onions to the *souq*, the market of winding alleys and surprise spaces where everything was sold. Whole carcasses of sheep were strung up in bloody repetition the length of the butchers' section of the market. Vegetables—okra, squash, peppers, tomatoes, eggplant and parsley—heaped the flagstones. Every vendor was shouting the name of his produce and price. Video cassettes looked anomalous in the shop windows of byways radiating from the market's central square. Ancient stone arches and stairways, some of them beckoning to a shortcut and some of them leading nowhere, spoke to the age of the town.

Bethlehem, and particularly its *souq*, was Nahalin's main connection to the larger world. Bethlehem was the place to buy and sell; the fact that it was the place of Christ's nativity was irrelevant to the hustling marketplace. From there, I took another bus back to Jerusalem.

F O U R

With the onset of the dry summer season, the battle between Palestinian and Israeli flared on the West Bank as well as in Israel. The Palestinians came up with a new tactic aimed at damaging Israel's heartland. They added the match to their primitive arsenal and began setting fires in the forests planted within Israel. Some of the forests had grown from saplings lovingly nourished by the first pioneering Israelis, who believed the trees would stand as a bulwark protecting their state.

In a borrowed car, I shuttled between the village and my apartment, waiting for word from the Najajras that they had found a place for me to stay. The idea of showing up with a suitcase had not broken Nahalin open for me, so I had fallen back on patience. I wondered whether I had picked the wrong place—some other village might be more compliant or at least easier to understand. But I also realized that I did have an attachment to Nahalin, albeit a tenuous one.

No fires were being set in the hills around Bethlehem, but the *shabab* in Nahalin had attacked the edges of the settlement of Neve Daniel and the kibbutz of Rosh Zurim. I did not see either foray, but I heard about each in some detail when I returned to the village. The young men were happy to supply the information, the only hitch being that the perpetrators were always anonymous. The eyewitness quality of their stories did not deter the Nahalinis from grammatical cover-ups by always referring to the *shabab* in the third person. No one admitted to being a member of the *shabab*. The gap of distrust was too wide, but on occasion it narrowed enough so that I heard some of the village's inside news.

"Four nights ago the *shabab* went up to Neve Daniel. They waited for a night with no moon so that they could hide. They know the mountains like a picture made in their minds, so they can walk in the darkness. The opposite for the settlers at Neve Daniel and all the settlements. They are afraid of the dark. This is why the settlers' lights are so many and so strong. They want to kill the night by cutting it into pieces with their lights. They know the *shabab* can swim in the dark mountains like fish in dark waves."

The young man with striking green eyes who was telling me this was named Fou'ad. He was a distant cousin of Fawzi and Farouk. Fou'ad and a couple of his friends were sitting on a stone wall, and they struck up a conversation with me as I passed. Fou'ad was particularly poetical.

"So the *shabab* went up in the dark and destroyed the new fence that the settlers from Neve Daniel put up around their field. This is a new field that widens their borders against the land of Nahalin. The *shabab* destroyed this fence before, but the settlers built it back. It rose from the dead, so we attacked it again and put it back down. Without the fence, it is easy for anyone to come and break the crops in the field."

On the same night, another contingent of Nahalin's youths set out for the lower slopes of the opposite mountain, the one cultivated by the Israelis of Rosh Zurim. Beneath their cow sheds, the kibbutzniks had planted fruit trees on what were once village terraces. The *shabab* carried knives, axes or whatever they could use to damage the trees. They spent two hours creeping along the bottom of a valley, dodging from rock to rock in case the soldiers at the army encampment detected them. They cut and broke some three hundred fruit trees on the lower terraces and escaped unseen.

In retaliation, the Israeli army brought a heavy-duty bulldozer to the high road to blockade it with boulders seemingly too huge to be rolled aside. This was the same spot the *shabab* had tried to block earlier. The Israelis topped their roadblock with the vagrant refrigerator shell the Palestinians had used first in their blockade. The soldiers added the mangled underbody of a car, the stubs of four wheel rims connected by a contorted metal plate. As soon as the army blockade was in place on the road a couple of hundred yards below Neve Daniel's resurrected fence, the *shabab* went up the mountain again and built a detour around it. They tore down part of a village wall and constructed two ramps of earth so that cars could swing around the army's boulders.

This blockade on the high road caught me by surprise one afternoon when I was giving Sa'ed, Fawzi's music-loving brother, a ride back to the village from a tiling job at an Arab house in East Jerusalem's suburbs.

We took the high back road from the main highway at Kilo Sabatash and were talking away happily, too happily, because neither of us saw what was ahead in time for me to stop. Parked across the road was the jeep of a squad of Haris al-Hadood, the Border Police. These were hardened soldiers. Many were professionals at fighting Palestinians, and many were Druze, Arabs who practice a unique religion that divides them from the Muslim world. The Palestinians dreaded the Border Police in general. This squad of soldiers had dragooned some of the young men from the village to block the *shabab* detour, once more turning the tables in the miniature war for the roadway.

The complexity of intifada politics was growing daily. Retaliate against the settlers by killing their saplings. Punish the *shabab* by punishing the village by blocking a peasant thoroughfare. Retaliate against the army with a detour. Retaliate against the Palestinians by forcing them to block their own detour and, in the end, irritating everyone in the village and raising the level of anti-Israeli sentiment a notch.

When I braked, the soldiers saw us. I started to back up, and one of them leveled his rifle at me. A basic rule of conduct on the West Bank was that if you ran, the soldiers shot, either because they did not want you to get away or because you had proved your guilt by running. I did not think this soldier would really shoot a foreign-looking woman, but I had no choice but to go forward. As I drove closer and they had a better look at Sa'ed, I realized how strange we must appear. They also saw the signs on the car that spelled out SEHAFI in black letters, declaring to potential stone throwers that I was a journalist, not a settler. I had not enough forewarning to untape them or to remove the checkered *kefiyeh* that I had spread on the dashboard to supplement the signs.

Not having encountered the Border Police head-on before, I wanted to panic, but I kept my composure. When they surrounded the car and began questioning me, I pretended I could not speak any foreign languages, only English, which none of them knew. I wanted to seem as ignorant and harmless as possible. Sa'ed, like many Palestinians who had worked in Israel, spoke Hebrew, so he translated for me. The soldiers stood around and discussed whether or not to arrest one or both of us—Sa'ed for taking a journalist into his village and me for trying to drive on an officially blockaded road. I kept saying that all I had done was give this man a lift when I saw him walking in the heat of the afternoon and that all I wanted to do was continue to the village and then back home to Jerusalem. This back road, I knew and they knew, was a most unlikely and inconvenient way to get back to the city.

Finally it was agreed that we could continue, but we had to take a different route. I continued to feign ignorance of the other two roads to the village, which by then I knew by heart. I got out a map from the car and spread it on the hood. One of the brawnier of the Border Police leaned over my shoulder and provided directions. I acted bewildered. He dug a pen from his pocket and used it as a pointer. He hesitated and then asked Sa'ed to translate a question: "Is it all right to draw the route in ink on the map?" I responded that of course it was. I kept a straight face, but inside I found the question strangely hilarious: here was a fellow who was going to blow my head off now asking politely whether he could mark my map. As Sa'ed and I drove the long way round to Nahalin, I was laughing at the ludicrousness of the whole incident.

Sa'ed was upset, though. "These soldiers can do anything they want to my village because they have guns. They order us around like we are children. If they did not have guns, we would have justice." He refused to smile.

It was Fawzi, as usual, who came up with the idea. If the Israelis were going to barricade the village, a countermeasure was in order. Why not flout the gut fear that every Palestinian had of Israel's soldiers and go traveling from Nahalin on an outing? Why not go on a picnic in the face of worry? I was delighted. It would give me a chance to see the Najajras outside the confines of the village. It might even be fun.

By the Muslim calendar, it was the first day of the year when we set out for a park near a town called Beit She'an, a couple of hours' drive to the northeast. The lake park was known as a place where Arabs and Israelis mixed peacefully, a place where we hoped the politics of the uprising could be forgotten for the day. It was in the Galilee near Tiberias, in Israel itself. To get there, we had to drive through the Israeli side of Jerusalem, back out onto the West Bank and then into northern Israel.

We took three cars. Fawzi drove his beat-up Peugeot, a relative of his drove another car and I drove a third. Everyone came— Fawzi with his wife and children; Ratiba in a black *thobe* with gold embroidery and a white head shawl; Sena and her sister, Adla, who was studying to be a nurse; Farouk; Sa'ed; and Shawki, who was ten years old. One of Fawzi's uncles also came along. He had just been released from the Ansar prison in the Negev Desert and bore an aura of gloom.

We set off in the late morning with Fawzi leading, first through Jerusalem and then eastward through sandy mountains inhabited by Bedouin nomads trailing their herds of goats from parched pasture to parched pasture. We continued to Jericho, a flat city edged by dusty refugee camps and irrigated banana plantations at the bottom of the Jordan Valley. We passed a couple of small Israeli settlements and the Mount of Temptation, an inhospitable rock where the fasting Jesus Christ refused the seductions of Satan. A monastery clung on the cliffs where Christ tested himself, and on the mountain opposite stood an imposing Israeli army communications post. It had a commanding view of the valley, much of which was within the limits of the West Bank, the same piece of occupied territory in which Nahalin and Bethlehem were situated. The Palestinians dreamed that this part of the Jordan Valley as well as the stony hills to the north and south of Jerusalem would become part of a state called Palestine. Gaza, the isolated rectangle of overpopulated and poverty-stricken territory on Israel's southern border with the Egyptian Sinai, also would be part of the imagined state.

The trip was going well. We had passed several roadblocks, but the soldiers had not bothered the Palestinians, asking only for their *hawiyas* and then letting them pass. Our mood grew lighter with each mile.

Sa'ed sat in the front seat with me, and other Najajras crowded the back. Mostly we played loud music, a selection of bad Western tunes and some high-pitched Arabic melodies, letting it blast at full volume as we sped down the hot road with whirlwinds catching up the dust from the dry land.

Sa'ed and I talked about another run-in he had recently had on the road returning from work. He and a second village laborer were stopped by the army. The soldiers handcuffed them and kept them for two hours, questioning Sa'ed about his work boots, Israeli army boots he had bought in a surplus-goods market in West Jerusalem. The soldiers were suspicious and hauled the two Palestinians into their jeep and then to the Basaa, the military and Shin Bet headquarters for the Bethlehem region. Four hours later they emerged from the former British fort, Sa'ed barefoot because his boots had been confiscated.

Farouk talked, too. He theorized about earning money now that the schools were closed on the West Bank and his dream of studying veterinary medicine indefinitely postponed. How was he going to live? What could he see in his future? He said he was thinking about working at construction jobs to save enough money to get a truck-driver's license. Underneath the gaiety of the day, he was not happy.

Without knowing it, we crossed back again into Israel. The Green Line, as the boundary is called from the color used on an armistice map, was not marked in any way. The Israelis did not want to call attention to a border that always caused political headaches. Who ultimately would control the territory on the West Bank, or even how much of it, was the question at the heart of the intifada.

The park at Beit She'an was abuzz when we arrived, mostly with Israelis sporting in a lovely series of lakes and waterfalls and picnicking. The Israeli women were wearing bathing suits or bikinis—costumes that utterly violated Palestinian propriety. I could only guess what Ratiba saw from the perspective of her all-covering *thobe* or what the men thought of these women whose flesh was so flagrantly naked.

The Nahalinis outwardly ignored the scene. We located a shady spot by one of the lakes and set down our food. Ratiba seated herself sedately and undoubtedly sweatily under a tree in her black dress and watched as the men and I went swimming, except for the uncle who wandered off by himself. He spent the afternoon sitting under a waterfall, trying to wash away his memories of the desert. Neither Sena nor Adla had been swimming before; they had never exposed their bodies to the freedom of air and water. But it was hot, and I was intent on swimming. I had dared to wear pants rather than a skirt that day. Knowing that I was already touching the line of decorum, and in the interests of not offending the Palestinians outright, I kept all my clothes on—pants, underwear, heavy T-shirt, even my belt and bracelet. But my swim in the turquoise water in the heat of the Jordan Valley afternoon was wonderful, and I stayed in longer than the others.

When I got out, dripping wet, I found Ratiba gone and the others upset. The police had taken Fawzi and Farouk away. I put on my shoes, watch and earrings—in a hopeless attempt to look less undignified—and rushed over to the park police station, where two Israelis had the two Palestinians cornered on a bench in a narrow room. They were all shouting at each other in Hebrew, and Ratiba was pressing at the side of the door. I assumed the two were being harassed because they were Palestinians.

The police released the brothers, but I demanded that one of the policemen come with me and apologize. An officer finally did arrive at the lake and made some excuses in Hebrew without showing any sign of contrition. The Palestinians were standing up, outraged and ready to leave, until Fawzi insisted that they stay because they had a right to enjoy the park. With my wet clothes clinging to me, I settled down to eat with the uneasy Palestinians.

It was only later, in the car on the return to Nahalin, that Farouk confessed with a laugh that he had called the lifeguard a donkey and said he would strangle him. The guard then called the police. The day had gone wrong.

F I V E

July baked the mountains dry and brought the grapes and the figs to the verge of ripeness. The wind rustled the yellow grasses on the hills, and the crickets buzzed. The dust on Nahalin's pathways was bone white. In the distance, a summer haze hung in the northeast over Jerusalem. Despite the somnolent feel of the hot, rainless days, Nahalin was tense. The intifada was changing the West Bank.

By summertime, the word *intifada* had gained recognition in the lexicon of geopolitics. Typical of Arabic's ornate grammar, the word derived from the eighth form of the verb "to dust" and meant "a shivering, a shuddering, a shaking off," much as one might shake the dust off a rug. The intifada had become a mass uprising involving the majority of the Palestinians in the Israeli-held territories in one fashion or another, whether it was by refusing to pay Israeli taxes, whittling slingshots, throwing stones at armed soldiers, burning tires, devising gasoline bombs from cola bottles and rag fuses, spray-painting walls with political graffiti denouncing the occupiers, tailoring outlawed flags, resigning from jobs in Israel, shutting shops every afternoon to present to Israel and the world a blank face of solidified anger, refusing completely to work in Israel, refusing to work in Israel on the days on which protest strikes were called, participating in unsanctioned political demonstrations, visiting sons imprisoned for these and other activities that the military government defined as threatening to Israel's national security, being shot for attacking Israelis, dying from Israeli bullet wounds and finally grieving the death of relatives and friends.

Some refused to describe the intifada as a war since the Palestinians were not employing guns against the Israeli Defense Forces' panoply of weapons, although stones thrown by athletic young men could kill, as could firebombs. The intifada was unlike any other popular rebellion of this century. The Palestinians had almost no guns because of a strict Israeli policy to keep them unarmed.

The Israelis were sending soldiers to the territories to do the job of riot police—squash unrest, stop protests and protect motorists. These were the soldiers of the Middle East's best army, men trained to face Syrian tanks and savvy Lebanese militiamen, not the Palestinian youths of the occupied territories, whose heavy ammunition consisted of rocks and whose gasoline bottle bombs, like those Deeb Najajra once manufactured, failed to explode more often than not.

The Israelis were fighting a war without the defined bounds that enable generals to marshal classic stratagems against enemy troops entrenched in stubborn positions. Instead, they resorted to unconventional tactics: firing at the *shabab* with plastic bullets and rubber-coated bullets, tear gas and marbles, dropping gravel from helicopters, beating suspects and breaking their bones, fencing off refugee camps, making massive numbers of arrests, dynamiting the family homes of Palestinian lawbreakers, fining homeowners for slogans painted on their walls and trying to force shops to stay open. Or they resorted to using live ammunition against the stone-throwing young men, sometimes hitting their targets with fatal accuracy and sometimes striking women and children. It was a war of shifting tactics, extemporaneous methods, a war of attrition in which each side was trying to exhaust the other on a front whose battle lines were moving through a hundred different villages, refugee camps and cities at a hundred different times.

The war also was odd because the antagonists, the population of Israelis and the population of Palestinians, continued to carry on partially normal relations. Although peace was being much talked about, no declaration of war had been made. Many Palestinians were still crossing the Green Line to work for Israeli employers. Israelis still administered the occupied territories, making the laws, enforcing them, issuing driver's licenses and other permits, collecting taxes, building roads and acting altogether as a harsh and circumscribing surrogate government.

The Palestinian organizers of the intifada were neither generals nor public figures but, rather, members of a shadowy group of political operatives who dodged the Shin Bet as they went. They were commanding their war via a series of leaflets, which were secretly printed and Xeroxed every couple of weeks and distributed through a circuitous series of messengers from city to city, neighborhood to neighborhood, refugee camp to refugee camp and village to village. The leaflets, signed always by the anonymous Unified National Leadership of the Intifada, provided the Palestinians in the territories with plans for how to rebel and antagonize the Israelis.

Although the Israelis caught some of the Palestinians printing the leaflets and shut down some presses, the missives continued to appear. Once the leaflets reached the street, their contents were passed by word of mouth from shop to shop and person to person. And, paradoxically, Israeli as well as Palestinian newspapers regularly published the directives spelled out in the leaflets as news, which of course they were.

By July, the intifada was entering its eighth month, and thousands of Palestinians had been arrested, interrogated and detained. Hundreds had been wounded by bullets or beatings. At least

150 more Palestinians were killed, according to Israeli army figures—although the United Nations reported that the number was
more than twice that—most of them struck by live bullets, some by
rubber-coated ammunition and some by tear gas fired at close range
or into rooms.

The intifada had spread beyond the obvious places—the
poor neighborhoods of Palestinian cities, the crowded houses of the
refugees and the winding alleyways of Palestinian marketplaces.
Using the cold measure of numbers killed, it was clear that the
village youths were battling most fiercely with the army; more were
dying in the countryside than in the camps.

This was how things were when momentous news came to Nahalin.
The Israelis had confiscated the second humped peak of Abu al-
Koroun. Within a week of the news, the army had staked off the land
with metal fence posts, and the Nahalinis knew what that meant.
Back in 1982 the Israelis took their first chunk of the mountain. The
villagers hired a lawyer, argued before an Israeli committee against
the confiscation and, not surprisingly, lost. The newly acquired land
adjoined the pine trees of the army encampment. The camp supported a core of young Israeli soldiers who were training to settle the
place eventually. The additional land gave the Israelis hegemony
over the entire summit of Nahalin's most prominent mountain.

As far as anyone could remember, going back to the time
when memories of long-dead generations mix with lore, the village
considered Abu al-Koroun its common inheritance. Although most
of the highest slopes of the mountain were not arable, the land was
used by Nahalin's shepherds, whose goats and sheep could find
sustenance in the scrubby plants sprouting between the boulders.
This land was crucial to Nahalin's definition of itself, as crucial as
its springs and gardens.

Various villagers gave me different figures of the number of acres that were staked off, although the precise amount of land was not the point. Nahalin's self-image had been chipped again, another piece of land had been chiseled from its valleys and ridges. The village *shabab* hung more flags, small and large ones, on the electric wires.

Not long after the confiscation I arrived at the Najajras' house high on the mountainside and saw women gathering near the village center. A demonstration was in the making. From my vantage, I could look down upon the old mosque, where the protesters were milling about.

When the army arrived, it came from two directions, down from its Nahal Gevaot camp on Abu al-Koroun and also down the long road sidling along the edge of the Valley of the Cow from the village of Husan. I was with Ratiba and her children when the jeeps appeared. Farouk disappeared downhill, wearing clean white pants and an eye-catching blue shirt. He had readied himself for an evening feast Ratiba was cooking for family elders who were due to preside over a reconciliation. Ratiba was ready to end a year's quarrel, whose origins were too abstruse for me to grasp, with one of her brothers. But there was no stopping Farouk from going with the *shabab*, not even for the minute it would have taken to change into less conspicuous clothes.

I stayed with Sena and the physically delicate Ahmed and watched from a rock outcrop near the house. We saw the gathered people and heard the warning whistles of the *shabab*, which carried through the valleys and bounced off the ridges. Women were climbing to their rooftops to watch with their children. Shepherds stopped, letting their sheep wander. Above, in the dome of the sky, the color was drained to a fragile blue.

The soldiers quickly and systematically cornered the *shabab* in an olive grove above the road from Husan. Two jeeps halted on the road, and the soldiers began firing canisters of tear gas. This tactic was of no use, though, because the day was windy, and breezes quickly dissipated the white gas that puffed from the canisters as they plowed into the earth or struck an olive-tree trunk. We could see the flash of Farouk's white pants among the trees. The *shabab* were slinging rocks at the soldiers but were hardly close enough to do much harm.

Half a dozen soldiers were kneeling on the road and shooting. We heard the loud pattering of their Uzis. I was holding onto Sena, leaning on her shoulders, frightened that someone was going to be killed.

Most strange to me was the elation rising from the Palestinians. Sena was yelling even as her brother headed into the fray— "*Yaa, habibi! Yaa habibi!* Oh, my dearest! Oh, my dearest!" She kept yelling almost joyfully with the arrival of each new jeep. She continued when the army opened fire on the olive grove where the *shabab* had taken up position. She kept yelling even as the army started shooting at her brother. She was more entranced than scared.

Fawzi, who arrived from work, calmly came over to watch with us. Ratiba had come out, too. Fawzi was sitting silently on the rock with his legs crossed. I asked him urgently why they were not afraid for themselves and for Farouk. He answered that there was no longer any space in their existence for fear.

"Life has choked us already so that we are beyond death," he said.

Observing the battle below with an almost casual eye, Fawzi explained that attempts to stamp out the uprising had not worked because the new generation of Palestinians leading the fight believed freedom from the Israelis was more important than death.

"The Palestinians are ready to die if they must," he said blankly, as if his statement were pure fact and courage and fear were irrelevant.

I could understand his words, but the feeling was alien to me. As Fawzi was calm, I was horrified. Watching the olive grove was like waiting for death in slow motion and perfect focus. We could hear the *shabab* yelling, calling on each other to attack as if the disparity in weaponry did not exist. We also heard the war cry of *"Allahu akbar"* rising from the grove.

Without warning, two big jeeps came barreling down the high road, having hastily cleared a way past their own roadblock, and stopped a couple of hundred yards above us. Sena, Ahmed and I lighted out for the house. All the while I was trying to cover my head with my hands, stumbling on the rocky slope while twisting my hair back so that the soldiers would not notice me. I feared that they would throw me out or, worse, cause the Najajras trouble. But I was getting a taste, albeit from a remove, of what it is like to be a Palestinian—surrounded, outgunned, outmaneuvered, invaded, helpless—those feelings that, twisted hard enough and long enough, turn into anger and then rage.

Within minutes, the soldiers below made their own attack, driving the *shabab* out of the olive grove and back into the village. We could see the soldiers firing and moving, grabbing people and beating them with the stocks of their rifles.

It was at this moment that Ratiba first and then other women lifted the skirts of their *thobes* and ran down the hillside to save the *shabab,* their children.

I joined the commotion, too, getting into a car with SEHAFI signs and driving down into the village. The main road was in an uproar, and it was littered with stones and the remnants of burned tires. Girls, their hands blackened from setting tires ablaze, came rushing up to show me how the soldiers had beaten their arms. A boy shouted almost incoherently about how the soldiers fired tear gas at him. An old woman reenacted how she was struck, forced to her knees and then down onto the ground by the soldiers. Another young boy was in tears because his father, a teacher, was one of three men the soldiers had just arrested.

Everyone seemed confused, including me. I had lost the ability just to observe the goings-on in Nahalin. I was trying to interfere, to show the soldiers that a foreigner was watching and to keep Farouk from harm's way. But when I got down into the village, he and the other young men had vanished. I spotted Ratiba with a clutch of other women on a pathway near the olive grove, but I couldn't get to where she was.

I was stuck among the army vehicles, alternately passing them at high speed and stopping to explain myself. I handed the soldiers my pink Israeli-government-issued press card and yelled that they had to let me through.

"I am sorry, you must get out. Who are you? You must leave," some soldiers shouted at me.

At one point, I was stalled on the road between two jeeps, unable to move either forward or backward. A soldier approached my car and examined my press card at length, checked the expiration date, demanded the correct pronunciation of my name and concluded by saying he had no authority to comment on anything. Only his commander did.

"Where is your commander?" I asked.

"Up there," he answered, pointing at the army camp in the pines on Abu al-Koroun.

Another soldier told me that no one had been hurt seriously, wounded by any bullet, and that the conflict was sparked because the village *shabab* had put boulders in the road to block army vehicles.

Nahalin's first big battle with the Israeli Defense Forces ended without bloodshed on either side. The three arrested men were released after the briefest questioning, their detention having been practically symbolic. But with this exchange of stones and bullets, the village entered the intifada in its small way.

Abu al-Koroun was not the only land being removed from the villagers' ever-dwindling property. Daher al-Matarsiya, the long mountain ridge running to the northwest above the Valley of the Cow, was to be the site of the largest settlement around, a new home for thousands and thousands of religious settlers. Talk of this had been percolating through the village, but it wasn't until the Israeli bulldozers arrived on the ridge that summer that anyone believed the inevitable. Daher al-Matarsiya, whose name means Backside of Matarsiya, had seemed too unlikely a place to build a settlement. The ridge seemed to be too close, sitting as it did halfway between Nahalin and Husan, less than a mile from either village. How could there be space enough for a new community of Israelis? The answer was that the Israelis intended to make the space habitable no matter what. Day and night a squad of soldiers guarded the two large bulldozers that began working one morning near the crest of the ridge.

If what the Israelis had in mind came to pass, the settlement was to have eight thousand homes stretching in apartment blocks from the edge of the Valley of the Cow to the cluster of trailers on the far ridge toward Jerusalem. The big settlement would take the same name as the existing trailer settlement, Betar, and it could eventually bring forty thousand ultra-Orthodox Jewish settlers to the site, ten times the number of Nahalinis. Religious city dwellers would be encouraged to move from Jerusalem with government housing subsidies to compensate for their taking up residence above the Valley of the Cow. I had a hard time imagining these people, dressed in their wide-brimmed black hats and black suits, known for their prayerful studiousness and curled earlocks, living on a mountainside far from their familiar neighborhoods in old Jerusalem.

A new highway was to be built to join the settlement directly to Jerusalem so that the settlers could whisk back and forth in a quarter of an hour and, more importantly, avoid having to drive past Palestinians in the villages, in the Deheisheh refugee camp and in Bethlehem. Betar was to be an island connected by an Israeli road to the safety of Israel proper.

For purposes of establishing the settlement, the Israelis had declared that between the villages lay one thousand acres of "government land." This land legally no longer belonged to the villagers of Nahalin, Husan and a third nearby village called Wadi Fukin. Nahalin was too dejected by its defeat over the land on Abu al-Koroun to contest the Israelis' unilateral declaration. But the villagers of Husan, who were losing a large part of their farmland and pasturage, had hired a lawyer, who fought the case for more than two years. At the end of 1985, the Israelis judged that the land was Israel's. The Palestinians had lost again within a system of land tenure that was awesomely confusing and easily manipulated.

It was a system under which the Palestinians had been regularly losing land and the Israelis gaining it, quietly winning the war for the ultimate prize. The Palestinians never had a state to provide protection for their land. The Israelis had governed the West Bank as well as Gaza since the 1967 war. Before the Israeli rule, the West Bank was occupied by neighboring Jordan, and before that it was administered by the British under an international mandate agreed upon in the aftermath of the First World War. Before the world war, the territory was a fragment of the Ottoman Empire, a far province under Turkish hegemony.

In Ottoman times, land belonged to a village if it was within shouting distance. A loud yodel was enough to prove who owned what. Under the Israeli occupation, proof depended upon a melange of land records and laws. Ownership was decided on the basis of Turkish documents from the time of the Ottomans, documents from the British administration, Jordanian documents and Israeli rules that had been implemented since 1967.

When the Israelis took charge of the West Bank, Palestinians had written titles to one third of the land. The Jordanians had been systematically registering the land so that the Palestinians would have clear proof of ownership. Otherwise, the proof rested on records of tax payments or on crudely drawn Ottoman-era deeds. The mountaintop land on which shepherds grazed their flocks was held in common by villagers.

One of the first things the Israelis did was to put an end to the registering of land in the names of Palestinians. The Israelis then began either buying or, more often, confiscating tracts of land for settlements, military bases and new roads. Palestinians could contest the confiscation of land before a committee composed of Israelis. When they did, they seldom won. The Israelis had two categories under which they classified land for confiscation—land for military use and land that was not being farmed. Military purposes, which included the broad category of Israeli national security, took precedence over other claims. Unfarmed land, even that used daily by shepherds, was termed vacant and therefore available to the state for whatever purposes it deemed necessary. The land on the ridge between Nahalin and Husan was declared Israeli government land on the basis of its not being farmed, even though the Palestinians had argued that their olives grew and their animals grazed there.

It was not long after the battle of the Valley of the Cow that I met with some of Nahalin's *shabab,* who had gathered at Deeb's house in the room with the posters. Deeb wasn't present but I expected him to show up. For the first time, the young men were somewhat relaxed around me. Ever since I had barged into the battle, I noticed what I thought was a thaw in the village's treatment of me. The more time I spent in Nahalin, the more I realized how many of the villagers I didn't know. But many of them knew or guessed, rightly or wrongly, who I was. After the battle, though, more people waved at me, and fewer boys reached down automatically to grab a handful of loose pebbles when they saw me.

The young men had plenty of time on their hands that day, as did all the men of the village, because the Palestinian leadership had called an *idrab*, a general strike during which all commerce was supposed to come to a halt for the day, all public transport to remain immobile and all workers to stay away from jobs in Israel. The strike left many Nahalinis stranded in idle protest against the occupation.

A few of the *shabab* in the room had been in the olive grove during the battle and were talking about it. They were all smoking cigarettes out of shared packs and passing a lighter around. They were still keyed up. One, whom I had not met before, looked at me sharply and asked where my notebook was—where was the proof that I was a writer? I had been trying to keep my notebook out of sight intentionally, so as not to make the villagers nervous. When I needed to jot something down, I did it inconspicuously, as if I were recording a proverb or a recipe, or secretly in the outhouse, as if I were taking my time. Or I would memorize what I wanted to write. I pulled my small notebook out of the pocket of my skirt. The group continued with its rehash of the battle.

"The problem was the distance to the road was too far. We could not hit them hard," one said.

"Then they started shooting," said another. "We attacked but then we had to run. We shouted at them that they were dogs; if they put down their guns and fought us like men, we would show them they were dogs. We laughed at them for hiding behind their guns."

If I had not seen the encounter, I would have thought they

were fabricating the extent of their courage. Up close, they did not look like fighters; they looked like teenagers or college students, wearing summer clothes and sneakers. One of them went to the hallway kitchen and came back with a pot of steaming tea and a tray of glasses. He served the tea around with the formality of a head-waiter.

After the tea was finished, I went for an inspection of the village with some of the *shabab,* who by then were willing to invite me along. It started as a suggestion that I take a walk with them and ended with a miles-long tour of the village's environs and outlying pathways, routes crucial for attacking and escaping army patrols. On the way down into the village, Deeb and Ahmed joined us.

Mustafa Ali, a lanky youth growing his first thick beard and mustache, strode along beside me and acted as a guide. He pointed to Daher al-Matarsiya, where his family's land had been confiscated and, with it, fourteen olive trees and ten plum trees. Now Israeli bulldozers were grinding a wide bench into the mountain slope, and Mustafa was prohibited from going to the land where he used to help his parents harvest olives.

"All I know is that they are surrounding my village," he said and put his hands up in a semblance of choking his neck.

The youngest in the group of seven was Fou'ad, the bright cousin of the Najajras who had trusted me from the first by telling me about the attack on Neve Daniel's fields. Fou'ad was fifteen and frustrated, like Sena, because the schools were not open.

"I want to learn, but it is *mamnua.* It is prohibited," he said, sliding into a mixture of English and Arabic. "The best students, the ones who want to succeed with their lives, are the ones who are being punished the most. The world is *maklube.* It is upside-down."

As we walked down toward the village spring, the *shabab* showed me what land had been taken by the army and by settlements. They named each spring, each ravine, each hollow, each wrinkle, each enduring pleat in the land that they believed was unfairly lost. All this was explained at a fast pace as we descended from the top of the village, not by the road but through the fields and groves. I had trouble keeping up because they were taking pathways that they knew in the dark. Fou'ad was so full of energy that he played a game of leaping from boulder to boulder alongside the path.

We reached the spring in the village and found dozens of Nahalinis lined up for water. Men had donkeys with plastic jerry cans lashed to their sides, women had square plastic jugs to carry on their heads and children held emptied half-gallon soda bottles. About three weeks before, the Israelis had cut off the village's piped-in water supply. No announcement was made, but the villagers thought that the cutoff was a warning to tell Nahalin to stay out of the intifada. The water would be restored in a few days, but until then the villagers survived as they had done in the past. Most were resigned to the difficulty.

"What can we do?" remarked a woman waiting to fill her can. "We can do nothing. The Israelis can do anything they want."

I drank from the pipe spout of the spring, bowing over the water as various Nahalinis watched. The water was clear and quenchingly cold. Mustafa plucked a couple of figs from a grove of trees below the spring, but the fruit was not yet ripe.

Another of the *shabab*, Mohammad, joined us among the fig trees. He was a short, agile youth with a prominently hooked nose. He showed off a rounded tin lettered with Chinese characters and a name in English. Called Tiger Balm, it was a perfumed lotion meant for rubbing aching muscles. Mohammad said it was excellent for cutting the effects of tear gas. Another antidote to tear gas that the Palestinians employed during the intifada was simply holding cut onions to their noses. Underneath Mohammad's shirt was the bulge of his *kefiyeh*, which he had wrapped around his waist and in which he had tucked his slingshot and some carefully chosen stones. In a minute, he could whip out his *kefiyeh*, tie it around his head like a hood so that he could not be recognized, find cover behind a boulder or olive tree and fit a stone into the leather pouch of his slingshot. He was prepared to do battle.

Unless their enmity and their stones were aimed at you, these *shabab* were not at all fearsome. They were polite. Mohammad stayed ahead of me to show me the proper path, and Mustafa followed behind, humming a snatch of an impromptu song, "The figs are not ripe, not ripe, not ripe, and when they grow ripe, the summer will end, the summer will end, the hard times will come, the winter will come, but the fig will stay strong, will stay strong, will stay strong."

We followed a path that skirts the Valley of Father Hair, a serpentine ravine at the base of Daher al-Matarsiya whose earth was planted with grapes and other fruits, and emerged at the road coming down the Valley of the Cow. A power line ran high across this road, and the *shabab* had hurled a Palestininan flag over it, one end weighted with a stone in a sock so that the cloth flapped as a permanent taunt to any army patrol passing beneath. It was too high to remove, short of hiring some daredevil team with a helicopter. A bit farther up the road was an outsize blue and white Israeli flag, flaunting the Star of David in the winds above the site where the bulldozers were working. We could hear the deep growls of the bulldozers' engines and saw a cloud of dust that had been kicked up into the air by their heavy treads.

Near the end of the valley Deeb had stopped to wait for everyone to catch up. He then pointed to each flag. "This is a Jewish flag, and this is a Palestinian flag. There is a war between them, between the oppressor and the oppressed," he said condescendingly as if no one else understood anything about the politics of the intifada.

We could see the canvas top of an army tent. We walked along the edge of the valley and up into the olive grove where the battle with the army had taken place. I was hot and tired by then. So was Ahmed, who had observed the battle rather than participate in it. He was limping along on one sandal, the other having broken a strap. While Ahmed tried to repair his sandal by hammering at it with a stone, the others experimented with hurling and slinging rocks at an imaginary squad of soldiers on the road a couple of hundred yards below. The youths had practiced arms, like all village boys who grew up hunting doves with slingshots and throwing stones to round up errant livestock. For the sake of the intifada, they worked on their aim during the long days without school. It was nigh unto impossible to get a rock as far as the road with any power more than a plink. Seeing this, I understood how fevered was the rashness that propelled the *shabab* into battle.

Deeb, focusing through his wire-rimmed glasses, tried with a sling he borrowed from one of the others. He failed. "This is not effective," he said. Deeb tried until he fumbled and the whole sling went tumbling down the terraces below. Nevertheless, the *shabab* believed they were doing serious battle with the army, just as the Israeli soldiers believed these youths with their slings were dangerous terrorists.

Deeb stayed in the grove to meet with other *shabab*, who were arriving one by one, their *kefiyeh*s making them look like they had rings of fat around the midriffs of their otherwise lean bodies. I went with Ahmed back up to the top of the village, where all seemed bucolic again. The afternoon sun bathed the ridges and valleys in a light finer than any I had ever seen before.

One night not long after the battle at the Valley of the Cow some of the *shabab* went up onto Abu al-Koroun and tore down the fence posts from the newly confiscated land. As a symbolic move—but one sure to aggravate the army—the *shabab* dragged ten of the metal poles back down the mountainside and deposited them by the big mosque, on display for the next Israeli patrol to come through the village. To save face, the army eventually would have to retaliate, to prove that it could control an inconsequential village near Bethlehem on the West Bank.

S I X

Nahalin was looking frayed after its baptismal battle with the army. The battle gave the village *shabab* a sense of being connected with the Palestinian world beyond the Valley of the Cow. With each morning's light, more anti-Israeli and pro-Palestinian slogans were sprayed the length of the main road leading to the village center. The most ancient walls received overlays of angry paint that clashed and overlapped. These graffiti shouted a message: FREEDOM IS COMING LIKE A GALLOPING HORSE. THE FUTURE IS PALESTINE. WE HAVE NO FEAR. The *shabab* who painted the walls were anonymous, their challenges went unsigned. But the expression of anger was real, and the army did not tolerate it.

Soldiers came through the village and ordered the Palestinians to cover the messages, using whatever color paint they had. Any male caught in the street, young or old, was a candidate for the task. Army patrols were coming through Nahalin with more frequency. The soldiers also made the Palestinians tear down the flags the *shabab* had hung.

By midsummer even the children were getting involved. A boy came up to me as I walked up the curving roadway toward the top of the village. He accosted me at the same spot where the children had flung pebbles at me when I was first in the village. The boy's hands were empty. He said that he wanted money to buy spray paint. Red spray paint. I shrugged off the request by saying that he should ask his parents, not a stranger in the street, that it was not proper to bother me with his problems. I sounded harsh and he looked chagrined but defiant. I did not know his name or his age, but I that guessed he was under ten and that he was a member of the Najajra clan.

From Sena Najajra, who had been enthusiastic from the start about my efforts to understand Nahalin, I had learned the basic demography of the village. She explained that Nahalin was divided almost equally into two major clans, the Najajras and the Shakarnas. These were two huge extended families whose members customarily married within the same clan, if not within their closer family of cousins. The two clans had a history of feuds and subfeuds, which arose sporadically and vanished only to arise again in another form.

The Najajras—with plenty of exceptions—made up the better educated and more progressive of the clans. The two clans were divided within the camp of Palestinian politics, with the youths of the Shakarnas siding with Yasir Arafat's mainstream Fatah faction of the PLO and those of the Najajras with Dr. George Habash's more radical Popular Front for the Liberation of Palestine, known in the village simply as Jebha, or the Front. The two PLO factions in the village, although associated with terrorism and irrationality in the West, were as standard as the Democrats and the Republicans in any small American town. Almost every adult, and many who were still children, joined or supported one faction of the PLO or another. The same held for almost every Palestinian community on the West Bank.

It took me a couple of months to catch onto this, though, because Palestinians did not openly admit their politics to strangers.

Belonging to the PLO was a crime under Israeli law. I was learning surprising things about the village by a gradual osmosis, absorbing bits and pieces of information in conversations. The Palestinian manner, polite as it was, was anything but direct. I was in for a stint of chattering and listening that would last over countless glasses of tea.

The Shakarnas had about six hundred men to their name and the Najajras about five hundred. Women and children, given their lowly social status, were not added when measuring clan size or strength. I wanted to know much more about the clans and the village's inner workings, but I continued to refrain from questions that might sound like those of a spy.

I had surmised the spray-paint boy was a Najajra because of the color he wanted. The color adopted by Jebha was red and that by Fatah black. Both colors were represented on Nahalin's walls about equally, with a dash of green signifying the small presence of Islamic fundamentalists.

Not long after my encounter with the boy, I witnessed my first confrontation over graffiti. It was afternoon, and I was at the house of Hanan Najajra, the kindergarten teacher who had been with me at Sheikh Deeb's. She was becoming a friend, someone with whom I could talk about the village. She was a sophisticated village woman, but she did not hide her words behind the formalities that many Palestinians used in defense as much as in courtesy.

Hanan's family's house perched on a slab of natural stone near the village entrance. We were sitting outside on another of the village's many concrete well tops, screened from the road by flowering shrubs and roses typical of the Palestinian penchant for decorative gardens. Hanan's two-year-old nephew, toddling around the top of the well, was the afternoon's chief source of amusement. He was passed around fondly by Hanan's brothers and then set on his feet and encouraged from every direction to play a game that consisted of running from one person's knees to the shelter of another's.

Cries of "*jaysh, jaysh,* army, army" suddenly rang through the afternoon. The child picked up the alarm. "*Jaysh, jaysh,*" he repeated, and across the village the *shabab* whistled.

Three jeeps full of soldiers drove into the village and halted on the main road. They dispersed quickly in bands, banging on doors along the road. We watched as the soldiers forced open a door on the other side of the road.

"That's Abid's house but he's not home," Hanan whispered with the omniscience that came from living in the same confined world day in and day out. "Only his wife."

Abid Musa Shakarna ran one of the vegetable stores, but he was not by inclination or background a village merchant. He was a veteran police official who resigned from his job with the Bethlehem authorities when the intifada began. His wife was a slim woman who had yet to bear children, a condition that was like a bereavement for a Palestinian. She appeared in the doorway, which the soldiers had surrounded. We could not hear what was being said, but the soldiers left after a minute and crossed the street, where they escorted a neighbor out of his house and sent him scurrying to look for paint. The man returned with a bucket and brush and started applying whitewash to the graffiti on the front wall of the former policeman's house.

"He was a policeman and now look what is happening. He is being treated like everyone else," one of Hanan's brothers remarked.

Down the road, a second squad of soldiers had ousted a bearded man from his lodgings. Hanan and the others laughed with a mixture of anger and scorn.

"That's the one we call the Nebi," Hanan said. *Nebi* means "prophet" in Arabic. "His brain is sick, and he thinks he is the prophet Mohammad, the founder of Islam. He talks crazy. Sometimes he talks about Allah, and sometimes he just talks nonsense," she said.

The soldiers had gathered around the man, who was shouting and nodding. Finally he shook his head vehemently and walked away. The soldiers stared after him, befuddled, and then went on to patrol the rest of the main road. When the jeeps left, the graffiti were gone, covered by a layer of newly splotched paint. They would be rewritten in the ensuing nights to the sound of epithets.

"The soldiers are animals," said Hanan with utter conviction.

"You can see," muttered one of her brothers, "these Israelis do not want peace. They want the land but they will receive a war."

"War," repeated another brother as he picked up the toddler again. "War," he said, and the child listened.

Despite the events of the intifada, the villagers went on tending their herds and their crops. Those who had vineyards were bringing in the first grapes of the summer season. Those with jobs in Israel were going to work unless a strike was called. What there was of a Palestinian economy was limping along on half days of business and sales to customers trying to save money. It was a hard time economically, even with infusions of money being smuggled from PLO coffers outside the West Bank. The PLO was making support payments to families with anyone in prison for political activism. The PLO and its factions also paid for lawyers to defend the prisoners in Israel military court, cases that were almost always lost. From within the West Bank, the leadership of the intifada was vocally encouraging Palestinians to kindle their own economy by starting home vegetable plots, like the victory gardens in World War II America, or home agricultural projects, like Fawzi's chicken farm.

Although it was not much of a boast, Fawzi's chicken farm

was the most modern economic structure in Nahalin. The only other enterprise of note was Abu Nimar's stone factory. Fawzi's farm consisted of rows of caged thoroughbred egg layers, an automatic watering system and drop-down egg-collection baskets. The seed money for the chickens came from Bethlehem University, which was trying to better agriculture in the villages.

Although the Catholic university was shut down by military decree, its staff stayed on, waiting and waiting. Some filled their time teaching outside the grounds of the locked university, participating in an underground educational system that was operating in most towns throughout the West Bank in improvised classrooms at homes, mosques, churches and any other buildings where lessons could be imparted secretly. But this out-of-bounds teaching was strictly illegal, and most villagers, even the brave ones, were afraid to go.

Brother Anton, the vice president of the university, and three professors came one day to look at Fawzi's project, a visit that was treated by the family with the gravity of a state ceremony. The house—with its discolored paint and peeling walls, old tile floors and cement outhouse with the door off its hinges—had been scrubbed and rescrubbed. Bunches of wild summer flowers were collected and set in big tin cans, new straw mats were placed on the floor and blankets pegged over the ramshackle closets. A feast of spicy chicken, noodles and rice had been cooked on the gas burner and made ready to be laid out on a table whose ricketiness was disguised with a white lace cloth.

Before lunch, the visiting professors, including the mannerly white-haired Brother Anton, toured the chicken house. It also had been carefully swept and prepared, although no one had taken the trouble to fill in the holes that rats burrowed in the dung-fertile earth, where they had their own feasts on scattered chicken feed.

As we all were dutifully examining the birds and their eggs

and the sturdiness of the cages, a rumpus broke out in a corner of the coop. I saw delicate Ahmed with a heavy stick flailing at something underneath the cages. The chickens were squawking in terror and beating their wings furiously against their cages. Ahmed, in chase of a rat, ducked around the corner and down one of the rows of cages still flailing with a quick grace that only he, a natural actor and dancer, could master. Finally he killed the rat. After delivering the mortal blow and a few extra to make the kill certain, he picked the rat up by the tip of its tail, his arm crooked delicately at the elbow like that of a modern dancer poised to begin a choreographed routine, and carried it out the doorway, past the dean and the professors. Everyone was politely impassive, pretending Ahmed's performance was not worth attention.

On the way back to the house, I took Brother Anton aside, literally leading him by his elbow to a place from which we looked out over the Valley of the Cow. We could see the ground being prepared for the Betar settlement. I told him what I knew, verbally sketching the future—ranks of new buildings marching along the ridge and thousands of settlers coming to live in apartments above the valley. Inevitably there would be battles, episodic but unending, between the arriving Israeli settlers and the inhabitants of the two villages at the top and the bottom of the valley, Husan and Nahalin.

"There is going to be bloodshed over this," I said.

"I know," he answered, and that was all.

I was appealing to him reflexively as one appeals to an authority figure, someone who could bring some sense to this relatively tiny portion of the struggle between the Palestinians and the Israelis for the land. That a high officer of Bethlehem University could somehow intervene was ludicrous, I later realized. After all, his university had been shut down before the intifada; Brother Anton did not have enough clout to keep his own institution running. We watched the bulldozers at work on the ridge before returning to the Najajra house for the sumptuous lunch.

Sena was the only woman besides me who sat at the table. The others served and then cleared the leftovers, which they ate standing in the kitchen with the children.

The conversation was mostly about hens and eggs. Fawzi and the others didn't have much to say about the intifada and Nahalin. When Brother Anton asked how things were, Fawzi answered carefully: "Things will get worse before the battles are over."

S E V E N

According to the calendar, summer had yet to change to fall, but a note of cold was beginning to glide into the deepening nights. A lonely wisp of white vapor would skirt an edge of the sky and then hurry over the horizon, as if sent to scout for the heavy nimbus clouds of the coming rainy season.

I had yet to find rentable lodgings. The man with the empty house told Fawzi he would rather keep chickens there than let it to a foreign woman. Clearly I was unacceptable no matter what. I fell outside the line of what was religiously tolerable. The man was not one of the Sufis, who were mystically easygoing about daily affairs, but one of the old-timers, who disliked any change from the traditional.

Women were not clean creatures in the eyes of the strictest Muslim men, particularly when they menstruated. I had a rude shock early in my time in Nahalin when I reached out to shake the hand of Abu Mazin, an older man who lived midway up the village hillside. His sons, including Fou'ad, who had come along when the *shabab* gave me a tour of the village environs, were bright and outgoing, always eager to stop and talk with me about American or Palestinian politics and culture. Their father, though, was not carefree about tradition. When I held my hand out to Abu Mazin, he stared and abruptly jammed his right hand into his coat. He met my handshake with the lining of his coat pocket so that he wouldn't have to touch me.

I continued to sleep in the houses of various Najajras. They passed me along every several days to another relative as if I were an exotic orphan. But the village was generally friendly, at least outwardly, to my comings and goings. I had learned enough Arabic to feel relaxed in most conversations, and while I missed the meaning of many words, I could follow the line of thought and express myself simply.

My guard against the unexpected was down. I thought all was going fairly well until one afternoon when I was sitting on the cistern top with Sena. She told me point-blank that a faction of the villagers had concluded that I was a spy for the Israelis. There was even talk that I was the blond Israeli who had been a member of the commando squad that assassinated Abu Jihad, Arafat's second in command, at his Tunisian residence earlier in the year. I was flabbergasted.

I waved at the view of Nahalin and asked, "Who would I be after if I were a spy? Abu Thinayn? Father Ears?"

"Why not? Abu Thinayn may be more important than you think," Sena said. She was joking back at me.

"Why didn't anybody tell me that this village had Palestinian leaders living here? Point out the house of Yasir Arafat. Point out the house of Abu Jihad," I kept joking.

It was sheer silliness to believe that the Israelis would post a spy in such an obscure village. Nahalin's *shabab* had not injured a single soldier, and not a single one of them had been transformed into a *shahid*, a "martyr," as the Palestinians reverentially referred to any who died in the cause of the intifada.

When we finally stopped joking, Sena looked at me and explained that one of the religious sheikhs had nailed a sign inside the large mosque that announced I was an Israeli accomplice. I had not been inside either of Nahalin's mosques, because I did not want to irritate the conservative sheikhs, who might take offense at a Christian infidel woman nosing around an Islamic sanctum. Almost as soon as the condemning sign was put up, though, it was torn down by the same young sheikh who had tried to trick me into speaking Hebrew when I was still new to the village.

Having been warned by Sena about the spy rumor, I knew that I had to try to squash it before it grew. I arranged a meeting with the *mukhtar*, Nahalin's equivalent of a mayor, the headman who served as an intermediary between the villagers and the Israeli authorities. He was a man known by every Nahalini and in whose house one of the four extensions to Nahalin's single telephone line rang, when the line worked.

I quickly returned to Jerusalem to marshal proof of my identity, which I had stopped bothering to drag around with me: a book I had written about traveling up the Congo River in Zaire and an assortment of reviews, including one written in Arabic in a British Broadcasting Corporation magazine. The Arabic review had already worked charms with Palestinians in Jerusalem, so I had a couple of dozen copies of it made. I wanted to make sure that as many Nahalinis as possible would see it.

The *mukhtar* invited me into his second-floor reception room, where I sat alone on one of a long row of meeting chairs. Abu Mukhles, the *mukhtar*, faced me, as did the coterie of advisers flanking him. I again was being treated like one of the men. Women served us Arabic coffee in delicate china cups, disappearing and reappearing with plates of deep purple grapes from the village fields.

The men shook hands with me and reseated themselves, saying little and thus forcing me to say a lot. They did not ask questions, so I launched into an explanation of my purpose. I said I wanted to write a book about the region near Bethlehem, a book about how Palestinians lived with the intifada and despite the intifada. I told them that many Americans did not know the difference between a Libyan, an Iranian, an Iraqi and a Palestinian, even though all but a fraction of Palestinians were keenly aware of America's support of Israel. The men nodded at my words.

One asked how long I was going to hang around the village. I answered that I wanted to stay for six months, nine months, maybe a year, that I did not know exactly.

A second man looked at me shrewdly and asked why it was that I did not have any children, implying that something must be wrong or strange or tricky about that. I answered at length, knowing it was crucial that these men believe that a woman might have honest reasons for not bearing children immediately. "In the West, in the United States," I said, "women can have a career first and then have a family later. Many are doing that now. It is possible to do both."

My explanation seemed to be grudgingly accepted, so next I handed around copies of the review in Arabic. The *mukhtar* read his copy slowly. He ordered another round of coffee and then stood up.

"*Ahlan wasahlan.* Welcome," he said.

The simple words rang like a blessing on my ears. I left feeling satisfied that I had salvaged my reputation, confident that no one could persevere in believing me an Israeli spy.

I went back up to the Sobiha neighborhood reassured. I told everyone that the *mukhtar* had given me an official welcome. I had passed a major test, or so I thought.

Planning to spend another night with Ratiba and her family, I was settling in for several hours of tea drinking and talking. Ratiba called me over to where she was squatting on the square of the porch at the front of the house. She had something to say, and my Arabic had improved enough that I could understand her if she repeated herself until I could disentangle the words in her quick sentences. Once I had a glimmer of what she was saying, I wished that I had not understood. She started by saying that Fawzi was her oldest son and therefore invaluable, the pillar of the fatherless family. Then, she continued, the neighbors were talking. They were asking questions about why I was staying so much with the family, why I slept there and whether I was a spy. Why else would anybody want to spend so much time in a village like Nahalin? I thought the question of why anyone would want to dally in Nahalin was my best counterargument to the charge. It should have been obvious that Nahalin was not fascinating enough to draw imported spies, but I was wrong. It was not obvious to the Nahalinis, who thought themselves important enough to merit a secret agent.

I knew enough by then to know the danger of village talk, rumors that went both ways, that someone was collaborating with the Israelis or that someone was organizing for the intifada. Ratiba didn't need to say another word, and she did not. She squatted beside me, squinting into the dusk. The most slender possibility that I could harm this family, whose members had embraced me, was enough.

Having overheard her mother's short speech, Sena intervened and took me down to the well top, where we huddled together on a rickety cot, wrapping ourselves in a blanket shoulder to shoulder. She told me not to listen to her mother, who always worried too much. Her mother, after all, had brought up a family with no husband, so she always fretted over one thing or another. Ibtisam, Sa'ed's wife, came down, too, as did Sa'ed. We were all squeezed together on the cot when Farouk noiselessly appeared from the dark. We had a miniature conference, whose agenda was to comfort me and convince me to stay.

Fawzi arrived at last and insisted that I stay. His argument was that the family would be facing problems of one sort or another with the Israelis anyway; therefore, the opinions of the neighbors were irrelevant. He said some of them, in any case, were collaborators, whose purpose was to make trouble for others.

I asked him why the village was split at a time like this. He explained that collaborators were in danger of being blackmailed by the Shin Bet if they quit their spying. They had begun for various reasons—to earn money, to get permission to travel or or simply to stay out of prison—and they would be devastated publicly if those reasons were revealed.

After all was said, I allowed my concern to wrench me away from the family, and I left well after the sun had gone down. I couldn't stay there for even one more night if other villagers were suspicious of me or if Ratiba was nervous. I didn't want to bring trouble to this family that had trusted me from the first.

I took the high dirt road, worried that some member of the village *shabab* might in the dark mistake me for a settler or a spy. It was ten at night, much too late for any person to be going about normal business in such an isolated place.

Everyone, with the exception of the army, avoided traveling late. Palestinians and Israelis feared each other, the Palestinians wary of army patrols and questionings or worse and the Israelis wary of *shabab* ambushes and stonings or worse. Since the intifada began, the only Israelis other than soldiers who regularly traveled the West Bank were settlers, and they usually carried weapons, including submachine guns issued by the army. Other Israelis, except for a rare reporter or businessman or religious tourist, stopped traveling in the occupied territories, stopped driving to Bethlehem to buy cheap meat and dine on grilled chicken, specialties of the town whose name in Arabic means House of Meat. They stopped going to Jericho to buy the bountiful fruit that grows in the sea-level heat of the Jordan Valley, and they stopped taking pleasure hikes to archaeological sites on the West Bank side of the Green Line.

Driving through the dark of the moonless night, I made it past the crags that stood above Abu Nimar's stone factory and could have made an excellent ambush point. I drove fast toward the main road, hardly slowing to swerve onto yet a new detour the Palestinians had made around the army roadblock near Neve Daniel's fields. I was almost at the junction with the main road at Kilo Sabatash when the car and everything around it was lighted in a glorious split second by a floodlight. I braked and sat bewildered behind the wheel.

It was the Border Police—two oversize jeeps of soldiers, defenders of all borders, both the clear-cut boundaries and the myriad other ones drawn between Israelis and Palestinians. With units of the regular army, the Border Police were responsible for enforcing calm along the edges of the West Bank's 20 refugee camps and its 150 settlements. They also policed Palestinian cities, towns and villages and guarded the roads on which settlers drove through Arab territory.

I had been unfortunate to have hit one of the Border Police's roving checkpoints at the wrong time, much too late at night, and with the wrong label, a red-checked *kefiyeh* on the dashboard. The *kefiyeh* signified that I was sympathetic to the Palestinians. The color, which I favored because it was highly visible to would-be Palestinian attackers, often signified a sympathy for the Jebha faction of the PLO. But it was too late for me to hide the cloth. In the backseat, I had the stack of copies of the book review written in Arabic. I guessed that I was in for trouble; how much I did not know. My mind raced to formulate an explanation, but I couldn't think of a good one.

A couple of soldiers approached each side of the car, and one spotted the Arabic writing. He let out a hoot and shouted to his comrades, who came running. They confiscated the stack and carried the papers gingerly to one of the jeeps as though they had discovered invaluable evidence. Another stood with his gun directly in front of the car to prevent me from bolting.

They had mistaken the reviews for *bayanat,* the leaflets written by the leadership of the uprising. I could only be a secret courier for the Palestinians, caught with the papers that were the lifeblood of the intifada.

"These are *bayanat?*" one demanded.

"No," I said, pausing before explaining something close to the truth. "I am a writer from America. These papers are about a book I wrote about Central Africa."

"Why are you on this road?"

"Why? Oh, I ate dinner with some villagers in Nahalin. That is the village down this road. I had to go around a roadblock, but I am in a hurry to go home to Jerusalem."

A book review in Arabic about the Congo River late at night? A stack of Xeroxes in a car on a back road that no one except a local could possibly know about? The Border Police were definitely puzzled. I could only hope that I had succeeded in casting doubt on their first guess.

I waited in the car. They radioed. They radioed more, to their superiors, I guessed. I assumed they were translating the article and ascertaining whether the Congo River might be the Jordan River, whether the dictatorship in Zaire might be Jordan or Israel, whether the words had ulterior meaning. I made no attempt to interfere, since any blustering might appear defensive. Finally a couple of the soldiers came back around to my window, handed me the reviews and waved me on, much to my relief.

By the time I was back on the main highway heading north past Bethlehem to Jerusalem, it was dangerously late. The road was empty. For the first time, I was grateful for the tall fence that caged off the Deheisheh camp and protected me from it. The last thing I needed after the hassles of the night was to be stoned by refugees.

I was in trouble enough trying to find safe ground. I had fled the village from suspicions that I was in league with the Israelis and ended up suspected by the Israelis of being in league with the Palestinians.

After this, I decided to stay away from Nahalin. I needed time to think about how I was going to deal with the village, and I felt aggrieved. Although I had been struggling to understand Nahalin, the villagers seemed intent on misunderstanding me. I was able to sulk for only a week, though.

I was in my Jerusalem apartment cooking stir-fried vegetables when the village came to me. I was enjoying the idea of eating something other than chicken and rice, while sipping a beer, which I would never do in the village, where alcohol is frowned upon from the depths of Islamic belief. I heard a tapping on the door.

"Min?" I yelled in Arabic. "Who?"

"Shin Bet," a man's voice answered in Hebrew.

When I opened the door, I found three Najajras. All three were dead tired, unwashed and underfed, although they still had the wit to joke.

Farouk looked as if he had lost ten pounds and not slept for many nights. Deeb was sick with some kind of pneumonia from sleeping out in the mountains to hide from the Shin Bet. With nightfall, the late summer chill crept into the rocky backbones of the mountains. Fawzi had lost his sparkle—the light had fled from his face. The three Palestinians were on the run.

Of course I invited them for dinner, but I was nervous about whether any spies might be following them, about what kind of trouble they might be in and about what kind of trouble they might get me in. I was also nervous about the very un-Palestinian fare. Meat was a mandatory part of any supper dish for guests, even if it was horsemeat. It honored one's visitors to serve meat. But I was caught absolutely meatless, having reverted to American low-choles-terol fare. When dinner was served, the Palestinian threesome went heavy on the soy sauce, trying to put some body into the light meal.

They began talking about what had been happening in Nahalin. Five nights before, several army squads had raided the village in search of Palestinians suspected of participating in the intifada in one way or another. Some villagers were roughed up and frightened, but no one was seriously hurt. The three men eating dinner with me were on the army's list. Soldiers had come to the Najajra house. Ahmed was taking his turn at the night-guard duty that the neighborhood had newly organized to watch for trouble from army patrols, the Shin Bet or attacks from collaborators who had been threatening other villagers recently.

At his post on the roof of Deeb's house, Ahmed had heard soldiers coming down from the high road. They were in jeeps with their headlights switched off. Ahmed picked them out from the darkness with his flashlight and impudently marked their progress with his beam. The soldiers were led by an officer who went by the assumed name of Captain Maurice, someone everyone in Nahalin recognized because he was the Shin Bet officer in charge of keeping track of the villages around Bethlehem.

The soldiers had gone charging after skinny Ahmed, and one walloped him on his back with the butt of his rifle, leaving a round bruise. Ahmed, the sensitive, dancing, rat-killing Ahmed, shouted and screamed. He ruined the clandestinity of the raid, enabling those who heard him to flee.

The soldiers trooped into the Najajra house and searched what little was there, opening the closets and scattering a pile of mattresses. They went up onto the roof, where they found young Shawki and demanded that he tell them where his brothers were.

They took him by his arms and legs, threatening to throw him off the roof into space, whereupon Ratiba lunged at them and ruined the gambit.

Some of the soldiers grabbed Sa'ed by his beard and led him down to the house of the *mukhtar*. The soldiers insisted that Sa'ed and the *mukhtar* join in locating the three men who were with me now. Captain Maurice wanted Farouk first of all, saying that the youth must report to military headquarters at Bethlehem. He also demanded to know the source of the money for the chicken farm, suggesting that it might be the illegal PLO. If Farouk did not show up, Captain Maurice implied, the consequences might be dire— soldiers might be coming every night, perhaps damaging the house or wrecking the chicken project. The *mukhtar* listened and then told the Israelis that he had no idea where the wanted men were. Sa'ed gave the same answer.

Soldiers had stayed at the Najajra house for most of the night while others searched other houses for more listed suspects. But none of the villagers cooperated, and the soldiers left without making any arrests.

The next day the army was back in the village, and the *shabab* attacked them from the olive groves. Farouk and a couple of other youths escaped after they were sighted by soldiers and chased for a mile down the long valley that slices away to the south of the village below the Rosh Zurim kibbutz and the Neve Daniel settlement.

At my place in Jerusalem, Farouk could hardly talk. He pushed his chair away from the table without half-finishing his plateful of vegetables. It was impossible to tell whether he was too exhausted by being hunted or whether his cultural standards made the food too unappetizing to stomach. Under other circumstances, I would have been amused at the sight of Palestinian villagers facing a supper of sliced vegetables.

Fawzi and Deeb guessed that Captain Maurice was searching

for Farouk in particular because the Shin Bet detectives had the idea that he knew something about a recent incident in Bethlehem in which two Nahalinis accused of being collaborators were beaten by other Palestinians. The safety of collaborators was a sensitive issue for the Israelis, whose control depended in part upon keeping a portion of the population pliable. That hypothesis would explain why the Najajras had grown so nervous about collaborators.

Farouk didn't say anything. After dinner, he went out onto the veranda to smoke a cigarette and look down the quiet night streets of Arab East Jerusalem, made far more quiet by the intifada. Few Palestinians walked about after dusk, since all the shops and restaurants were long closed and no one wanted to be on the street alone when one of the regular army patrols passed. Deeb, Fawzi and I huddled around the kitchen table. Fawzi and Deeb were lighting cigarette after cigarette, Deeb coughing from being out in the mountain night. Most Palestinian men smoked as if they had no idea it could kill them. But they knew about the hazards of smoking and said that they didn't care, that the times were so difficult it did not matter when they died.

When Farouk returned, I put cushions from the sofas onto the floor for the three men. It was not a breach of etiquette to let them stay on the floor so long as I slept in another room. In any case, I could not turn away people who had invited me to eat and sleep in their homes.

Fawzi sat up with me at the kitchen table. His mind was awake. I asked him why the army was chasing him, too. I could guess that Deeb would be a likely suspect for the Shin Bet, given his record and the opportunities offered by the intifada for further rebelliousness. As for Farouk, I had seen him throwing stones at soldiers, an offense that by itself merited arrest under the rules employed by the Israelis. Fawzi, caretaker of handicapped children, was more difficult to understand.

He began by talking about himself. Fawzi's stare was introspective. His eyes looked to be a solid black when he concentrated. Only when he laughed did light come into his eyes, and he wasn't laughing that night.

Fawzi recounted that he was the first Nahalini to attend Bir Zeit, a Palestinian university north of Jerusalem known for its advocacy of Palestinian rights. He brought ideas with him when he returned to the village and, in order to disseminate them, formed what he called a social club. At its zenith, the club had two hundred members, whose purpose was "to make the village progress."

"We were trying to change the way people thought. The people have been occupied in more than one way, by the Israelis but also by themselves. We worked against problems caused by some of the religious sheikhs, such as the ones who tell the people they can cure a disease if they are given a sheep. We worked against the idea that religious magic can drive off sickness. We worked for women's rights, the right for them to have their own minds. We worked to make people understand that Allah won't solve all their problems."

Fawzi's words did not surprise me. As I had gotten to know the Najajras, I assumed they were more involved in the deeper affairs of the village than they let on. They were different from many Nahalinis if only because they didn't pray at either mosque. Fawzi, it was turning out, was one of the few men in the village who dared to flout Islam.

Fawzi went on to explain that he was forced to dispense with his club after the intifada started. "The Israelis ordered it shut for what they called security reasons."

"Did they explain what the security problem was?" I asked.

"No."

"Did you ask?" I asked.

"No, because they wouldn't have told me anything. They said that it is enough for you to know that what you are doing is against the state of Israel. They said that if they said any more, they, too, will be endangering Israel," he recounted. "Their thinking goes in a circle with no room to spare for the Palestinians."

Fawzi paused, then said, "The village is boiling, not just because of the *jaysh.*"

I nodded, waiting for him to tell me what he wished.

"When you first came to the village during Ramadan, we did not tell you everything that was going on. We were beginning a campaign against the collaborators. These are the people who report to the Israelis. The *shabab* one night wrote their names on the walls of the village, saying that they must go to the mosque and repent."

Fawzi continued with the story. No collaborators renounced their quisling behavior.

"They thought Jebha was responsible for writing the names on the walls. Maybe we were. But they were responsible for worse things. For giving our names to the Shin Bet."

Without coming out and saying it, Fawzi seemed to be telling me that he was a leader within the village intifada, a member of Habash's faction of the PLO.

"The struggle between the collaborators and the others is hot. Four houses have had their windows broken, three belonging to collaborators and one belonging to their relatives. These are the bad people in the village, not the correct people."

"In America, we call them the good guys and the bad guys," I told Fawzi.

"The village is not so simple," he replied. "If you are not a collaborator, you will protect someone in your family who is. That is why we have so much trouble. The families protect their members."

Fawzi explained to me that within the two major clans, there were six subclans or *hamulas*. So tightly intricate was the web of familial relations in the village that an insult or injury to a single villager immediately multiplied throughout his larger family, his *hamula*, to uncles and cousins, sisters and aunts, grandsons and grandmothers. A problem for one made a problem for many, whatever the truth of the matter.

The village grew more complex the more I learned, not less so, as I had once expected. I found myself trying to separate familial from political motives even as I was trying to understand both.

After Fawzi went to bed, I was sleepless. I thought about the last thing he had said. "I will go to prison because I do things differently. So for six months"—the standard detention time for political prisoners—"I will be gone."

I worried that the Shin Bet might have followed Fawzi's car into town or that some clever agent might recognize his license plate. I felt sick with helplessness, unable to do anything, to prove to Captain Maurice that Farouk, whatever he had done, was a gentle youth and to prove that these Palestinians had ideals. I stayed up late waiting for another knock on the door, the tread of footsteps on the stairs, the men coming to take the three away. When I finally got to bed, I twitched at the sounds of the night, the normal sounds of street cats fighting and the wind jostling through the upper leaves of the jasmine bushes in the front garden. I was harboring wanted men.

Other than the inner jangling of my nerves, the night passed peacefully. In the morning, the three left in the old, white Peugeot that Fawzi had bought to drive to work in Jerusalem and to make egg deliveries. They had decided to go home to Nahalin and face what was to come.

After another week, I returned to the village and immediately went up to Ratiba's house, finding there only the women and Shawki. The women were tight-lipped, their faces somber. They weren't afraid of my being there, though. The talk of my being a spy had passed for the time. Rolling up the sleeves of his shirt, Shawki showed me bruises on both his forearms, where he said the soldiers had grabbed him. Sena told me that during the raid the soldiers had woken her from the bed where she slept in an inside room. They prodded her with a wooden club. Captain Maurice entered the room and demanded to know whether she knew who he was. She said, "Yes, you are Maurice."

"Captain Maurice," he corrected.

"Maurice," she repeated.

I was starting to see that the whole family might be blessed or cursed by the same streak of stubbornness.

Ratiba was miserable. She was hunkered down on the cement floor of the visitors' porch, asking blindly, "What can we do? *Shou bidna nsawi?* What can we do?"

It was not Farouk who was arrested immediately, though. It was Deeb. He was last seen by his relatives when he left for Bethlehem with a friend in a car and was dropped off at the El Amal Cinema. Using the single telephone line into Nahalin, Captain Maurice called the village *mukhtar* the same evening to say the Israelis had detained Deeb and still desired Farouk. Deeb was on his way to the Negev prison.

After Deeb's arrest, Farouk stayed away from the family house, sheltering in the caves near the Ain Feres spring below the village. He appeared from time to time, looking worried and thin. As the weeks went by, he began saying he was thinking about allowing the Israelis to catch him.

"If they take me, I have nothing to tell them. If they don't take me, I have to live in the mountains forever. I will have no chance of going to school. Even if they open the schools," he said.

Fawzi decided it was safe to carry on with his job, driving to Jerusalem and back every day. Since Captain Maurice had not taken him yet, he was beginning to think the authorities really did not want him.

E I G H T

Given all that was going on, I resolved to stay away from the high Sobiha neighborhood and the original Najajras for a while. I didn't want to give Ratiba anything else to worry about. Fortunately, other families were willing to offer me a place to sleep. Hilmi Najajra, a brother of Ratiba who lived in the bottom half of Nahalin and had none of her worries, invited me to stay with his family.

Grape season was nearing its end when I first visited Hilmi's house, which sat on the same rise as Hanan's near the low road leading out of the village to the Valley of the Cow. I carried my suitcase, which had grown heavier because I was packing clothes for the cooling nights of late summer, to the house and up a fine stone staircase. No one was there, an odd situation, because Hilmi had a large family. I was descending the stairs, wondering what to do, when one of Hilmi's girls saw me and ran around a corner of the house. I heard Hilmi yelling for me to come. I found him in his element, with his six children and his wife attentively crowding around. Hilmi was directing the production of *dibes*, a grape brew that is like a Palestinian maple syrup. Surplus grapes were plucked from their stems, ground, sieved and then boiled.

A short man radiating energy, Hilmi was stoking fires beneath two blackened caldrons of grape syrup and was stirring one and then the other with a hefty slat. Children were being dispatched to bring wood from a pile chopped from the trimmings of thick old grapevines and were being sent into the house for one thing or another. One of them was ordered to fetch a glass and spoon so that I could be given a sample of the *dibes*. The nearest thing to it I had ever tasted was grape soda, except this was viscous and stuck to my throat. I gagged but quickly assured my host that his *dibes* was delicious, which it was if properly eaten—that is, dipped from a bowl with bread.

Hilmi, who worked as the chief handyman at a girls' school in East Jerusalem, was a creative man. He had designed the facade of his house with an artist's eye. In the front was a garden shaded by grapevines, embellished with tangerine and promegranate trees and topped by a dovecote containing cooing doves. A walkway of polished stone led around the garden to a distant outhouse or back up the steps to a wide porch with ironwork railings. Inside, the space shrank into three rooms and a kitchen, a house simpler than its setting. On the walls were pieces of Hilmi's sporadic artwork, stiff portraits of relatives and graceful renderings of Arabic calligraphy.

I was swept into Hilmi's family. His oldest daughter, Nura, was eighteen, through with high school and living at home with no expectation of progressing to university studies. She was stuck at home, waiting to marry, and was delighted to have someone around other than her siblings. The other children were younger, and Hilmi's only son was under ten, too boyish to throw a stone, much less a rock, more than a hundred feet or so. This was one family that had no *shabab*, no activists, no troops for the intifada.

Hilmi himself was devoted to his family and as apolitical as could be imagined in this land where politics were indivisible from the history of every stone. He wished only that Palestinians and Jews could live in peace.

"I work so that my family can eat," he said with enthusiasm.

"That is enough. I don't want to be rich. Rich people don't sleep well," he said.

"Why?" I asked.

"Because they are always trying to count their money," he continued in a light tone. "They start at one, and they stay up all night to get to six hundred thousand or six million. If they can't count it all, then they imagine they have lost it. No, it is better to be poor like me. I count my children, I get to six and then I can sleep."

From Hilmi's veranda, it was easy to see the main roadway. More layers of mismatched graffiti had grown on the village walls. Some had been splashed with such varieties of lettering and paint that they resembled murals by an abstract artist. On the pavement were black marks where tires had been set ablaze. The electric wires were strung with stones on strings, sticks on strings, cans on strings, shoes on strings—a collection of counterweights for Palestinian flags that had been flown and torn down.

Despite the changing face of the village and the efforts of the shabab to make a stand like their peers in other villages, Nahalin still lagged somewhere well behind the several front lines of the intifada. Neighboring Husan had been under strict curfew for more than a week, after its shabab stoned the security chief of the little Betar trailer settlement. They smashed a window of his passing truck with a rock that struck him in the head and cracked his skull. A squad of soldiers was stationed on the roof of a Husan house, from which they could survey the village and the whole Valley of the Cow. One young man from El Khader, down the road, had been shot by soldiers during a disturbance. He was dead, a shahid. Another from the village of Battir, north of Husan, had also died from army bullet wounds and become known as a martyr to the intifada. The shabab of Battir also regularly stoned Israeli trains on railroad tracks that skirted their village.

Nahalin was relatively calm and Hilmi's house safe from the intifada. After the *dibes* was finished boiling for the day—it would be stewed the next day as well—we retreated into the house for tea and dinner and more tea. The house had no heat except for a portable kerosene cooking stove, whose circular flame was excellent for warming your hands but nothing more. Most of the family ate and slept in the same room, creating a communal warmth that far outstripped the stove's. Hilmi's wife, a quiet and obedient woman when Hilmi was around, served a steaming platter of rice and stuffed cabbage on a low table. We sat on mats on the floor, crowding the circumference of the table, and scooped away with bread until we were full.

Hilmi rose before the evening tea was poured and, without saying anything, hurried into the next room. No one paid any attention, but I was perplexed until I saw that he had started praying, prostrating himself and softly repeating verses from the Koran, his attention directed hundreds of miles away, to Mecca. He was reciting passages from the holy book. A devout Muslim had to pray five times a day no matter what the circumstances. The prayers were a form of both self-discipline and worship.

The room where we ate had the usual set of tall closets arrayed along the length of one wall. A spacious double bed dominated one end of the room and a cabinet television set the other. The television was turned on at dusk and stayed on through dinner and the evening news programs. When it came time to sleep, the parents of the household occupied the bed, and the younger children fell asleep in a tangle of mattresses and pillows laid on the floor at their feet, soothed by the drone of the television that kept playing, sliding from news to an outdated Egyptian movie. The nights were too chilly for anyone, other than a fugitive, to sleep outside anymore.

I slept with the oldest three daughters in a second room.

Nura had a cot against one of the walls. I shared a well-used mattress on a straw rug with Rula, a lanky girl of thirteen. We each had a hard pillow, and we shared a blanket that had absorbed the musky smell of sleeping bodies.

Rather than sleep, Nura wanted to talk, so I sat with her on the cot while the others slumbered. I was trying to get accustomed to the villagers' sense of privacy, or lack of it. My habits kept telling me that I needed a room of my own, a space without noise or other disturbances. Of necessity, I learned that I could fall asleep under most circumstances. Nura told me in whispers about how she had run afoul of village propriety.

She was good-looking, with a regally straight nose and full lips, but she hadn't married because her father and uncles had yet to endorse a groom. She was not allowed to talk to any young men, much less violate the deepest of customs and select her own husband-to-be, although she had landed herself in trouble by trying to do just that. She had fallen in love. Now she was stuck in the house until the time when she would be taken away from her family to become child rearer and servant, if not companion and lover, to a husband with whom she might never have had a lengthy conversation before the wedding.

Three years before Nura had fallen for one of the young men of Nahalin. First, it was considered untoward, even shameful, to fall in love. By not waiting for family approval, she had put her personal desires ahead of the opinion of the elders of the family. Second, the man who had caught Nura's eye was considered lazy, since he had no steady job and had not finished his studies. Knowing the odds were against him, he came to propose anyway and was rejected. The young man stalwartly tried and was rebuffed again. Since then Hilmi had kept a fierce eye on his daughter's comings and goings.

Still enamored, Nura had smuggled notes to the man via a woman friend of hers, refusing to let the love slip away. She sat on the veranda in the afternoons often in tears, and her heart became a great source for village gossip. And then one day it was broken when she learned that her not-so-faithful go-between was engaged to her young man and would marry him within the month. I tried to comfort her, telling her there were plenty of other men in Nahalin, better men, who would not turn and marry her friends. I didn't tell her I thought most women in the village put up with far too much bad treatment.

Almost every dawn in the house started the same way. When Hilmi woke, his wife scrambled from the warmth of the bed to heat tea. The mornings had turned cold, like the nights. She started baking rounds of bread from dough she had made the night before and got the girls up for the chores.

Hilmi left for work in his fifteen-year-old pickup truck, after stopping in the village center to take on workers bound for construction lots in West Jerusalem's growing Israeli neighborhoods. The dashboard of the pickup was emblazoned with Arabic lettering that asked Allah to watch over Hilmi and the truck. He was able to make a few extra shekels a day this way to feed his children. Hilmi was well off compared with other villagers, who worked at sporadic construction jobs for daily wages as low as thirty shekels, a sum translating into fifteen dollars. Hilmi had a steady income as well as a bit of land. He was respected in the village. Although he did nothing to support the intifada, not even seeming to approve of it, he had a reputation for honesty. He got along with everybody. Hilmi was a man who would never spy on his neighbors. As Hilmi's guest, I earned the tolerance of the village children. Some still eyed me in the road, but none stooped for a handful of ammunition.

As soon as Hilmi was gone, the females of the house began their work. The brunt of the housekeeping fell on Nura and Rula. To begin with, the mattresses had to be hauled together and precisely restacked in two piles. The blankets were then collected, folded and also restacked. The same with the pillows. Every pot, pan and cooking utensil used the day before had to be scrubbed to a state of perfection. Every inch of floor in the house had to be washed.

They toiled for hours. Rula carried a mound of kitchenware down the stairs to an outside sink by the garden. The taps gave cold water only. With a bit of soap, a rag, a worn pad of steel wool and the increasingly timorous sunlight of the season, Rula attacked the dishes, emerging later with stacks of gleaming glasses and pots.

Rula had a broad nose and thick lips that left her open to the taunts of other children. They, as well as their parents, were pridefully conscious that theirs was a handsome people with aquiline features and lustrously dark eyes. But Rula bore up under everything, it seemed. She showed off her pair of white sneakers, which her mother bought for her when there was talk of the schools reopening. But the schools stayed closed, except for interludes of a couple of weeks here or a couple of weeks there, and Rula refrained from sullying her good shoes for village purposes.

Since there was no school, the entire family hung around the house after the chores were finished, waiting for Hilmi to return and begin with the grapes again. But a sudden distraction occurred with the discovery of a blooming *narjes*. I was led by the children into Hilmi's front garden, where they grouped to stare at something in the ground. I stared, stood and did not see anything in particular.

"It is a *narjes*," Hilmi's son said as if that should make me understand.

"A *narjes*," he repeated emphatically.

"A *narjes*?" I repeated questioningly.

His sisters giggled. Rula pointed to a diminutive blossom a couple of inches off the ground. I still did not understand.

"I see a little flower," I said.

"Smell it," Rula suggested.

I bent over double in order to get my nose to the ground, and then the miracle of the *narjes* flower revealed itself. The blossom smelled like eighty-proof honeyed perfume.

After the *narjes* was fully appreciated, this smidgen of sweetness in the hard landscape, I decided to take a stroll to Hanan's house, not far from Hilmi's, across a boulder field. I asked Nura to come along. She told me she could not; the rule until she married was that she was not allowed to parade around the village unless escorted by a trustworthy relative.

Hanan had agreed with only a touch of bemusement to teach me the rudiments of Palestinian embroidery. In decades past, no well-raised Palestinian woman was ignorant of the intricate patterns of stitching used to decorate the long *thobe.* The designs, passed from mother to daughter, from aunt to niece, from neighbor to neighbor, were highly stylized. They derived from myths and fables and often incorporated some motif from the environment—a rose, a flower, a bird, a deer, a bird in a tree—patterns repeated a hundredfold in minute cross-stitches. The overall pattern for the dress, though, was simple. A *thobe* is little more than a rectangle with two long sleeves affixed to it. The needlework consisted of six long bands of embroidery running the length of the skirt and a square of solid embroidery defining the bosom. The stitching was often resplendent in threads of crimson, gold, blue and green.

A *thobe* took weeks of labor for an able embroideress to complete, and the finished one was a source of utilitarian pride. A well-made dress had a roomy pocket at the neck, where women stashed their money and valuables during trips. Many women had one *thobe* they stored in the closet for special occasions and another they wore daily and, often, nightly, as a working dress, nightgown and market dress. It was a garment worn unvaryingly through the cold of the winter and the heat of the summer. A good number of younger women were experimenting with Western fashions—some even wore pants—but the older village women stuck with the time-tested *thobe.*

I had a grandiose plan of eventually trying to embroider my own *thobe,* so I began with a rectangle of black cloth, a ball of red thread and Hanan's guidance. I had forgotten my childhood embroidery lessons, and my fingers, accustomed to manipulating pens or playing erratic chords on computer keyboards, had to relearn the cross-stitch. But I had a strong motive; I wanted to attract the attention of the older women, who I predicted would be delighted by my clumsy efforts.

"Keep the thread above the needle," Hanan lectured. "It goes more quickly that way. Over two stitches and then down twice," she advised me until I completed a neat diamond of stitch-work and was praised for pulling the thread well and tightly.

Hanan was an odd village woman. At the age of twenty-five, she had not married. To be single at that age made her an old maid in the village's judgment. She supported herself with her job at the kindergarten in the village center. She previously had worked teaching Arabic studies at a high school, but she lost the job for reasons that were never made entirely clear to her. It might have been because a cousin of hers was arrested for political activities. The kindergarten work was frustrating because the advanced teaching degrees she had earned at Bethlehem University were little use in handling fifty-five children in a couple of bare rooms. The children had no toys with which to play or learn. She and a colleague invented games and stories to compensate for the dearth of props. Hanan was a village woman caught between the past and the present, a present in which women from peasant families could get a university education and attempt to escape the traditions into which they were born.

Hanan never looked as if she lived in Nahalin in a poor

house with no bathroom or bathtub. The family washed in a tin tub with jugs of heated water. Hanan always looked as if she could have been strolling down some Paris boulevard, slim, poised, exactingly dressed, meticulously coiffed and her eyebrows shaped to perfect arches. She wore gold earrings shaped like birds with detailed feathers. But she was by no means on the Champs-Elysées. She walked every morning to the kindergarten, down the dilapidated main roadway. She stepped gracefully over the potholes that had not been filled, the rubbery-stinking soot from burned tires and the animal dung. She ignored the shouts of dozens of playing children and the graffiti.

Hanan and I were walking down this stretch one afternoon when she told me that she was nervous about being seen too much with me. She did not waver, though, when I offered to stay away from her house. She said I should not be intimidated by fears. Villagers, even some of her neighbors had asked her about me and what I was doing. She brought this up as we were heading for my second appointed meeting with the *mukhtar*. I had arranged it because of yet another rumor that was circulating on the insatiable village grapevine that I was spying for the Israelis. By that time, I was somewhat inured to the accusation. I was realizing that no matter what I did, I remained the best piece of gossip to come Nahalin's way for a long time. I also heard that rumors were going around the entire West Bank to the effect that the secret police were disguising themselves as journalists to catch Palestinians off guard. True or not, the rumors were hard to deny. The Shin Bet could forge an American passport easily enough.

But I kept coming back. That was what, I had to keep reminding myself, would make people trust me in this village so set in its secluded ways.

Hanan continued with our conversation as if there were

nothing to worry about. She told me that despite her degrees and her job, she was not free, or liberated in the Western sense, to do as she pleased.

"Things have changed for women in the village, for the younger women. But things are still traditional," she said.

"What do you mean?" I asked. "Traditional. What is that?"

"It means that women must follow the men. They come after the men and must follow the rules of the men. It is more important that a man eats, so he eats first, and then the women eat. The men do not cook. They wait for the women to bring them their food. A married woman does not earn her true status of respect until she has given her husband a son, not a daughter."

Palestinian men frequently went not by their surnames but by the names of their eldest sons: Abu Mohammad—Father of Mohammad, for instance. The same for women: Imm Fawzi—Mother of Fawzi. But never were they known by the name of a daughter, however wonderful or outstanding the girl might be.

One of the more trivial mannerisms illustrating the status of women was the habit many men had of not bothering to use an ashtray. They smoked and flicked their ashes on the cement or stone floor, followed by the cigarette butt. Women cleaned the floors reflexively, washing them every morning and sweeping away dust, mud, food crumbs or ashes several times throughout the day.

"Being traditional means that unmarried women—married women, too, but they are too busy anyway in the house and the fields—cannot be seen talking to men, even casually chatting the way we could at the university. In this village, everybody knows, or at least has heard about, what everybody else is doing. It is impossible to do anything without the whole village knowing.

"You never escape your family. You are never alone," Hanan summarized.

This was true not only because everyone minded everyone

else's business, as was the case of small towns everywhere, but also because the villagers tended to intermarry. Family trees grew into an involuted jungle. In every byway of Nahalin, there was bound to be someone closely related to Hanan's family.

"I am more free than Nura," Hanan said as we walked, "but I have never been free like you to go places where no one dictates what you do, what you say or what you wear. Many people here think that women's minds are weak. Here, even now, I am getting pressure because I refuse to wear a scarf over my head. It offends the very religious ones. They want all the women to dress like fundamentalists. Not everything is going forward with the intifada."

One day I was embroidering with Hanan in her family's spare four-room house. With evening, Hanan switched on fluorescent lights, which were cheap but gave a harshly white glare. Most of the village houses were lighted the same way. Also in the sitting room were several teenage boys from the neighborhood, who were the right age to be termed *shabab*. Hardly a single young man had not done something to aid the intifada, even if it was only throwing nails in the road to puncture Israeli tires. The group at Hanan's was talking about Betar. The settlement had been growing steadily, and a minor skirmish had occurred a couple of days earlier. Some *shabab* had climbed up to the entrance road to Betar and set the dry grass there on fire. Soldiers came down with flashlights to look, but the Palestinians had vanished. The exploit was described to me in the third person. The group at Hanan's knew the details but mentioned no names. The *shabab* had done it.

At Betar, the first blocky buildings were staring down at the village through empty squares where windows would go. The laborers who were chipping the stone and mixing the mortar for Betar were Palestinian West Bankers, men willing to work anywhere for a wage. These workers were brought each day under military escort from Hebron, which was far enough away that they were not familiar to the people of the Bethlehem region. At night, the army stood guard.

As we embroidered, the young men talked about politics, about the Palestinian state and what form it might take. Should the Palestinians settle for a state no bigger than the West Bank and the Gaza Strip, or should they dream of a state that extended all the way across Israel as well, from the River Jordan to the Mediterranean Sea? Would it be possible to include the Israelis with the Palestinians in one combined nonreligious state that permitted citizens of all faiths? There was a consensus that any one of these hypothetical states was better than none. Almost anything looked better than the occupation.

When the evening news came on the television in the next room, we learned that a bus had been firebombed in Jericho. The details were not out yet, only that Israelis had been killed on the West Bank. A vicarious thrill, a sense of victory, transformed the young men's mood. Their fervent wish was that it was soldiers who had died on a transport bus. Everyone in the room agreed that Israelis serving in the army should be prepared to die. The Palestinians had no pity for the army. Later, when the news came that a settler woman and her three children, as well as a soldier who tried to rescue them, died in the bombing, the villagers maintained that Israelis, particularly settlers, would have to die in the intifada.

As I was walking back to Hilmi's later in the evening, picking my way by the light of a half-moon through the field, I heard popping that sounded like live fire coming from beyond the Betar settlement in the direction of Husan. I was becoming used to the possibility of gunfire, but Nahalin was at a safe remove from the shooting. It was less than two miles, a distance that could make all the difference in the superheated round of daily events.

At Hilmi's, the girls brushed and braided my hair and played with the tube of cream I used to keep my lips from cracking in the sun and the night cold. While we were playing, the children spotted the silver cross in the pocket of my skirt.

"I am a Christian," I explained. I had been purposely carrying the cross to prove that I was not an Israeli.

"But I thought you were an American," one of the girls stated in bewilderment. I said that the two were not mutually exclusive, but I was not certain that my point sank in. An American seemed a strange creature filled with power, not like the familiar Christian Palestinians who were living in Bethlehem.

One dawn, once Hilmi's household was awake but before the sun had risen high enough to warm away the chill of the mountain night, I decided that my hair was unbearably dirty, gone too many days without a wash. The kitchen had a spigot of cold water, and I had no other choice. Nura poured cupfuls of cold water over my head as I lathered the shampoo and shivered. All the children watched with glee at the sight of me, for all my strangeness, getting soaked in the sink as any one of them would. Afterward Nura doused me with cologne, her brother awarded me two pieces of spearmint gum and I was ready to go. My plan was to walk down to the village spring with Nura that morning, but I learned that her father had heard about our intention and prohibited her from going. He had left for work.

"I can't go," she said. "You go but I can't. My father doesn't want me to see any man. Even if I am with you, he won't allow me."

That same morning I washed my pajamas. When I returned from the walk, I found that Rula had waited until they were dry, collected them from the railing where I had hung them, folded them without a wrinkle and laid them on our mutual pallet.

NINE

The morning of my first day of olive picking began badly. At half past six, while I was still deep in my dreams, Hilmi's wife slammed open the door to the room where I was sleeping with the three eldest girls of the family.

"You are late already, and you have not even gotten up," she yelled at us. "Your grandmother is already in the olives. She is old and sick, and she has started working while you all are lying there sleeping. Shame. Shame. Shame."

The last thing I wanted to do was get up, but I did, and with alacrity. I was not happy at being rousted, but I was pleased that I was being treated like everyone else. It was another step toward understanding how the village worked. With autumn, almost everyone helped bring in the olive harvest, except for men preoccupied with jobs.

We dressed and rushed out of the house, the four of us and Hilmi's young son, who had been asleep in the adjoining room. With the accusation of sluggardliness ringing in our ears, we went without breakfast, an uncommon experience in this village, where I usually was not allowed to move without first stopping to enjoy a glass of tea. We took with us a plastic bag of bread, tomatoes and cucumbers, as well as a plastic jug of water, for the days were still hot even though the nights were cold. It was the end of September, and the season had barely begun. Although the olives were still green in the trees and bitter to the taste, they were ripe enough that if you squeezed one, it produced a viscous white oil.

The trees we were to pick were in a grove a good distance out from the village, near the foot of Abu al-Koroun. They were on a wide dirt terrace among other trees of the same age, forty years. That meant they had been planted about the time of the first Arab-Israeli War. They were not old in comparison with others on the West Bank, but they were substantial trees, the years beginning to accrue in the gnarls of their trunks. The leaves of the trees were a dusty green, having survived another rainless summer.

There are millions of olive trees on the West Bank, and I had been wondering how each family knew which trees it owned and which it did not. The terraces were not regular, the groves were not fenced and the trees made no rows. All the trees looked the same to me, some larger and more gnarled, but not memorably so. I learned quickly how ridiculous was my puzzlement. For once you harvested an olive tree, you remembered it. A tree of any significant age, in a good season—and this was turning out to be a good year for olives—would bear thousands upon thousands of fruits. The more venerable the tree, the more time-consuming its harvest.

The grandmother, Halima Najajra, was at work when we arrived. She was stout and unflagging despite a rheumatism that made her knees ache with every step and every bend. And she was wearing the customary and cumbersome black ankle-length and wrist-length *thobe*.

Two tasks went into harvesting an olive tree—picking and gathering. Both were simple. The pickers climbed into the trees, with or without the help of ladders, and plucked the olives off the branches to shower them by the tens, by the hundreds and, ultimately, by the thousands onto the ground. The gatherers stooped, sat, squatted and crawled as they collected the olives into plastic buckets. The buckets were emptied into gunnysacks and filled again.

Our work began happily enough. The children were singing songs and everyone was talking. We were joined by five more of Halima's grandchildren, who came down from different houses.

The lyrics of one whimsical song went "Your hair is like an umbrella, and your eyes are like an airplane on the attack."

But as the sun rose and the day gathered heat and the olives kept raining down from the hands of the pickers, I began to realize that this was not just work, it was hard work. The olives had to be picked up one by one from among the dried clods of dirt left from the plowing of the terrace, which was still done by donkey power. This particular terrace and a line of others were covered also with clods of dried cow dung from the time two years earlier when Rosh Zurim, the ridgetop Israeli kibbutz closest to the village, let slide a river of liquid manure from the lake by its cow barns. The kibbutz claimed the manure slide, which damaged a swath of Nahalin grape fields, was accidental. The villagers believed it was not.

Whether the clods were dirt or dung made little difference to me. Every time I gathered a hundred olives, another hundred lay before me. With the others, I sat, then crawled, then squatted, trying impossibly to find a comfortable position.

The first hour I found fascinating. The second hour, less so. The third, monotonous. The fourth, numbing.

The monotony was briefly broken when Naim Najajra showed up to help a little and talk a lot. He was Ratiba and Hilmi's youngest brother. Naim had a mind bubbling with thoughts. He was in his late twenties and still unmarried, a rare state, because he wanted to find a woman who could share his mind as well as the home he was building while the elementary school where he taught remained closed.

Naim had such a surplus of time that he dreamed up and was

executing an elaborate color scheme for the inside walls of his visitors' parlor—pink triangles inset with bluish cloudlike designs. He wanted some day to study for a doctorate in philosophy. But he was far from that, his university studies stalled by the intifada. One of his courses was interrupted in the middle of analyzing Joseph Conrad's *Heart of Darkness*. This book was the first thing he talked to me about when I met him. His face lighted up when I told him I had read the book.

"Joseph Conrad had an excellent mind. This book is a story within a story within a story. We were studying it page by page, watching how he was using his stories to talk about the human condition and the human soul. But we never finished," he said.

When he stopped by the olive grove, though, Naim had American politics, not English literature, on his mind. He had been listening to the news about the latest presidential debates.

"Bush sounds to be smarter than Dukakis," Naim said as he began picking olives from the lower branches. "But neither of them sounds so smart. It brings a question to my mind. Why is it that there are only two political parties in the United States? It is such a large country. Israel is a small country, and it has many political parties. I think it would be a good idea for the Americans to have more parties. Then I think about the West Bank and the fact that it is not allowed to have any parties or any elections. I also think I think too much. The human mind may not be capable of understanding why the world works as it does."

A cousin of Naim who had also strolled down to the grove was listening and interjected, "You are sounding like you swallowed a radio today."

More clever than us that day, Naim and his cousin managed to find excuses to leave the grove without putting in more than a few handfuls of work. They left us with the midday heat, by which time we were all tired of olives. The youngest girl had scratched her leg from climbing in the trees, and Nura's fingers were bleeding from holding onto the scaly bark of the olive branches. We paused for a short while to have our lunch and to quench our thirst with great gulps of warm water from the jug.

By early afternoon, I had lost my notion that harvesting olives had a romance to it. The more ancient the tree, the more magnificently outflung its knotted limbs, the more bountiful its fruits, the more work it demanded.

That day we picked three trees and filled two waist-high sacks with olives. When we finished the last tree, Grandmother Halima made no bones about quitting. She took an empty sack, spread it on the ground and lay down flat on her back, groaning as she straightened each joint. She put an empty plastic water bottle under her head as a pillow and ordered one of the boys to go fetch the donkey to carry the olives. My back ached, too, so I followed her example.

Many Palestinians had started picking earlier than usual, before the customary wait for the first wintery rain to wash the trees clean. The harvest was a serious business, for olives and olive oil could be worth as much as one hundred million dollars a year, one third of the West Bank's produce. The greener olives produced less oil, but the West Bankers feared that the Israeli authorities might make good on recent threats of preventing them from harvesting and taking their olives to the presses if their villages were causing too much trouble.

Already the village of Bidya, a relatively large community on the northern West Bank, had the clamp put on its olive harvest. This punishment came after the village *mukhtar*, who was widely hated by the villagers for engaging in the sale of local land to Israeli settlers, was gunned down in his car. To keep its hold on the West Bank, Israel had to try to protect Palestinians like the Bidya leader who cooperated with its policies. In at least ten villages, soldiers had interrupted the harvest either by imposing curfews or by simply ordering Palestinians out of their groves.

The harvest began in October and continued into November as the olives finished ripening from green to green-purple to purplish black. The villagers harvested every day until their family trees were clean, and then they moved to the trees of their extended families. In every direction, up the slopes and down the ravines, women and children, grandparents and younger men were working on the trees, hauling ladders from terrace to terrace, filling gunnysack after gunnysack with sorted olives. It was a time for cooperation, at least within the clans. The Najajras helped the Najajras, and the Shakarnas helped the Shakarnas.

It was in the olive groves that I made my first acquaintance with some Shakarnas. One afternoon when I was trudging back from the groves, I was overtaken by a man and a woman, both of them dapperly dressed. The man carefully tapped me on the shoulder as I was walking. When I turned to him, he gave me a half bow, finished a flourish with his arm and said, "Abu Marwan here. Professor of geography at Arrub Institute." He was wearing a green sport jacket and gray woolen pants. His hair was cropped to a military-looking bristle. He bowed in the direction of the woman. "Imm Marwan also. Headmistress at Nahalin girls' school for elementary and preparatory students," he said. Imm Marwan, his wife, was wearing a flowered dress and patent-leather shoes. Her hair was tucked away behind a scarf.

Abu Marwan kept chatting all the way back to the village and his house. "This is the longest summer vacation we have ever had, and it's not even summer anymore," he said, sarcastically referring to the closed schools. "This olive picking is the only work we can do now. I have gone from professor to laborer. What will come next?"

Imm Marwan broke into the conversation. Most village

women stayed quiet when their husbands were talking, but she was an exception to the rule. "If our students are not allowed to study," she said, "this is the worst thing that the Israelis can do to hurt us. The Palestinians cannot live without schools. The minds of our children will be lost."

I agreed. The closing of the schools was hard on the Palestinians, since the one thing they had, even when they were made refugees, was their education, their learning, their ability to make money as professionals in the rest of the Arab world. They worked as engineers in the Gulf sheikhdoms, as bureaucrats in Jordan, as doctors in Saudi Arabia; but they often were unable to find suitable jobs on the West Bank, where the economy had been kept technologically underdeveloped during the times of occupation. Because of their learning and their wandering, the Palestinians sometimes were called the Jews of the Arab world.

"What can we do?" Imm Marwan asked, shrugging.

Abu Marwan invited me into his house, which nestled in a walled garden on the road leading to the top of the village. The visitors' room was a glassed-in space furnished with mats and pillows on the floor as well as upright chairs. I took off my shoes at the door as was polite when entering a Palestinian house where mats were furniture. Abu Marwan stretched out easily on the cushions and began talking very seriously while I sat stiffly in a chair.

"I have noticed that you are always with Najajras," he said. "Why do you ignore the Shakarnas? We are half of the village. Do you think the Shakarnas are bad?"

Flustered, I answered. "Oh, no. I want to understand everyone in Nahalin. It is a mistake to think I don't want to talk to Shakarnas. It is only that the Najajras were the first people I met."

"The Shakarnas are good. You see them going to the mosque," he said.

Abu Marwan himself was not on the religious extreme, but

he was dutiful about his prayers and about going to the mosque on Friday, the holy day. He always wore a tie, which made him stand out from the other prayer goers, who were wrapped in their long robes or cloaks.

After this talk, I made a point of visiting Abu Marwan. I also went olive picking with his family, a day that was relatively easy because ten people worked together. A woman brought us tea from the village, balancing the glasses on a tray all the way down a wide ravine. With many hands, a big tree could be picked in the inspiring speed of one hour. It was later in the season, and the olives were turning darker.

I listened to Abu Marwan as we gathered olives from sacking spread around the bole of a tree, a slight improvement from sitting on the dirt. Two boys in the branches above were sending down a plump rain of olives on us and all around us.

Abu Marwan said that olive trees could grow to be five hundred years old and that they were called the tree of the poor because they did not need constant manicuring. They grew by themselves, bearing fruit each year. He said they were known as the trees especially blessed by Allah.

He talked about the elections coming up in Israel rather than those in the United States.

Although as a West Banker he could not vote, he said he was rooting for Yitzhak Shamir for prime minister. His reasoning was not without its logic. He wanted the more conservative Shamir to beat Shimon Perez because he thought having the right wing in power would make matters for the Palestinians worse, bringing stricter military measures and more settlements, and therefore further inflame the intifada and force change ultimately. That, he argued, would be better than the current state of limbo. He quoted a proverb: "Being anywhere is better than dangling between heaven and earth."

Also with us that day was Abu Marwan's father, a white-bearded man dressed in a loose brown suit cinched with a wide leather belt in which he had stuck a pruning saw. Everyone respectfully waited for him to direct the group from tree to tree.

The old man pruned as we went, his sawing making a patient sound and sending olive-wood dust down onto the gatherers and into the hair of the children who were not wearing head scarves. Overhead several jets whined by, tearing the soft sounds of the hillsides, flying past on training exercises or perhaps heading north to Lebanon on one of the bombing runs made sporadically against Palestinian guerrilla bases. The war in Lebanon was different because the Palestinians there fought with guns, grenades and rockets—not with stones like the West Bank *shabab*. The most recent air raids were reprisals for a suicide car bombing that killed Israeli soldiers in southern Lebanon. The jets were so high they were invisible.

As we worked, I sensed something of what it means to be tribal, something of human collectivity, an unquestionable feeling of belonging to a group with a common and vital purpose. Olives into the bucket, olives into the bucket, everyone with the same intent, gathering the olives into hands, then buckets, then bags, many into one.

"If only the Jews and the Arabs mixed like olives," Abu Marwan remarked.

Abu Marwan was my entrance to the Shakarna side of the village. I met more Shakarnas later in the autumn when I was walking toward the top of the village past a couple of shops. The ones I met at first were among the leaders of Nahalin and were more open than many of their relatives.

"*Faddali,*" a deep voice said from inside a vegetable shop. "Welcome. Enter."

I went to the door of the shop and peered inside, but at first I could see little in the gloom. The voice belonged to Abid Musa Shakarna, the childless police detective who had resigned in the first wave of the intifada and whose house was near Hanan Najajra's. When my eyes adjusted to the cool shade of the shop, I saw Abid, a large, strongly built man, sitting at a desk that looked as if it could have come from a police station. At the rear of the shop, two men were playing backgammon and two others were watching over their shoulders. Crates of grapes, onions, potatoes and apples lined the sides of the shop, and a counter was heaped with used clothing, a mercantile afterthought among the vegetables. The foursome at the rear glanced up and then riveted their eyes again on the board as the dice clattered against the inlaid wood.

"I am Helen," I said, addressing myself to Abid.

My eyes had adjusted to the light, and I could see his squarish face, blunt nose and eyes that were unusually blue. I was struck by how much he still resembled a detective despite the wooden boxes of squash, carrots, pears and figs that replaced the filing cabinets of his former office. He had positioned a desk in the middle of the space and on it put the shop scales. When he was paid for a bunch of vegetables, he slid open the top right-hand drawer with a quick expertise, deposited the coins and slid it shut immediately, as if it contained investigative reports or other secret documents.

Despite his demeanor, Abid turned out to be talkative, particularly about his problems. I was learning that almost every Palestinian had a grievance and, more often, a litany of grievances.

Abid had been one of six Nahalinis who resigned en masse from the Bethlehem police force at the behest of the intifada leadership, which ordered all the Palestinian law-enforcement officials working for the Israeli military government in the occupied territories to quit their work. Many other Palestinian policemen did the same, refusing to work for the same govermental apparatus that was fighting the intifada. They were blackballed from taking any jobs over the Green Line in Israel. Abid, who was a senior detective, had little alternative but to employ himself.

"I am a poor man now," he said. "I sell old clothes and eggplant for a few shekels. It is enough to live on. I have no car. I have no luxury, but this is not why I am unhappy. What do I have to look forward to in the morning when I get up? Selling vegetables? My mind is as dead as an eggplant. Backgammon, the throw of the dice, that is the only intellectual challenge that I am witness to, day after day. But I have become like the other Palestinians. There is nothing more the Israelis can take from me. If they want to take my house, that would be all. And if they want to take it, what can I do?"

As Abid was holding forth, a deep explosion rocked the shop. I was caught by surprise. Abid did not budge.

"The settlement," he explained.

The Israelis were beginning to blast into the bedrock of Daher al-Matarsiya. The explosions would become more frequent in the coming months. I had stopped jumping at the sonic booms from the Israeli fighter planes that periodically ripped through the sky, but the blasting was closer and louder.

The vegetables had resettled in their crates when Abid Musa's mother came to visit, setting herself down in a chair by the desk. She was large, dressed in a heavily embroidered *thobe* and the skin of her face was wrinkled like that of an elephant. But her expression was that of an angel who had been working in the sun rather than sitting on a cloud. When she greeted me, a hundred wrinkles danced upward from her mouth to her eyes.

"Welcome," she said, as if she had known me all her life. "Welcome."

Looking at Abid, she questioned, "Where is the coffee for your guest?" Custom dictated that I be served as quickly as possible.

"I have sent for it. I have not delayed," the son promised his mother.

Children came with small handfuls of shekels and left with bags of vegetables. When the coffee arrived, the old woman announced that in the coming year she was planning to make the hajj, as Sheikh Deeb had. First she would cross the bridge into Jordan and then take a bus the long thousand miles south through the deserts of Saudi Arabia to Mecca. Well in advance, she was relishing the journey to Islam's most sacred place. She still had to wait through the autumn, the winter and part of the coming spring.

"When I make the hajj, I will do my duty to Allah, and I will smile," she said.

We drank our coffee in silence. Not talking, leaving gaps of time in a conversation, was permissible according to the Palestinian etiquette. I was not accustomed to it and tried to come up with something to say. I inquired about the woman's other children.

She discovered that I had not met Mohammad, her eldest son, and immediately escorted me several dozen yards up the road to a second shop, which I had also passed many times on my walks through the village.

The man standing behind the wooden counter exuded dignity. The shelves around him held tins of meat, packages of paper diapers, bags of candies, bottles of cola and plastic jugs of syrup for dilution into orange or lemon drink. On the floor by a steel freezer containing milk and ice cream were sacks of staples like rice.

This was Mohammad, better known as Abu Jafer, heir apparent to the chieftancy of the largest of the Shakarna subclans. His *hamula* had one thousand people. Even though Abu Jafer was in his late thirties, his hair and beard already were graying, and he had risen to take on the role of settling disputes, overseeing *sulhas*.

Rather than resort to an outside system of courts, Palestinian villagers for many, many years dealt with their own disagreements. A *sulha* was a meeting convened to find a compromise, and the man presiding had to have the respect of his clan. Abu Jafer had gained that at an early age.

When he was not settling arguments or tending his store, he taught English in Nahalin's school. His mastery of the language was all but perfect.

He immediately took me upstairs to the large room in his house where he held *sulha*s and drew me into conversation. Several of his seven children listened respectfully. He knew who I was and said he had argued with other villagers about my purpose in Nahalin.

"Why would the Israelis send a spy to Nahalin?" he asked himself. "The answer is they would not. First of all, they have enough Palestinian spies who report to them, and second of all there is nothing of note to spy upon here."

He told me the suspicion would never completely fade away, though, no matter what I did. I argued with him, saying that since everyone in the village had been able to observe my modest conduct and had no basis to believe that I was asking troublesome questions, the suspicion would die a natural death.

"You are smart. You are educated, but you cannot forget that these people in this village have their own patterns of thinking, and those patterns are not for you to change. They have their perspective and their beliefs. Many will never understand what a single woman does walking around Nahalin. This is not something any father would approve of his daughter's doing. It is not the way of villagers."

Abu Jafer's words were not news to me, but his bluntness made me think. I had to me more careful. As if he were reading my thoughts, Abu Jafer started talking about me.

"This must be hard for you, a stranger coming to a strange

place with a strange language, wanting to discover and finding it is more difficult with each step, because with each step you sink deeper into a world you will never be able to comprehend. At the best, you will be able to see a little of it, and in order to do even that, you will be lonely, and you will have to suffer a little. You Americans are not so accustomed to suffering as we are. You endure suspicion and we endure occupation."

His words were so much to the point that all I could do was nod.

"This is a war we are living in. You are watching it and we are sitting in it. It is a war that is easy to see when the army is firing bullets, when blood darkens the ground, when the *shabab* attack the Israeli cars, when shattered glass wounds soldiers or mothers. It is a war that is easy to see if you are a bird flying over the West Bank and looking down at the ground. Everywhere, from the north to the south, you see the mountains are changing, the hills that once were stones or fields are not growing wheat; they are growing apartment buildings for the Israeli settlers. It is a war that is easy to experience if you are a Palestinian and you daily face the Israeli regulations, if you cannot go anywhere without your *hawiya,* if you cannot build a house without a permit, if you cannot plant a vineyard without a permit, if you cannot dig a new well without a permit, if you cannot own a book if the Israel censor disapproves it, if you cannot teach the name of Palestine in the schools, if you cannot go to Jerusalem to work and also sleep there, if you cannot drive down the road without soldiers stopping you and searching your car. The Palestinians use stones, and the Israelis use regulations, which make no sound when they hit you."

T E N

In mid-October, the Shin Bet grabbed Farouk, hauled him away with an escort of soldiers and that was that. The first day went by and the second without word, without even a hint of what the Israelis were doing with him. By the second day, a murky cloud of anxiety had settled on the Najajra compound. No one knew where he was or how he was being treated. Was he being interrogated? Was he being beaten? Was he breaking down and confessing to acts he may or may not have committed? Did the Israelis take him because they thought he was soft and would give information, never having been imprisoned before, or because he might know something about the beating of the collaborators in Bethlehem?

Ratiba refused to eat anything except a piece of *taboun.* She chewed the bread grudgingly, as if its taste were repugnant. She squatted for hour after hour on the floor of the guest porch with her head between her hands, sunk in distress, while the rest of the family and assorted relatives sat around on the chairs and worried out loud. Shawki came in from the yard of the compound and reported that the rabbits also were refusing to eat; they had never been fed by anyone other than Farouk.

The details of how he was arrested were discussed and rediscussed. At one in the morning, Farouk had come back to the house from the mountains where he had been hiding for weeks. Sena fixed him a good breakfast, and he changed his clothes, putting on his best jacket because he sensed something might happen. Then he went to sit with Sena in the shade of a couple of young olive trees by a stone wall, a nook the Najajras used as a place for thinking or just getting away from the interminable public hubbub of extended-family life. They talked.

"I told him all my problems," Sena said. "He is my best friend. He is the person I tell my confidences to."

Farouk went back to the house to rest. The family believed that one of the neighbors saw Farouk enter the house—one of those families they suspected of being collaborators—and secretly reported it to the Israelis, maybe by hastily driving into Bethlehem or maybe with a walkie-talkie the Shin Bet had provided.

Shortly before midday a long Mercedes *service*, a taxi with West Bank license plates rather than yellow Jerusalem ones, came crunching down the gravelly lane to the Najajras' house. The men inside the Mercedes were wearing *kefiyeh*s like Arabs. But they were from the Shin Bet. They shouted that they wanted Farouk to come out. Three jeeploads of soldiers pulled up within minutes, and the soldiers surrounded the house. Farouk came out and found himself facing Captain Maurice.

"I want Farouk Najajra," Maurice said.

"I am Farouk," Farouk said.

Maurice looked startled, suddenly face-to-face with his not-so-fearsome-looking quarry. "Show me your *hawiya*," he ordered.

Farouk gave him the *hawiya*. Maurice took it, compared the photograph on it with the person and nodded.

The Israelis handcuffed Farouk, wrapped his jacket over his head so that he could not see, bundled him into one of the jeeps and left.

Ratiba shouted after the disappearing jeeps. "Remember, you are a man and they are dogs."

Afterward she had nothing more than a promise she had made to her son. She had told him when he was in hiding that if he were imprisoned, she would try to buy him a calf on his return. This was no small promise, for calves were expensive, costing several hundred dollars.

Fawzi asked me to help find his brother. I did whatever I could, starting at the old Arab mansion in East Jerusalem that headquartered the International Committee of the Red Cross. It was the one organization whose delegates were allowed to pay regular visits to the jails where the thousands of Palestinian political prisoners were kept.

A clerk at the front desk, who spent her days listening to the miseries of one desperate family after another, told me matter-of-factly that the Red Cross probably would not be able to see Farouk for two weeks and might not even find him before then. The Red Cross was not allowed to visit prisoners for the first fourteen days of their arrest, although the organization was supposed to be notified of all arrests within twelve days. Making matters more difficult, the delegates of the Red Cross who visited prisons were mired in nearly limitless work.

It was explained to me more than once that there was little the Red Cross could do to expedite anything. If luck was with Farouk, one of the delegates might locate him by chance within several days. If luck was not with Farouk, it could be longer. If the Israelis decided to question the prisoner, all bets were off. He could be held for months without anyone seeing him except special Red Cross officials assigned to visit the innermost part of the prison system, the interrogation cells.

I was told, like everybody else, to wait, which I did not do. I took my address book, filled with names of important people—diplomatic officials, officials at international relief organizations, human rights experts and accomplished lawyers—and started telephoning. I extracted promises that inquiries on Farouk's behalf would be made of authorities in the military government and the highest-ranking personages in the Red Cross. I had hope, a lot more than Farouk's family; I was new to the Israeli detention system.

I kept going back to the Red Cross. Five days after Farouk was taken, no information had turned up. This was normal, I was told again. As the days wore on, all anybody could tell me was that Farouk had not been located in any of the "general sections" of the prisons, where the mass of political detainees were held. This negative information indicated that he might be in one of the interrogation sections. In the press of the intifada, with the army's having detained so many Palestinians—most of them young men but ranging in age from thirteen-year-olds to septuagenarians—prisoners were hard to locate.

I went back to the Najajras' to unhappily report my lack of progress. I found Ratiba alone in the house. She was sitting on one of the cots and crying, not hard, just so the tears were seeping out of her eyes.

She was repeating the same thing. "But where is he? Where is he? I don't know where he is."

I sat next to her and tried to comfort her. I noticed how hard and stubbed her hands were, calloused from fieldwork and housework, the plain tasks of living in Nahalin. The doors to the closets were hanging open at sloppy, dejected angles, a breach in the usual cramped orderliness of the Najajra house. When I went outside, I saw three dead chickens in a neglected heap by the door to the hen shed. A dome of gloom had settled over the house and the compound. Others in the family had gone to Husan and Battir, seeking information from those Palestinians whose sons were in prison and might know something about Farouk. I remembered how different things had been when I first met this family. It was early summer, before the intifada, and the Najajras were sitting in the sun-filled guest porch on the same battered furniture, but laughing about a silver balloon that had drifted down from one of the kibbutzim, a balloon with Hebrew writing on it floating near the ceiling.

Back in East Jerusalem I visited the office of Jonathan Kuttab, a Palestinian lawyer with a degree from the University of Virginia Law School. He was a member of the American Bar Association and had practiced on Wall Street, specializing in leveraged leasing, before returning home. I went looking for advice on what to do about Farouk. Since his return, Kuttab practiced law in both Israeli courts and the military courts in the West Bank that heard the cases of political prisoners like Farouk. He was a witty man who did not mince words.

"The first thing you have to get through your head is that the system here does not intrinsically resemble the American one. On the surface, it might look somewhat similar. You have a judge; you have a prosecutor; you have charges against the accused, or rather, sometimes you have charges against the accused. If the charges are deemed of interest to Israel's national security, they can be kept secret. It is impossible to practice law rigorously when you, acting as the defendant's lawyer, cannot see the sheet of charges against him because revealing them would allegedly damage the security of Israel. Practicing law in the military courts is like playing tennis with your eyes closed. Basically it comes down to one simple reality: the law is what the Israelis governing the West Bank make of it."

"What can be done?" I asked.

"Not much. Send him a letter in prison. Tell him his family is well. I myself can't get much done. I argue for the record. I argue to get sentences reduced. I almost never win a case."

If the Israelis wanted somebody, they took him and kept him. If they had a prisoner for eighteen days without charging him or bringing him to trial, they could renew his detention with the approval of a military judge appointed by the military administration. The judge came to the prison, and the prisoner was brought before him there, often without a lawyer to represent him. The judge usually decided whether to renew the detention on information supplied by a military prosecutor. The prisoner had little or no chance to argue about what was happening.

Additionally, the Israeli authorities on the West Bank had implemented "administrative detention," a method under which Palestinians could be imprisoned without charge, evidence or trial for six months. The reasons for the arrests and imprisonments were not made public but kept in a secret file, again based on the argument that the information could endanger Israel. Most administrative detainees were suspected of pro-Palestinian political activity, and most ended up, like Deeb, in the Ansar Three prison in the Negev Desert.

It was two weeks after Farouk was arrested that Fawzi came to me distraught one afternoon to tell me that he had heard some bad news. Soldiers had beaten Farouk on the high back road immediately after they arrested him. A farmer had witnessed the beating and, after ten days of worrying about what he had seen, had come to Fawzi to tell him. No one had yet been able to locate Farouk, neither the Red Cross officials nor a lawyer from Bethlehem whom Fawzi had hired.

Fawzi persuaded the farmer to tell me what he had seen. The man, who was leery of getting involved in anything involving the Israeli army, agreed to talk if he came disguised.

I met him on the guest porch of the Najajras' house. He entered from one of the rooms dressed in a long gray peasant's robe. His head was wrapped in a thick white cloth, allowing only the narrowest slits for his eyes. He talked without hesitating, though.

"I am a farmer," he began. "I was working in my field, building a wall from stones. Then I saw army cars coming up the road, and I decided to hide."

The farmer said he had watched from behind his wall as the jeeps came to a halt about midway between the village and the main road at Kilo Sabatash, somewhere near the detoured roadblock below Neve Daniel. The jeeps seemed to be out of sight of everything except for terraces of grapes and almond trees. He said he was about fifty yards from the scene.

"I looked at the soldiers and I saw them stop," he continued. "I saw they had a young man who was handcuffed, and his head was covered. I saw them take this person from the car to the road, and I saw them beat him with their hands and boots and sticks. This lasted from ten minutes to fifteen minutes; I could not say exactly. I was not thinking about the time. When they took him from the car, he was standing, but then he was thrown to the ground. He was wriggling from side to side as they beat him. I think he was trying to prevent them from hurting him. I saw them hit him on the neck, but I could not see so clearly where exactly they were hitting him. It was his whole body. About fifteen soldiers were there, and most of them were beating him. Sometimes they were taking turns. They also were shouting ugly words at him: 'Your mother is a cunt. Your mother is a prostitute.' He was screaming. After the beating, they ordered him to go back to the jeep, but he was not able. I do not think he was able to stand on his own. Two soldiers picked him up and threw him in the back of the jeep. After they threw him in the jeep, they left.

"After I saw all this, I stopped working, and I came back to the village, and I learned that it was Farouk who had been arrested."

After the farmer finished talking, Fawzi's face was like a stone.

Fawzi told his mother nothing of this news, for fear that she would become gloomier than ever. I left an urgent note at the Red Cross headquarters in Jerusalem, saying that Farouk might be injured. But the atmosphere in the old mansion was, as always, one of overworked helplessness. As I became more frustrated, my empathy for Farouk and his family grew.

Finally, after the first week in November passed, I heard that the Red Cross had seen Farouk. It had taken eighteen days to find him. He was in the interrogation section at the Dahiriya prison, a place established in a village near Hebron, and it had a reputation for harshness.

"We saw him," one of the Swiss Red Cross delegates told me over the telephone. I met the Red Cross man later under the pines in the garden of the old mansion so that he could tell me the details. Journalists, Red Cross delegates and international aid officials all assumed their telephone lines might be tapped by the Israelis. We found a couple of chairs in a secluded corner of the garden.

"The word is that his health is good," he told me.

"What does that mean?" I asked, knowing that Red Cross delegates were accustomed to seeing scores of battered, beaten and broken prisoners daily.

"It means he is not suffering any major injury. His bones have not been broken. He has not been permanently damaged. And his mood is good."

"What does that mean?" I asked.

"It means that although he is being grilled by the Shin Bet, he is holding up. It means that he did not break down in tears when the Red Cross representative got in to see him. Many times when they have been with the Shin Bet, they start crying the minute they see the face of someone from the outside, someone who gives them an idea of the outside world."

The interrogators at Dahiriya were notorious for their painful methods of extracting information and confessions, including beatings, humiliations, freezing showers and confinement in coffin-like boxes. The worst part of the news was that he was under check *maftuha,* or open check. That meant he could be held for a six-month period of questioning even if no indictment had been issued, and the period could be lengthened.

There were by now almost nine thousand Palestinians in Israeli prisons or detention camps. The vast majority were not common criminals. Their offenses ranged from throwing stones to belonging to the PLO. All the prisons and holding centers were crowded.

Dahiriya was where many of the Palestinians arrested for joining the intifada were initially detained and questioned. The general section was reported to be bad, and the interrogation section a black hole that was the Shin Bet's province, off-limits even to the army officer in charge of the prison. According to the common wisdom, only a very few prisoners stood up to the Shin Bet and refused to cooperate. The only way to escape the interrogators and their methods was to sign a confession written in Hebrew.

Dahiriya had about twenty rooms, ten small cells and half a dozen tents to house prisoners numbering in the several hundreds. The rooms were dim, their windows covered with metal shields. A typical room was six yards by nine yards and held about fifty Palestinians, who had barely enough room to lie down and sleep on thin mattresses. The prisoners had to relieve themselves in a bucket, one per room, that was emptied at the whim of the soldiers on guard.

The prisoners ate on the floor where they slept, a scant menu whose highlight was an occasional bit of corned beef or a piece of fruit that had to be shared. When a soldier entered the room, the prisoners had to leap to their feet, face the wall with their hands behind their backs and answer in Hebrew. *"Ken,* Captain. Yes, Captain." If a prisoner did not follow this routine, he was beaten.

I gleaned this information from affidavits of former prisoners and from reports by Palestinian and Israeli human rights groups. Other than the Red Cross and lawyers and sometimes families of prisoners, outsiders were not allowed in any part of the prison. But the government did permit inspections by critical observers on occasion. A month after Farouk was arrested, Neta Goldman, an Israeli lawyer and member of the Association for Civil Rights, visited Dahiriya with a group of colleagues. She was shocked by what she saw when she looked into a cell.

"When they opened the door of the cell, it was like a deep, dark hole," she said. "It was so stinky we could hardly breathe. The smell was horrible."

Fourteen prisoners were confined in the cell, which she estimated was not more than fifteen square yards of space lighted by a single bulb. The only other light came through peepholes in the cell door.

On November 9, which was an intifada strike day to mark the beginning of the twelfth month of the uprising, more information came in from the Red Cross about Farouk. I met again with one of the delegates, who confirmed that Farouk had indeed been beaten by a group of soldiers upon his arrest. But the beating was not what he first complained about. He was unhappy with his handcuffs, which hurt and had been on a long time. He complained about the behavior of the interrogators, who were "questioning him thoroughly with accompanying blows." But he did not make an urgent request to see a doctor; he was managing better than most under Shin Bet questioning.

"He did not seem to be near a psychological breakdown, not the total breakdown that other prisoners have," the Red Cross man said. "He asked us to take a message out that he needed warm clothes, a visit from his lawyer and clean underwear. They don't give these guys underwear, and they are limited on washing."

When I took these new details about Farouk to the village, I found the Najajras grim. On the way there I passed the house of Intisar, Ratiba's eldest and married daughter. She was sitting on the wall of her garden, which she lovingly tended so that flowers and shrubs bloomed almost year round. I greeted her with a good morning, and she broke all the rules of Palestinian politeness. She berated me for saying the morning was good. "How can the morning be good when Farouk is being interrogated?" she asked and resumed staring at her plants.

The mood at Ratiba's was just as bad. Sitting on the house steps, Sena was desultorily tossing stones at the trunk of the fig tree, which was dropping its leaves on the hard autumn ground.

"What can we do now?" she asked without expecting an answer. "The Israelis have taken my brother. What do we have left? Chickens."

Shawki came around from the cellar kicking at the leaves. He went inside without looking up.

E L E V E N

The leaves were also falling from the venerable fig tree in the compound of Abdel Hafith Mustafa Najajra and his wife, Miriam, two
old Nahalinis who lived alone near the center of the village. Having
put concerns about Farouk aside temporarily, I went to visit the
couple after I heard that Abdel Hafith was considered one of the
most dedicated of the village Sufis. I wanted to learn more about this
mystical branch of Islam and its twig that grew in Nahalin.

It was midafternoon when I knocked on the metal door in
the wall protecting the compound. Miriam opened the gate and, as
if she had been expecting me, waved me into a compound that
looked as if it had not changed for decades. Abdel Hafith was
unloading sacks of olives from his donkey. He turned to look and
continued with his work as if there were nothing unusual about a
foreigner walking into his house.

The compound was enclosed by several slightly askew one-
room buildings. One housed the young donkey; another served as
a kitchen and another, with an ancient stove, as a winter bedroom.
The main room was a stone building sheltering under the fig, a tree
that in Sufi belief was inhabited by spirits called *djin*. Spirits or no,
the place had an otherworldly sense, a sense of deep peace.

But this calm in which the compound floated may have come

from nothing more than the fact that the couple lived by themselves, without the usual clamor of the extended family, since all but one of their children had migrated to Jordan. They had reduced their habits to simplicity.

Miriam, a delicate woman whose face had weathered with the seasons, led me inside and told me to sit on a mat, bringing a pillow for me to lean on. The room was plain. Several aging chairs were pushed against the walls. On the arms of the chairs were piled a few suitcases, in which Abdel Hafith and Miriam stored what they needed. An old cupboard in one corner looked as if it had not been moved in thirty years, the mirror on its front so antiquated that it shimmered rather than reflected.

Miriam fetched me water from a jug on the windowsill, and she brought a plate of almonds, which she shelled for me by cracking them with the butt of her hand against the hard floor. The palms of her hands were painted deep orange with henna, a ceremonial dye women used to beautify themselves for weddings and other occasions. She said little to me, so I talked as best I could, telling her who I was and what I was doing. She smiled, brought me a ripe green apple on a plate with a knife and then got up to change her regular white head scarf for a longer white shawl. Ignoring me, she unrolled a small rug, knelt and began her late-afternoon prayers. I was left with the apple, afraid to cut into it for fear of interrupting the sanctity of the moment. I sat frozen like a child afraid to talk in church and listened to her recitations from the Koran. After about five minutes of this, while she was still in the middle of her reverie, she stood and quickly turned her head toward me and demanded, "*Kooli.* Eat." She went right back to her prayers, while I sliced the apple and ate.

Abdel Hafith had gone to the old mosque across the roadway to pray. When he returned, he came to sit with us. He and Miriam were both very tired. They had three hundred olive trees and had been picking for eighteen days without cease.

Abdel Hafith had a closely trimmed white beard and wore a black embroidered skullcap and patched pants. He was short and compact. When he sat, he crossed his legs and his hands, and grinned, revealing a gap between his front teeth. Miriam, tired as she was, got up from her mat and and went across the compound to make a pot of sugared tea.

I talked to Abdel Hafith about the great prophets and the great religious figures.

"Moses, Abraham, Solomon, Jesus, Mohammad," Abdel Hafith said, "all of them are accepted by Islam. Islam does not throw any of them away. It accepts them. They all taught the same faith, but they had different ways according to how advanced their people were. Mohammad is the last prophet and the final prophet, but he is not the only prophet."

Miriam returned with the tea, bending slowly to pour it because of rheumatism. She did not complain. Sufis strove to raise their minds above the ensnarement of worldly affairs so that they could comprehend the divine.

Their sect is a branch of the Sunni Muslims, who prevail in the Islamic world. The Palestinians of the West Bank—except for the Christians concentrated in Bethlehem, East Jerusalem and Ramallah—are Sunni. The Islamic fundamentalists, who began to thrive in the West Bank with the unrest brought by the intifada, had yet to make more than a minor appearance in Nahalin. Elsewhere they were becoming a force to be reckoned with, a core group of believers with a vision of an Islamic state of Palestine.

Like everyone in the village, Abdel Hafith and Miriam had been affected by the Israeli occupation, but they were among the least angered by it. The Israelis had not altered the village's religious practices, and as for the land, the Sufis could remain above that.

Abdel Hafith had land on both Abu al-Koroun and Daher al-Matarsiya that had been taken by the Israelis. He lost fifty olive trees. But he took a forgiving stance.

"All Jews are human beings. If God wants to give the land to any people, it is all right. All this land belongs to God."

From that day on, I treasured these two Sufis. Their compound was a place where I could always find refuge from the daily chatter and anguish of the village.

During the harvest season, Nahalin took on a sense of accomplishment, as every afternoon donkeys and horses appeared out of the olive groves, from the ravines and mountains, their sides harnessed with metal racks laden with bags of olives. The smaller donkeys wheezed under the weight. The village almost achieved a festive sense despite the intifada. Any feeling of accomplishment was rare, what with the schools closed, the economic hard times caused by the political strikes, and the intifada continuing without tangible result, except for the growing numbers of the dead, wounded and imprisoned.

As the olives were being harvested, clouds began to form up in thick ranks across the sky. The first rain came one afternoon, falling on the olive groves. The villagers stopped where they worked among the trees and whooped with joy at the cleansing rain. It was the first in more than seven months. The olives were washed in the trees.

Most of the harvested olives were taken to nearby presses, where their coveted oil was extracted. I set off for one of these presses with Hanan Najajra and some of her relatives. As we bounced along in back seat of a pickup truck loaded with bags of

olives, she taught me how to sing a harvest song that bragged about
how great the olives were from one's own locality:

Eladal ouna o eladal ouna
Zaytoun biladi ahmal ma aykuna
Zaytoun biladi ma ahla habato
Ma ahla shaklo o ma ahla nbato
Wa al alim koulou birid aklato
Wa alakla mina ahsan ma aykuna.

The song meant this:

My country's olive trees are bountiful,
My country's olive trees have the most beautiful olives,
The trees are beautiful and the olives are beautiful
And all the world wants to eat them,
And to eat them is better than anything.

I was singing with Hanan and her mother in the backseat of
the truck heading for Surif, a neighboring village with an olive press,
when we were stopped by the army.

It was Israel's election day, which meant the Israelis did not
want any disruptions; the army had marshaled reinforcements to the
West Bank. The territory was "sealed off" so that no Palestinians
could cross the Green Line that day or the following day, which was
the anniversary of the Balfour Declaration, a potentially incendiary
date for Palestinians trying to wrench free of Israeli hegemony.
Journalists of any sort were banned from the occupied territories.

A barrier manned by twenty soldiers was blocking the crossroads. They halted the truck, and the commander—a tall Israeli with
dark hair and ruddy European looks—ordered everyone out of the
truck. He was wearing a red beret.

"*Kull,*" he said in Arabic, "all," motioning with his gun to prove that he wanted everyone out of the truck. But since women were a second class of people, in their own society and also in the eyes of the soldiers fighting the intifada, we three stayed in the backseat, hoping to be ignored as women so often were. The commander ordered the three men from the front seat and made them heave the sacks of olives out of the back of the truck, untie them and reach down into them to prove that the harvest was hiding no weapons or other anti-Israeli contraband.

Then the commander came back to the side of the truck and said in Arabic, "When I said everybody, I meant everybody."

We stepped down onto the edge of the road and tried to stand as noiselessly and inconspicuously as possible. But after a while, Hanan's mother moved toward the rear of the truck so she could see what was happening. She was a small woman, about five feet tall, aging and stooped. A soldier stepped forward and lifted his rifle, although he did not aim it. That was enough, though. She scuttled backward, making herself even smaller and saying with a village accent, "*Kull emleeha. Kull emleeha.* Everything is good. Everything is good."

The search in the back of the truck continued, and then the soldiers ordered the men to lift the seats inside the truck and open the glove compartment. "*Ifta. Ifta.* Open. Open."

I was hoping they would not notice me. But the commander in the beret inevitably approached me and asked, "Who are you?" in excellent English.

I told the truth, an American writer. But not wanting to cause the Palestinians trouble, I also told him I did not know these people and only was getting a lift from them to the press, where I wanted to watch oil being made. Then, because of the date, he asked me whether I knew who Balfour was. Knowing how important an event this was in the history of Israel, I replied carefully that Balfour was the British foreign secretary who in 1917 declared that the British cabinet had approved the concept that a Jewish homeland should exist in Palestine. The declaration was the seed of the Jewish state. I did not want to get into an argument about the fuller text of the declaration, which stated that the rights of the Arabs in Palestine must simultaneously be upheld.

The commander nodded at my response but told me I would be prohibited from traveling to Surif. He then ordered all six of us to wait on the road until a higher commander could arrive and assess the situation. I stepped forward and argued delicately. I said he must let the Palestinians go on their way since the problem seemed to be with me rather than them. After several minutes of this, he waved them away. Hanan made a loyal effort to remain with me, and I hissed at her, hoping the soldiers would not hear, telling her that she must leave for her own good.

The Palestinians departed for Surif with the olives, and I was left, an errant writer in the occupied territories, with a squad of soldiers on election day. They told me to come over to their camp by the road, where three Israeli settlers had stopped to drink coffee with them. The soldiers were from Nahal Gevaot, the army base in the pine trees on the shoulder of Abu al-Koroun. They were young, serving their initial three-year stint in the army. Before they were dispatched to the West Bank, they had been posted in southern Lebanon. The afternoon temperature was dropping, and one of the soldiers had crawled into a sleeping bag. I asked him what Lebanon was like. He answered. "It was not a game. This is a game."

I sat, and as the minutes passed, my impatience grew. I asked the commander why I was not allowed to see olive oil made. He said only that he had orders to restrict the movement of Palestinians and journalists. But as the minutes turned into half hours, I became anxious. I muttered and stared into the distance at Surif, a pretty village adorned with a minaret. Two hours passed before the commander relented and waved down a passing van and told the Israeli driver to give me a lift to the Kfar Etzion kibbutz and the main road back to Jerusalem. He said I must keep going until I had crossed back over the Green Line at Jerusalem.

The driver, wearing a knit skullcap that was the emblem of the ultra-religious nationalists settling the West Bank, welcomed me. But once we were half a mile past the roadblock, he ripped the cap off his head, let out a sigh of relief and said, "Lucky I got by that one."

He had been born in Libya, a Jew who had come to Israel at the age of eight with his family and was now living in Tel Aviv and making his living buying grapes in Hebron and selling them back in the big coastal cities. He was wearing the skullcap to disguise himself as a West Bank settler, knowing that would make it easier for him to pass the army checkpoints. He did not want to interrupt his trade merely because of the army's nervousness.

The grape dealer dropped me on the main road, and I thumbed a ride with a car of Israelis who were all wearing skullcaps in earnest. They were staunch admirers of Shamir and were fervently hoping for his electoral success. The driver, an American from one of the settlements south of Kfar Etzion, was singing, "We Shall Overcome." The Palestinians I had left on the road to Surif could have been singing the same protest song.

When the driver finished his verses, he broke into a speech about how everything was going to get better: Israel was still a young country, a baby, that had yet to grow larger and stronger; the Palestinians then would have to leave. I did not debate with him, since he had been kind enough to give me a lift as far as Bethlehem. Instead, I mused on the fractured cast of characters playing out the West Bank's bloody drama.

Just south of Bethlehem, we passed the Deheisheh refugee

camp. The settlers left their windows rolled down, something I never did for fear a refugee might hurl a rock at me. They discussed the relative merits of closed and open windows.

"It's six of one, half dozen of the other," the driver said. "If they hit you with a rock hard enough to break the window, you get flying glass in your face. That can be as bad as a direct hit. But if they're throwing Molotovs, the best bet is a closed window. You pray that it will bounce off."

I got out near the long road curving around the northern flank of Bethlehem and up into Manger Square, where the Church of the Nativity stood on the site of Christ's birth. The town's main taxi stand was nearby. What I did not know was that the entirety of Bethlehem was on strike in solidarity with the outlying suburb of Beit Sahour, where two Palestinians had been shot the day before. Nothing was operating, not a single taxi or bus. I started walking into town and found it practically deserted. The shops were shuttered and the streets empty of traffic. I came upon three merchants sitting out on the sidewalk in front of a closed souvenir store and sipping Arabic coffee. They explained the situation and I explained my plight. One fetched his car and chauffeured me back to Nahalin, generously risking getting stoned by driving during a strike.

The mood everywhere seemed bad. As we were driving to Nahalin, I observed more jeeps on the road than usual. The army was making a series of raids to clean out the villages, to get rid of flags and graffiti, to demolish houses built without permits and to make arrests as part of an effort to break the momentum of the intifada.

As we approached Nahalin from Husan, we ran into a bit of trouble. An overloaded flatbed settlers' truck was heaving around the bends into the village, belching exhaust smoke. The truck stopped abruptly. It had been stoned. The driver got out, spotted a Palestinian in an olive grove above him and, taking an outdated wooden-stock rifle, fired six shots at the Palestinian, who had instantly disappeared.

The Bethlehem merchant quickly turned his car around, and after the truck had continued hastily up toward Kfar Etzion, I walked into the village. I arrived at Hanan's about half an hour after the others returned from Surif.

The next morning it was clear that the election had been won by Shamir over the more liberal Perez. The news rolled over the village like a wind, ruffling people a little but not making any deep impressions. The general attitude was that both Perez and Shamir held the same fate for the Palestinians, because neither intended to allow them a real state of their own, unencumbered with qualifications, soldiers or settlements.

Most of the fall I had been staying at Hilmi's, but the following day, Balfour Day, I accepted an invitation to sleep at the house of Intisar, Fawzi's oldest sister, the woman who had been so gloomy about Farouk when I tried to greet her in the morning. She was pregnant and exhausted from the constant mischievousness of her three boys. Her daughter, on the other hand, was quiet and gentle and already, at the age of eight, had learned to serve tea and sweep the house—a miniature model of the ideal village woman. Sena came over to spend the night with me, and we slept in the main bedroom of the two-room house.

Intisar's husband was absent because he was working in Jerusalem, and as it was impossible for him to commute daily from the village, he slept there illegally during the week. But he was not alone. Thousands of other Palestinians were similarly forced to disobey the Israeli law mandating that no Palestinian from the occupied territories may spend the night in Israel without special permission.

Many slept locked in dismal shacks so that no one would notice them.

The boys were raucous, playing their version of cowboys and Indians—*jaysh wa shabab.* The weapons for this game were rocks for the *shabab* and sticks, representing military clubs and rifles, for the army.

One of the boys told his mother that he wanted to be an Israeli, not a Palestinian, that he preferred the role of the army. She asked him the reason, and he replied that the Israelis were stronger, and he wanted to be strong. She disputed him, saying that one day the Palestinians would have their own state and their own flag and would become the most courageous people on earth.

TWELVE

During the autumn, I usually came and went to and from Nahalin on the old village bus. Abu Sayal always refused to take my fare, maintaining his hospitality. Besides me, the only person who did not pay to ride to Bethlehem was the village fool, a young man named Basam who wandered about shaking everybody's hands and bombarding them with effusive, half-comprehensible greetings. He was endlessly good-natured, and the villagers treated him gently, shooing him away only when he was too cloying. He loved to ride the bus, so Abu Sayal let him on board for free. He would stand staunchly at the front of the bus, holding onto a railing and watching the scenery with pleasure as the bus made its routine circuit to the Bethlehem market and back.

The more time I spent in Nahalin, the more I realized that nothing about the village was as simple as it looked. Even when things appeared to be going well, I waited for something to go wrong. At any moment, any one of the villagers I knew could be arrested and thrown in prison. I could be accused by some villager of some purported misconduct. I had learned that I couldn't always gauge what was behind the Palestinian politeness. I didn't know, and often I couldn't guess, what the villagers were thinking. Some, like Hanan and Fawzi and Hilmi, trusted me. Others, whom I didn't know, still stared at me when I walked through the village or waited for Abu Sayal to start his bus. All the while the intifada never let up. No one knew what it would bring.

The longer I was in the village, the more modest I became in my attire. Midcalf skirts revealed too much leg for the more traditional Nahalinis. When I visited older people in Nahalin, the women would hasten to cover my legs completely with a towel or blanket, even if I had on stockings. The longer I stayed with Palestinians, the more sensitive I became to the sight of bare flesh. My own wardrobe, baggy and lengthy as it was, looked more and more risqué to me, so I decided to buy a real dress.

One morning I took Abu Sayal's bus to Bethlehem and the market. I walked down in the early morning to the village center. Nahalin was white and gray in the early light, and the sound of heavy drilling at the Betar settlement site was drifting across the valley. A couple of loud blasts had already punctuated the morning. On the bus, Basam was standing at the front, and several women dressed in their *thobes* for a shopping expedition had taken seats. I sat with one of them and pulled out the length of black cloth with its thin line of embroidery that Hanan had helped me with. It was out of my hands before I could take a stitch. The women passed it around, admiring it and criticizing it for the mistakes I had made. One, then another and another, furiously stitched away at the pattern, as if they could correct it once and for all.

I looked at these women next to me, and I saw how different we were. My hands were uncalloused; my skin was not weathered; my feet were not toughened by decades of trudging through fields of thorns and stones. They had spent their lifetime scrubbing, hoeing, stooping, picking and giving birth. Their bodies were as solidly square as their *thobes*. Their breasts were stretched flatly down their bosoms from nursing child after child. And their faces looked with a skeptical stoicism upon a world that promised no pleasant surprises. These women were tough. The intifada had made them tougher.

As I was watching the women, Sheikh Deeb made his way to the bus, cane in one hand and a large pot of honey in the other. He sat down across from me, smiling to himself meditatively, his ears sticking out beneath his turban. He told me he was taking the honey not to Bethlehem, but to the larger market in Hebron, where he expected to get a good price. Honey in the cold months was a luxury. We talked about Deeb, his grandson, imprisoned in the Negev, but there was little to say. We shook our heads and waited for Abu Sayal to climb into the driver's seat, adjust his *kefiyeh* and edge down the roadway, stopping to pick up women waiting on the village outskirts. At the archway in El Khader, Sheikh Deeb got off to catch a ride south.

Abu Sayal parked in his customary place by the derelict cinema. Palestinians sat randomly on the littered steps. Some ate kebab hot from the grill at its usual place on the sidewalk. I walked up past the meat market to the section of the *souq* where a row of tiny shops sold long dresses. The shopkeepers hung the dresses out on high poles so that they looked like multicolored banners. The dresses all had the same cut—long and shapeless—although they came in every color imaginable, from chartreuse to lilac, from black with gold filigree to white with orange swirls. I chose a solid blue one and held it up to my shoulders to make sure it was long enough. It was. The hem touched my instep. As I was imagining how decorous I would look in the dress I had just bought, the sound of gunfire ripped through the babble of the marketplace. The army was shooting at the *shabab*. Without missing a beat, the shopkeepers clanged their metal doors shut, having scurried inside with any shoppers who were nearby. I was whisked into the dress shop with three other women and the shop's owner, a middle-aged man.

The store was cramped and without electricity. We stood in

the semidarkness and listened for more shooting. There was none immediately. We peered through chinks in the door.

"Watch out for the tear gas," the shopkeeper said offhandedly. He did not panic, having survived scores of tear-gas attacks in the Bethlehem market. No one else seemed to panic either. The women cursed the soldiers under their breath, but they were calm like the shopkeeper. Not being so accustomed to tear gas, I was alarmed. I also feared more gunfire from the soldiers none of us could see.

We then heard the thick thumping of tear-gas canisters being fired somewhere in the vicinity of the meat stalls. The gas came seeping into the shop, not much, but enough to make us all gag. My eyes burned as they never had before, as if someone had thrown pepper in them, and my stomach cramped as if I would retch. I pulled the top of my jacket across my face and cringed in a corner. The Palestinians stood stoically still. Slowly the gas dissipated. The shopkeeper opened his door, and we walked out into a market that had resumed its bustle. I wanted to imitate the nonchalance of the Palestinians around me, but I couldn't, and I headed for the bus as fast as I could, uncertain whether more shooting would follow.

On the road leading to the cinema, a gang of *shabab* had rolled out tires from some impromptu depot and set them ablaze. Choking black smoke filled the street. A squad of soldiers, all of them with their backs up against the wall of a building, were firing into the smoke. I dived into a side street and circled around to the bus, hoping fervently that Abu Sayal would be there. He was poised at the wheel, not wanting to desert his passengers, who were arriving coughing and panting. A final pair of women clambered aboard with boxes of fruit on their heads. Abu Sayal did an expert turnabout and headed away from the smoke, the *shabab* and the army. Basam, still at his station at the front of the bus, waved farewell to the scene. The man making shish kebab waved back. He had not moved during the commotion but had tied a cloth over his face and kept turning the spits of meat on the grill.

Back on the bus to Nahalin, I felt much safer surrounded as I was by hefty village women, some of whom filled out every inch of their *thobe*s with squared, muscular limbs. I looked in their faces and saw calm, a patience that came from many, many days of having no choice but to work. No soldiers were going to bother an old blue bus filled with peasant women. We rode inconspicuously past the Deheisheh camp, where the fence had been reinforced with more barbed wire and the army tents opposite had grown in number.

The Israelis were concerned about a potential source of trouble. The Palestinians' congress in exile was planning to convene in Algeria to publicize the intifada and demand a state of Palestine, with what effect in the occupied territories nobody could predict.

At the El Khader arch, two jeeploads of Border Police were tarrying as if they expected trouble. But the village was quiet. At Husan, foot patrols were marching along the roadside in squads of six, and in each squad one soldier bore a backpack with a heavy radio, from which sprouted a six-foot antenna. Squawks and radio orders in Hebrew encompassed each squadron in a cloud of noise, separating the soldiers from the village through which they walked. They soberly watched the Palestinians on their porches, and the Palestinians soberly watched back, both waiting for something to happen.

This went on day after day, except when violence flared, when a tire was lighted, a barrage of stones thrown or shots fired. Everyone was accustomed to the unease, to the undercurrents of tension that played through the mountains like the wind, sighing and blowing and sometimes seeming to drop to a dead stillness. I had ceased being startled by the sight of soldiers with submachine guns, by roadblocks, by the fact that there was a war going on.

* * *

In Nahalin, I moved from house to house, always confident that if no place was to be found, Rula always had space on her mattress. I knew my way around the village and its clans, at least superficially. I could recognize the names of the six subclans and guess at the shifting politics going on beneath the surface politeness. I knew who was active with the *shabab*—almost every young man—and I knew who favored Fatah, Arafat's faction of the PLO, and who favored Jebha, the ideologically more radical faction. As I had learned, political philosophies tended to follow clan lines. I had identified the houses of a couple of known collaborators and steered clear of them. I did not put two and two together, though, and conclude that I was associated with the Najajra clan and, therefore, with the Jebha faction. I also paid little attention to Hamas, the Muslim fundamentalists who wanted a strict Islamic state run according to unbending religious principles. Hamas had about a dozen members in the village, but its influence was on the rise.

Nahalin was not getting any less tense as the intifada continued. The *shabab* had finally managed to tie a Palestinian flag to the top of the mosque's minaret. The flag flapped colorfully and defiantly. But the whole minaret was dwarfed by the metal tower of a construction crane that had recently been erected on the Betar site.

The weeks wore on, and little changed except that intermittent rains were falling, rains that soaked into the dirt and turned it dark. Occasionally the clouds parted and the sun warmed the earth. It was on just such a sunny day that I returned to the village from Jerusalem, carrying with me medicines and books for some of my friends. I tried driving in first from Kilo Sabatash but found the army had been hard at work refurbishing the roadblock, closing off the *shabab* detour permanently by bulldozing a wide pile of dirt up against the multi-ton rocks, the refrigerator shell and the upturned car chassis, which were already in place.

As I was turning back, I paused for a few minutes to watch a shepherd herding his long-haired goats in a rocky field below the new Neve Daniel houses. It was a warm afternoon made strangely moody by half-white, half-blue clouds lingering in the autumnal sky. The branches of the leafless fig trees stood out gray against the sky.

I had noticed soldiers everywhere on the way out. It was a Palestinian strike day, to protest the demolition of houses in the occupied territories. Because of the strike, most West Bankers were not working in Israel but were at home waiting for trouble to come along. Aware that more rocks were thrown on strike days, I did not take the next most obvious route back to the village. I avoided the villages of Husan and El Khader, where the Palestinians did not know me well, as they did in Nahalin, and drove around past the settlements to Nahalin's south. At Kfar Etzion, I was struck by the anomaly of an old white-bearded Palestinian wearing a white head-cloth and riding a white donkey along the newly paved black road that runs between the kibbutz and the neighboring religious settlement. I was aware of details that afternoon, or I thought I was.

At the turn into the valley by Abu al-Koroun, I met a woman I knew. I had a chat with her and admired the embroidery of her dress. All was auspicious. I continued down the road and looked for, but could not see, the flag on the minaret of the mosque. Was it down? I wondered. Had the lack of wind let it flop out of sight? But I did notice a smaller flag on a rough pole stuck in a rock wall perpendicular to the road about halfway down from Abu al-Koroun. Near the flag I came to a line of rocks across the road. I stopped and, without thinking, put the car in neutral and got out to move a few of the rocks so that I could go on to the village. I had my SEHAFI sign on the windshield and the red *kefiyeh* across the dashboard. I was thinking that I had nothing to worry about since most people in the village would recognize me. Besides books for Sena, I was bringing rheumatism medicine for Halima, the Najajra grandmother with whom I had worked in the olives. The books and medicines were on the passenger seat.

Without warning, rocks began hitting the car, the road and all around me. Hard. I was being ambushed. I twirled around and rushed for the car. More rocks came but they missed me somehow. I leapt into the driver's seat and reversed crazily down the narrow, windy road under a further hail of rocks. Coming out from behind a grove of olives on the right and from behind boulders on the left were *mulethamin,* translated as "wrapped ones," *shabab* with their faces covered in black-checkered *kefiyeh*s so that only the slits of their eyes were showing. They chased me and stopped only when it was obvious I had outdistanced them.

Once out of range, I stopped. I was trembling, shocked by the attack and by the realization that these were Nahalinis, *shabab* from Nahalin, behind the *kefiyeh*s. This was the village where I had spent so many days and nights, where I had tried again and again to prove that I was not an enemy, that my aim was to learn about the village not to injure it. I couldn't tell who had ambushed me, and I didn't know why they had done it. I only knew that if I kept retreating now, these *mulethamin* would be convinced that I was frightened. And I was, but I couldn't show my fear, or I might not get back into the village. I also believed that my attackers would soften when they realized I was returning to Nahalin with no ill intent.

I rolled down the car window and waved the red *kefiyeh*. I shouted that I was a journalist. Some of the *mulethamin* walked toward me a little and then beckoned, making big welcoming motions with their arms, that I should come forward. I did, pulling back abreast of several of them. I said again that I was a journalist, and

I motioned to the books and boxes of pills, saying I was bringing medicine to an old woman.

Someone grabbed my *kefiyeh,* and rocks came battering down on the car. The windshield was hit but it didn't break. The *mulethamin* were attacking from the olive trees, and I went again into a maniacal high-speed reverse until I was once more out of range. The masked Palestinians stood on the road and glared at me. I sat in the car, more frightened than I had been since I first set foot on the West Bank. I wasn't going to drive forward into the same trap again, but I also wasn't going to retreat. I was in a quandary.

Then, as if in answer to my dilemma, three villagers came walking up behind me from the direction of Abu al-Koroun. I didn't recognize the trio of men, but they knew me by sight, as many villagers did. They tried to calm me, telling me not to be afraid. I was still trembling; my left leg was shaking on the clutch pedal. Two of the villagers stayed with me in the car, and the other went and talked to the *mulethamin.* He returned with the *kefiyeh,* and all three got into the car. We drove to the ambush point, got out and moved the rocks, drove past the ambush point, got out and carefully replaced the stones. The *mulethamin* had blended into the landscape. I asked my newfound benefactors who my attackers were, but they didn't tell me.

"I told the *mulethamin,"* one benefactor said, "that they made a mistake just now, that you are good. It is up to them whether they believe this. It won't help you to know their names."

We made it into the village, and my benefactors went their own way. I headed for the the house of Naim Najajra, the schoolteacher who was Ratiba's youngest brother and who had helped so merrily and briefly with the olive picking. The driveway to Naim's place was narrow and led to a courtyard protected by the houses of relatives. I pulled hastily into the driveway and brought the car to a screeching halt, startling Halima, who had been basking in the sun on a blanket in the courtyard. I told them what had happened, and Halima told me that the army had riled the village the day before. Soldiers had come upon the flag on the minaret and had ordered a young man to climb up and tear it down. They had fired tear gas through the whole village to keep the *shabab* indoors and then had sped away. The ambush I chanced upon could have been laid by rankled *shabab*. But whatever the reason, I was still upset.

Halima was upset, too. She brought out coffee. I had to drink two cups of the strong stuff before my hands ceased shaking. At first, I spilled from the cup. Halima then hefted herself inside and brought out a platter of leftover lunch, chicken and rice, and tried to get me to eat it. The village hospitality never ceased, but I could not eat anything. Naim came out from his house. Halima and he tried to coax me to go sit in his cloud-painted guest room, where I could feel safe. I refused.

Slowly I was becoming angry. The fear that had shaken me was transmuting into an anger that came from deep inside. The bunch of villagers who ambushed me could have killed me. The windshield could have shattered into glass-sharp shrapnel. A rock could have struck me in the face. Had they wanted to kill me? Were they just trying to scare me off? I didn't know.

I had a taste of what Israelis felt when they traveled the West Bank. Transmitted along the arc of a rock being thrown, the Palestinians' anger was personal and deadly. When it was concentrated on you at a close range, it was fearsome. There was nothing accidental about it. You were the target. But what made me even angrier and what hurt me was that I was not an Israeli settler. Although all the Palestinians in Nahalin might not be convinced, I had done nothing to harm them.

Hussein Najajra, an Arabic teacher and relative of Naim,

came out into the courtyard, and I made a speech to him about the need of the American people to understand the Palestinians and that this stoning of my car was not helpful.

He agreed. "Whichever people did this, they were stupid," he said.

Halima again offered me food. "It is a shame that they threw stones on you," she said.

Sena arrived in the courtyard, having already heard what happened. She hugged me. "Helen," she said, "this was unnecessary. This was not good. You should not stop coming to Nahalin."

I gave Sena the books and Halima the medicine. By then, I had calmed down enough to think ahead. I was again flooded with fear. Naim's courtyard made a temporary sanctuary. I guessed there must be *mulethamin* in ambush on any route I would try to take out of the village, but I couldn't stay cowering in this courtyard in a village that was on edge.

A single stone was tossed at me as I backed out of the driveway and headed for the other side of the village, the neighborhood where Hanan's and Hilmi's houses were and where I was well-known.

On the way, I saw another bunch of *mulethamin* milling around on the main road. Some were rolling tires toward the Valley of the Cow. My impulse was to yank the car around and head in the other direction, but that would only have taken me back to the place of the first ambush. I proceeded, and the anonymously wrapped figures let me pass. I could recognize none of them. As I was weaving down the road, avoiding the *mulethamin,* one stepped out in front of the car. As I stopped, he pulled his *kefiyeh* aside. It was one of Hanan's brothers, and he said it would be OK for me to drive out the other way if he came with me.

"It's Jebha on this side of the village. We like you," he said.

I hoped he was telling the truth. One of their tires was already burning. The *mulethamin* had laid down a strip of nails across the road, which they directed me around. Just outside the village, in the high olive grove where the *shabab* had fought the army, *mulethamin* had gathered in colored garb. Others stood in the open with rocks in their hands. One of the leaders ordered the *shabab* to come quickly, and they came, some carrying clubs. They surrounded the car, and for a moment I wondered whether this was another, more terrible trap. But nothing happened and I drove forward, out of the village. The *shabab* ran along both sides of my car to ensure that nobody on high made a mistake. I was not to be stoned by this faction of the Palestinians. Jebha approved of me and Fatah had not.

Rocks were the starkest of weapons. There was nothing to them; there was no elaboration; there was no apparatus between the thrower and the target. Rocks were direct, much more so than guns, which could be fired accurately and cleanly from a distance. Rocks were primitive, employed for millennia before mankind developed tools and weapons.

The *mulethamin* could have killed me with their rocks, and I wanted to know why they wanted to. I wanted to talk to them. I wanted them to explain to me the depths of their paranoia and anger, an ugly mix, I was sure. I wanted to understand.

The warm afternoon had passed, and the evening chill had been settling on Jerusalem, where I was holed up, shaken and writing notes about what had happened. I was wondering why, or how, the *mulethamin* had failed to kill me. They were close enough. Maybe they were momentarily unsure. Maybe I was lucky. Or maybe they just wanted to terrify me or warn me. I planned to see Fawzi and get an explanation.

The next day Fawzi came to see me.

"I am sorry," he said. He said that I had been caught in a rending fissure between the village's Fatah and Jebha factions.

"I talked all last night to people with importance about what happened. I said that you were writing about the village and that this was a good thing. The world needs to understand that Palestinians live like human beings. They listened. We agreed to send representatives from each one, from Fatah and Jebha, to Jerusalem to ask questions about you. To find out if you are straight."

Readily I agreed that the investigation should proceed, but I had plenty of doubts. I had no idea who would be judging my integrity. I assumed members of the underground leadership of the intifada would be my arbiters, but I did not know them. Or if I did, I did not know their clandestine roles. I was jittery.

"The problem you had was not because of you," Fawzi continued reassuringly. "These people who attacked you thought you were against them because you were spending too much time with the Jebha."

A lesson had been learned the hard way. From then on, I vowed to make friends with more Shakarnas, with anybody who might think I had been taking sides.

I had been blind to the obvious. I lost another layer of naïveté. *Bucolic* was no longer a word that occurred to me when I thought of Nahalin. Complex, yes. Difficult, yes. Hospitable, yes. But what was behind the smiles? Had one of the masked stone throwers previously invited me onto his guest porch and plied me with tea? How was I to know whom to trust?

I asked Fawzi if any of my attackers would speak to me.

"No," he said flatly. Clearly this was not something that could be talked out within the village.

I asked whether I had ever been in any of their houses.

"Perhaps you have by chance," he said, offering no clues to their identity.

Fawzi was perturbed not just by my account. He hated seeing the village fighting itself. "We should put these things away. Now is not the time to be fighting inside the village. The fight is much larger than just our village. It is not a game that we should be playing now. We have to be more serious. The enemy is not you, and it is not the other Palestinians."

Talk had been bouncing around Jerusalem that the different Palestinian factions were rubbing against each other on the West Bank as a whole, trying to gain ascendancy in the national and international arenas.

I was going to have to prove my neutrality on yet another level. I gathered once more proof of my writing and my identity. A few days later I was summoned by telephone to an office in East Jerusalem. Fawzi was not there. Two men whom I had never seen before were seated at a table. One was tall and thin with a sharp face. He did the talking. He started by asking me the details of the stoning. He paused and looked at me hard.

"Do you know who I am?" he asked.

"No," I said.

"Tell me everything, because I will be hearing the other side. Others saw what happened in Nahalin. I will be hearing the truth. Any lies will finish you."

I was telling the truth, but that did not stop me from squirming in my chair. I had no idea what my attackers might say, and it seemed that my questioner was from the intifada's leadership. What would happen to me if lies about me went up through the Palestinian ranks?

After a few more questions about my motives for traveling on the West Bank, he ended the questioning abruptly. "That is enough. Go now and do not remember what I look like. Do not tell anyone about me."

I said that I wanted only one thing, which was to talk to some of those who had stoned me, disguised or not. I wanted to make them realize I was not the enemy.

"If you have told me the truth, they will understand," he said. "Don't make the mistake of asking me too many questions."

He rose as I did and walked stiffly toward the door, as if something in his legs caused him pain. He opened the door and closed it quickly behind me. I heard a lock click.

Back in my apartment I waited to find out whether I was doomed or saved. Four days after the meeting he telephoned.

"You have done excellently. Now don't worry. You will be safe everywhere you want to go around Bethlehem and the area. You have my word. I am the man from Fatah."

He hung up. I took this cryptic message to mean that he represented Fatah and could guarantee that members of his group would not bother me. I suspected the ambushers had been among them.

THIRTEEN

Back in the summer, King Hussein of Jordan had astonished the Arab world by severing his country's longstanding economic and legal ties with the West Bank, links that had survived the Israeli occupation. The king set off a furor. Palestinian nationalists demanded that the PLO seize the opportunity to step into the theoretical void, and right-wing Israelis called for immediate annexation of the whole territory. But nothing changed; the Israeli military remained indisputably in charge.

By autumn, the Palestinians had decided to take dramatic action. Their congress in exile, the Palestine National Council, which met every few years to determine policy for the Palestinian movement, agreed to convene in Algeria and declare an independent Palestine, a state that would include the West Bank and the Gaza Strip. Yasir Arafat was to preside and the leaders of the PLO factions attend. The luminaries among the "outside" Palestinians were to be there, those who lived in exile. The "inside" Palestinians, those from the West Bank and the Gaza Strip, were not attending; Israel would not give them travel permits. But there was no guarantee they would not try to raise an uproar at home.

As mid-November and the Palestinian congress approached, the Israelis adopted a preemptive tactic, clamping down on the West

Bank and the Gaza Strip with more military force than ever. The occupied territories were sealed off from the rest of the world. The regular checkpoints—like the one between Jerusalem and Bethlehem—were beefed up, and additional ones were established at important intersections. The Israelis temporarily cut telephone lines to areas where they predicted trouble; they combed through the angriest villages and arrested potential dissidents. To punish suspected troublemakers and their families, the army blew up their houses in the northern and southern regions of the West Bank. They sent out squadrons of soldiers to see that Palestinian flags were torn down and the omnipresent wall grafitti painted over yet again. Hundreds of thousands of Palestinians in refugee camps were placed under curfew, which meant they could not leave their homes morning, noon or night.

The Israelis did not want any news of trouble to add to their problems, so they again banned journalists from the West Bank and the Gaza Strip for the duration of the meeting. The Israelis feared massive protests and celebrations by the Palestinians locked within the occupied territories while their exiled leaders debated in Algeria about the status of Palestine. Israel and Jerusalem were closed off to Palestinians from the territories; the Green Line was a closed border.

Wanting to be in Nahalin during the potentially inflammatory meeting, I decided to remain in the village illegally. I chose to be locked in rather than locked out. Since returning to Nahalin after the ambush, I had been staying again at Hilmi's house. Filled with young children, it was a neutral place. My being there could not antagonize anybody.

The weather had turned frigid, and the rains were coming with frequency, building into downpours from clouds that blanketed the sky from ridgeline to ridgeline. Everyone seemed to have a cold or the flu. The stone house, like all the others in the village, had no central heating; its walls absorbed the cold and dampness from the rains. The kerosene burner was kept by the dinner table, but it provided little heat. Hilmi sat by the burner and chafed at not being able to cross into East Jerusalem to work.

For the first time, soldiers were stationed at the village. As part of its preparations for the Palestinian meeting, the army had set up two nuqtas, or "points," as their observation posts were called, one on the roof of an empty house at the top of the village above Ratiba's place and the other on the craggy rocks above the stone factory on the road to Kilo Sabatash.

Fifteen soldiers manned the nuqta above Ratiba's house, where I went to visit one morning, taking narrow paths that hid me from their sight. The house was still in a state of gloom. Sena, Ahmed and Sa'ed had gone to the Dahiriya detention center to visit Farouk three days earlier only to find that he had been taken somewhere else.

"The guard just said he wasn't there and we had to leave," Sena told me.

As we were discussing Farouk's plight, we saw six jeeps passing through the village and heading up the high road along with a bulldozer. We were paralyzed, wondering whether the bulldozer was meant for demolishing some home. We waited, listening. Hours later word spread through the village that the army had reinforced the blockade on the high road and had also plowed one across the road to Husan. The only way left out of the village was up past the army base and the Gush Etzion settlements.

The night before the debate in Algiers was to culminate in a proclamation, I was invited to stay with Hani Awad and his family. Hani had worked as a highly paid crane operator in Jordan for many years, but he quit his job rather than stay and be forced to serve in the Jordanian army and never again be allowed to reside in the West Bank.

Visitors came by the house in the late afternoon, including

a couple named Hassan and Inam Shakarna and their three young boys. I took an immediate liking to them and they to me, and they suggested that I share their house with them. They also had a couple of unused rooms beneath their house that I might rent. The rooms needed some paint, they said, but they contained a sink and running water. When Hassan and Inam rose to leave, I contained my enthusiasm and promised to come by within the week, after the political situation quieted. I also knew by then that anything might happen in Nahalin, for the good or the bad, and that I should not count on their offer. On the other hand, Inam was the youngest sister of Abu Jafer and probably would not have volunteered to shelter me if the Shakarna clan was opposed. Perhaps the man from Fatah was already smoothing my way.

The weather turned colder than it had been the previous night, and we had dinner on a mat in the bedroom, where it was warm, in the space between the cupboards and the foot of the bed of Hani and his wife, Siham. Next to that bed, with no space between, was the bed for their boy and infant girl.

They made me eat more than my fill, forking choice pieces of beef at me after I had eaten a bellyful of stuffed squash. And when it came time to sleep, the generosity did not cease. Hani insisted that I sleep with Siham. He would sleep on the floor mat. At this point, my instinct for privacy rose to the surface. I insisted that I would not sleep with his wife but in the salon, the room they used for guests in the summertime. I had seen a solitary sofa there. Hani maintained that the salon was too cold, much colder than the bedroom. More important, he insisted, this was not the Palestinian way of sleeping, that people liked sleeping together. I still was not swayed from my purpose of achieving a night alone. Hani changed his argument.

"What if it is the middle of the night and a dog comes?" he asked, a dog being generic for anything loathsome or fearsome.

I said I was not afraid of dogs.

But he tried again. "What if the army comes? Won't you be afraid to be in there by yourself?"

I said I was not afraid of the army either and added that soldiers, if they came, would find me no matter which room I was sleeping in. He was forced to realize that nothing would budge me. It was terribly cold on the sofa, so cold that I dreamed someone had put frozen coins in my socks.

Hani left before dawn to drive to Ashdod near Israel's coast, hoping to get to his factory job there. Before long, he returned to the house. The remaining road out of the village past the army base was blocked, too, this one by soldiers.

No Palestinians could move from one district to the next. The villages were being isolated. An army helicopter passed overhead twice, low. The date was November 15, the day that the Palestinian council was expected to announce the formation of the independent Palestinian state.

I walked down to Hanan's and stayed as she and her sister were rolling stuffed grape leaves, as nonchalantly as if this were any other day. In front of the house was a row of brightly colored jugs. These heavy plastic jugs were everywhere in the village, filled with olives that had been sorted for eating, then cleaned and slightly mashed so that they could soak in a seasoned salt broth that brought out their taste. With the olives curing, there was time for other culinary pursuits.

I sat down on a low bench with Hanan in the little aisleway by their kitchen. From Hanan's, we could see the soldiers on the high rocks. They had been up there all day, sitting, walking back and forth, watching the village through binoculars. They, too, were waiting for the news and the reaction. We had heard rumors, and then radio reports in the morning, that a state had been declared and that a declaration of independence had been drafted. But nothing seemed to be happening, so I settled down with the women and learned how to wrap grape leaves.

It looked easy until I tried. Using your right hand, you smoothed a leaf onto your left palm, took a clump of seasoned rice and spread it in the middle of the leaf. You folded up the bottom two lobes of the leaf, tucked in the edges and rolled it like a miniature cigar, tightly enough that it would not fall apart when it was wedged with other leaves in layers in a pot and cooked.

I was getting the hang of how to force the rice to stay inside the slithery leaves when shouts rose from an olive grove near the village center.

Some *shabab* ran past the house, and one yelled at us. "It is a celebration. The leadership has ordered a celebration for the state. Palestine."

About forty *mulethamin,* their heads and faces masked by cloth sacks with eyeholes cut in them, came marching in two files out of an olive grove. They were dressed from head to toe in solid colors, those of the Palestinian flag—each one in red, black or green. And they were all carrying Palestinian banners. At the head of the procession, one carried a Palestinian flag measuring six feet across. The others carried flags that were smaller but still large enough to land them in prison if the soldiers chose to swoop down and make arrests.

They were organized. First they went to the village cemetery and paraded up a small hill to the mausoleum housing the tomb of a village lord from the century past. From this prominent spot, the *mulethamin* waved their flags and cheered and sang. The soldiers above were watching all the while, pacing back and forth along the line of rocks, lifting their binoculars so that the afternoon light bounced off the lenses and sent sharp flashes down the valley, but they did nothing more. The soldiers were not reacting. The *mule-*

thamin then marched the length of Nahalin, carrying ladders and tacking flags to every pole along the way, and rallied back at the village center near the mosques. Some younger Nahalinis ran along the streets with cans of spray paint, writing political graffiti anywhere they could. One of them painted a Star of David in big red marks in the middle of the street and then painted a swastika on top of it, defiling the star with the symbol of hatred.

The soldiers still did nothing except move back and forth along the cliff. The afternoon deepened. A white banner proclaiming independence was raised at the center of the village. I was sure the army would charge. Everyone was. The *shabab* built a bonfire, and three *mulethamin* climbed to the roof of the kindergarten building with a loudspeaker and made speeches: "This would not have happened without the intifada. This is Palestine, according to us. We have made it ourselves."

People sang the most popular of the nationalist songs— "Biladi, biladi, biladi, Laki hubbi wa fouadi . . . My country, my country, my country, To you my love and loyalty . . ."—performing an off-key but exuberant rendition of the tune. Young men, arms linked, performed the *dabke,* a Palestinian dance with energetic kicks. People were clapping, their hands high in the air. Hundreds had come by then—grandmothers, men, children. People passed out RC Cola and sweet wafers, the Palestinian-village equivalent of champagne and caviar.

This was the first party the underground leadership had officially allowed since the intifada's outset. It was also the first time the army had not moved in immediately to squash demonstrations of Palestinian nationalism. As policy, the army was suppressing the smallest demonstrations and using live ammunition if necessary. Beneath the celebratory hullabaloo, the tension was still there. Every person was watching for the army. When the electricity was suddenly cut off, the village fell into darkness and people scattered.

"The army is coming," some shouted. I froze, trying to make up my mind which way to try to run—down through the olive groves or into a nearby house. Everyone else was trying to make the same decision.

The lights came back on, and the villagers looked around nervously. But the army had not moved and the party resumed.

From the roof of a building opposite the kindergarten, other *mulethamin* lighted fireworks that shot glitzy tracers of color into the evening sky. The soldiers still did not come down as hope spilled through the village.

Women hugged each other as the crowd got drunker and drunker on the idea of independence. Men hugged each other. Children ran around the fire, applauding with a holiday glee. The youngest villagers might not have understood what had happened, but they recognized the wondrous import of the event.

The declaration of that independence was written by a Palestinian poet, Mahmoud Darwish, and read in Algeria by Arafat. Translated from Arabic, it proclaimed in part:

> The National Council declares in the name of God and in the name of the Palestinian Arab people, the establishment of the State of Palestine on our Palestinian land, with its capital holy Jerusalem.
>
> The State of Palestine is for Palestinians wherever they might be. In it they will develop their national and cultural identity. They will enjoy full equality in rights. Their religious, political, and human dignity will be safeguarded under a democratic parliamentary system based on freedom of expression and freedom to form parties, wherein the majority will take care of the rights of the minority

and the minority will respect the decisions of the majority. It will be based on social justice, equality and nondiscrimination in public rights on the basis of race, religion or color.

The framers of this new, abstract state called for an end to the Israeli occupation and agreed for the first time that Israel had the right to exist on the condition that Palestine would also exist.

Nahalin's *mulethamin* wired the big flag from their procession across the middle of the street, declaring their independence as concretely as they could. Night fell, and the villagers drifted back home to await the next day. The army never came down, apparently under orders to keep the inevitable celebrations as cool as possible. They uncharacteristically avoided confrontation.

Since journalists had not been able to penetrate the West Bank that day or night, almost nothing was reported to the outside world about the hope that welled from the Palestinians. The intifada had accomplished something even though Palestine remained a state of mind rather than geography.

The only obvious change that occurred the next morning was the disappearance of the soldiers from their *nuqtas*. The crisis was over. The big flag hung in place, and now that the West Bank was again open to traffic, life resumed its routines. But the atmosphere was charged. The villagers seemed to lift their feet higher and hold their heads more proudly.

I took the village bus to Bethlehem and saw that the hillsides were layered with what looked like gold, from the light shining through the terraces of grapevines whose leaves had curled and turned translucent. In places, the leaves had fallen, revealing the gray tendrils beneath. The only road open was the one that led past the army post. But Abu Sayal, his white *kefiyeh* crisp with the morning, pushed his bus up the steep rise to the shoulder of Abu al-Koroun, confident as a rider on an aging but faithful horse. As the bus reached the ridgeline, I noticed that the road was lined with young pines planted by the Israelis, and the trees were thriving in the stony landscape.

F O U R T E E N

The offer from Hassan and Inam to rent me rooms beneath their house did not fall through. I arrived at their door with some extra sheets in my suitcase, and we went together through a mint garden and under a pair of olive trees to a doorway beneath the main house. Hassan was carrying a key befitting the entrance to a medieval castle, a black iron instrument on a chain and weighing half a pound. Far too large to fit in a pocket, it was typical of the keys used for all the village's older locks. The double doors of heavy painted metal were grander than the interior, two whitewashed rooms divided by a cubbyhole, where a sink was bolted into the wall.

The previous tenant was a flock of sheep. Despite the fresh whitewash, the rooms smelled of the mustiness of livestock. But when I opened the windows, a cold late-November wind from the mountains scoured the air. Hassan moved a wooden bedstead down from above, and Inam brought blankets. I added a wicker chair and table from the Bethlehem market, a small rug, a kerosene stove, an Arabic coffee pot, a small teapot, cups and spoons. I hung my dresses on nails pegged into the wall and folded my other clothes in a cardboard box under the bed. The view, crisscrossed with laundry lines and interrupted by rooftop water tanks and angular banks of solar heaters, took in the southwestern side of the village. I could see the village's minaret and the valley winding around the knoll below the village toward Ain Feres. I had two and a half rooms with a view. I also had privacy.

Proving that my privacy was by no means inviolable, Inam came scurrying down through a sudden rain at midday with her rambunctious sons while I was still organizing my several possessions. She invited me for chicken and rice in their spaciously designed and meagerly furnished house.

Hassan and Inam were poor. He was an architectural engineer and had spent his earnings from a good job in Saudi Arabia on his house. He never earned enough once he returned to the West Bank to buy amenities. He owned a couple of beds, a set of closets, some stuffed chairs and two tables. The house upstairs was half empty. Hassan had yet to find a job commensurate with his education. He was working as a laborer, hauling concrete and carrying stone, using his muscles to implement designs that he could have engineered himself. He was forced to depened upon day labor, the toughest, least well paid and least steady work there was. Each morning at dawn Palestinians would arrive at Jerusalem's no-man's-land and wait to be hired by building contractors. The Israelis cruised through the lot, looking for the strongest men. Even young men were often left without work. In addition, the strike days cut into basic wages. Hassan was making sometimes as little as three hundred dollars a month. His training was irrelevant. His tall muscular build was what mattered in the eyes of his employers.

When Hassan returned from abroad with his savings, Inam was fifteen, a schoolgirl in Nahalin. Her father agreed readily to the proposal from Hassan, who was from a respected village family. She was a desirable bride, a pretty girl with light skin, freckles and long, curling hair. Inam had powerful family connections, too, being the sister of Abu Jafer, who was moving toward the day when he would preside over Nahalin's largest *hamula.* Inam was given no choice in the matter of her marriage. She showed me pictures of her wedding; she was engulfed in white frills, and her mouth was painted a bright red, but she had little expression on her face.

When we talked alone, she told me that she was not unhappy with marriage, only with the circumstance in which it had left her, half educated and with children who consumed her every minute. When she was not worrying about them, she was worrying about money, yearning for furniture and pretty dresses that would have taken an engineer's salary to provide in any quantity. She was smart, and she wanted to continue her studies, perhaps in nursing. But that eventuality was beyond any horizon she could see at the moment, at the age of nineteen.

It was not until the day I moved in that Hassan and I carefully edged into the subject of how much rent I would pay. Polite to a fault, Hassan had not raised the issue directly. The setting of the rent was arrived at by discussing the cost of refinishing the old well alongside the house, an oblique means of addressing the family's need for money.

"Not that you need to pay for the well," said Hassan, who went on to repeat that if he had money, he would not take a shekel in rent from me, in the way of Palestinian hospitality.

I finally suggested a generous sum by village standards, more than one hundred dollars a month. It was agreed upon immediately.

That night, after being taken around to be introduced and reintroduced to the neighbors on each side, I took a private ceremonial pleasure in closing and bolting my door. I folded my clothes as neatly as a Palestinian and snuggled into my narrow bed, alone. By candlelight, I took some notes, and then I enjoyed my solitude. I felt safe. Certainly Abu Jafer, with all his influence on the Shakarna side of the village, must have approved the arrangement his sister made with me. Abid, the retired police detective, must also have given his brotherly go-ahead. The Najajra clan, I knew, would never cause me trouble, and I also had the assurance from the man from Fatah and his operators that I would be watched over. That night I was as pleased as I could be. I had managed to move into Nahalin, into its very middle, about halfway up the hill from the village center and the mosques.

I lay awake and listened to the silence of the mountains. The rain had stopped, and no noises came from the streets or the houses. People were asleep, the men resting for another day of work or another day of workless frustration, the women resting for another day of washing and cooking and the *shabab* resting for another day of unpredictable events.

Some neighbors had stabled a donkey beside their house. It slept fitfully and brayed at odd interludes. It sounded to me as if the beast were voicing all the village's woes bound into one gaspingly repetitive expression. The donkey's braying ended abruptly after minutes while the village seemed to suffer without cease through summer drought and winter rains. Nahalin, now that I had pushed so hard to find a place to live here, was not the quiet hamlet I had hoped it would be in my earliest and most farfetched imaginings. It was a hard little village, stony and uncomfortable, beset by troubles that welled from its internal squabblings and came flooding over its horizons, a village of small-town gossip plagued by global problems. But I had somehow found a niche, and my own troubles in the village promised to lessen.

I slept happily under a pile of blankets, inhaling the smell of sheep that permeated the plastering of the walls, until a blast of musical chants from the main mosque startled me from my slumbers.

ALLAHU AKBAR U MOHAMMAD RASUL ALLAH. GOD IS GREAT AND MOHAMMAD IS HIS PROPHET.

It was the predawn call to prayer, recorded and played over

loudspeakers from the high balcony of the minaret, a call that used to be chanted at a shout by a mosque attendant. The chanter, a muezzin, has been replaced at almost every mosque by electronic equipment that automatically sounds the call to prayer five times a day. I had heard the chanting many times before, but I had never slept so close to the mosques.

The smaller mosque quickly joined in with a mimicking counterpoint, so that praises to Allah collided and then mixed with each other, filling the darkness with a jangled harmony. Only the most serious Muslims rose to pray at that hour. Most Nahalinis kept sleeping. Only in the month of Ramadan, when many villagers fasted through the daylight hours, were the mosques filled with worshipers obedient to the first call to prayer.

Within a few nights, I learned to pull a pillow over my head and fall back to sleep without heeding the amplified supplications from the mosques. That night, though, I got up and quietly un-bolted my doors so that I could look down on the cold village. Wrapping a blanket around my shoulders, I stood shivering in the clouded night and soon crawled back into my bed. I had intended to luxuriate and sleep into the morning, ignoring the habitual early rising of the various families that had hosted me since my arrival in Nahalin. But when the morning had hardly turned the clouds gray, Inam, with children trailing, was knocking on the door. I vaulted out of bed, pulled on a skirt and sweater, straightened the covers on the bed and answered the knock, knowing that I had no choice but to hospitably open the door. When I did, they all four trooped in cheerfully. The boys examined each of my scanty furnishings with delight, as if the possessions of a foreigner were magical. Immediately I went into the second room and squatted on the floor by the kerosene stove, which I began pumping.

"Welcome. Sit down. I am making tea," I said, imitating the Palestinian way.

"No, no, no," interjected Inam. "We came to invite you for breakfast. You must come up."

I did, feeling that I never would be able to repay any of these villagers for their insatiable hospitality. I had not forgotten that several weeks before a band of disguised *shabab* had stoned me twice, but I had found trust again, this time within the Shakarna clan.

Disguises were among the array of tactics employed by both Israelis and Arabs as they struggled against each other. I also played with disguise, by adopting longer and longer skirts to comply with village fashion and by donning head scarves to comply with the codes of Islamic fundamentalism.

The original disguise of the intifada was the simplest, that of the *mulethamin* who wrapped their heads in *kefiyeh*s. It worked to protect them from being identified when they confronted Israelis. The masks made the Palestinians look ominous and larger than life, more threatening because no one could see their young and sometimes adolescent faces, only the glint of their dark eyes.

The disguise worked for the *mulethamin* unless they were seriously wounded and taken to a hospital, where Israelis were monitoring who was being shot. They demanded from reluctant Palestinian doctors the names of wounded *shabab*, whom they would often then imprison. Lightly wounded Palestinians tried to stay away from hospitals so that they could remain anonymous. Within this province of disguise and identity, a macabre struggle often took place over bodies. If a Palestinian youth died of his wounds, the army tried to seize the corpse so as to control the funeral and limit its attendance to close family members. Otherwise, corpses easily became the focus of angry Palestinian crowds. *Shabab* sometimes stood guard at hospitals waiting for the death of a compatriot so that they could spirit the body away before Israeli soldiers arrived to do the same thing.

Members of the Shin Bet were quick to employ their own disguises. They commandeered from Palestinians cars with blue or green West Bank license plates and drove into Arab neighborhoods wearing checkered headcloths. They arrested Palestinian suspects, raided businesses that had refused to pay taxes and surveilled neighborhoods. They also used the trick of posing as journalists by pasting press signs on their cars or vans. This, of course, made life more difficult for me. I didn't want to be mistaken for the Shin Bet and stoned again.

I also didn't want to incur unnecessary anger from the Palestinian fundamentalists, who were on the rise by the fall of the first year of the intifada. Hamas, the most militant arm of the Muslim Brotherhood, was becoming a force in the intifada. The PLO factions looked moderate by comparison. Hamas had little tolerance for other religions, and it was willing to enforce its beliefs with violence. In a strange period of cooperation at the outset of the Palestinian uprising, Israel had encouraged the growth of Hamas as a counterweight to the PLO. That ended, though, when Hamas burst out of control to become a player in the uprising, and Israel banned the organization.

In the village, more and more young Nahalinis were joining the Hamas movement, convinced that bellicose Islam was the answer to their frustrations. This was different from the gentler beliefs of the regular Sunni Muslims and the otherworldly Sufi Muslims, who separated their religion from their politics. For the militants of Hamas, Islam and its most dogmatic codes of conduct were inseparable from the struggle against the occupation. They believed that power flowed from Islam. If traditional values were reinstated, the dignity and power of the Palestinian people would also be reinstated. Violating Islam was tantamount to thwarting the quest for power.

A woman wandering about without family was an insult to Hamas's sensibilities. So the stronger Hamas grew, the longer grew my dresses. In a further effort to compensate for my maverick behavior, I took to covering my head in the village and making sure my dresses brushed the ground. I also stopped wearing a belt, so that my waistline was not outlined. Step by step, I was looking more and more like a village woman, rectangular and staid.

My village guise protected me from the scrutiny of a squad of Israeli soldiers who were making a house-to-house search exactly like the one I had seen several months earlier. I again was at Hanan's, but this time the soldiers decided to search our side of the road. By the time we realized what was happening, the squad was striding up the narrow roadway toward the top of the well top, where we were sitting as usual. It was too late for us to maneuver. Hanan's brothers went inside the house, a way of proving that they were minding their own business, not out looking for trouble. The women stayed where they were. Hanan was embroidering, and her mother and sister were sorting apples from a sack, separating the good from the bad, the ripe from the unripe. I cautiously backed my chair into the shade by the corner of the house, pulled my scarf over my forehead and stooped forward like an old woman. I cast my eyes on the ground in hopes that their blueness would not be evident. If necessary, I could whip out my passport, but for my sake and for the sake of Hanan's family, I did not want to have to explain why I was dressed like a Palestinian. It would have taken more than a few words.

As I crouched in the shade, the soldiers filed directly into the house. Hanan went in behind them. I heard a splintering sound and a crash but no shouts, so I presumed that no one was being hurt. A few minutes later, they all came out, the five soldiers and the three Palestinians. The soldiers went to the next house, one pausing to glance questioningly at me before following his comrades.

I went inside with the Palestinians to survey the damage. The soldiers had pulled both doors to the closet in the visitors' room off their hinges and thrown them on the floor, revealing the contents—an assortment of fabrics and yarns, a sewing basket and folded clothes. The soldiers had grabbed some sweaters and thrown them about the room, whose only other furniture was the neat line of simple wooden chairs for guests. In the next room, where some of the family slept, the soldiers had slashed a mattress in half so that its wool stuffing eddied around our feet.

"Why did they do this?" I asked Hanan.

"To see if we were hiding anything dangerous," she said.

"Like what?"

"Oh, I guess they wanted to find weapons or PLO literature. But they never find anything like that in Nahalin."

We watched from the windows of the guest room as the soldiers filed from house to house, entering finally Hilmi's home. I knew the house contained one young boy, females and a strict Hilmi, who would allow nothing dangerous to go on. But the soldiers went in, and the children came scurrying out with their mother onto the veranda. We heard the sound of pots and pans clattering onto the cement floor of their kitchen.

My dress and scarf might have fended off Israeli soldiers and it may have mollified Hamas, but it did little to allay the suspicions of a group of young men who hailed me while I was walking up the hill toward my rooms. They were sitting in an empty shop that had been converted into a rudimentary repair garage. A car was up on blocks, and they were positioned to its side around a kerosene stove on which they were brewing coffee.

I went and sat with them, although I had not met them before. The young men began asking me questions, particularly a large, square-faced one and a second one, who was wearing a red T-shirt that announced LIVE FOR TODAY.

"What do you think about the situation?" the big one asked.

"I think the time is hard, but the people are strong," I said diplomatically. I sensed that this was going to be a quiz of my politics, and I trod delicately. I also sensed that these men might be some of the group who had stoned me. Something made me edgy. I was not in danger. We were sitting peacefully a few yards from the roadway, where villagers were coming and going. But there was something hard in the eyes of those I was sitting with. Inwardly I prepared myself to make every effort to convince them of what I was doing in Nahalin.

"What do you think about Fatah?" the one with the T-shirt interjected impatiently.

"Fatah is good," I said.

"What do you mean?"

"Fatah is the group that follows the path of Yasir Arafat, and Yasir Arafat founded the PLO. Arafat is the first among the PLO's leaders," I said, trying to dodge the question.

"Arafat is good?" he asked.

"Yes, Arafat is good," I answered, not wanting to aggravate my listeners. I did not idealize any of the Palestinian leaders, although I had come to understand their common goal. I had grown continually more convinced that the sooner a separate Palestinian state was created, the sooner the violence would abate. If it did not, the Palestinian struggle could continue endlessly.

"The state will come," I offered.

"When?" the big one asked.

"That is the question," I said. "No one knows. One year, two years, five years, ten years. But if the state does not come, the Israelis will have a bigger problem. They will have to kill or get rid of all the Palestinians."

My questioners nodded uniformly.

"Why are you here in Nahalin?" the big one continued with his line of questioning.

"Because I want to understand the problems of the Palestinians, and Nahalin has all the problems. There is the problem of the land, the problem of the settlements, the problem with the army that has a base here above the village, the problem with the economy. The people are poor, they have trouble finding good work and the fields don't provide enough to live on. Nahalin has no telephone that works; it gets no help from the government for its roads; its school has been closed for more than a year; the children are forgetting how to read. Look, you can see for yourself the biggest problem."

I pointed to Abu al-Koroun and to Daher al-Matarsiya. "That land is gone. More settlers are coming. Nahalin is surrounded." I thought my speech was convincing.

"But why do you need to live in Nahalin? Why can't you just get your information and leave? Why do you stay here?" the one with the red T-shirt said.

At this point, I gave up on the niceties of the discussion and tried using my best piece of brute logic. "Listen to me, please," I said. "If I were a spy, I would not be in this village. I would be in a village where important Palestinians lived. I would be in a village where the *mulethamin* truly are giving the Israelis a headache. I would be in Husan, where they throw stones at the settlers; I would be in Battir, where they attack the train; I would be in Deheisheh, where they have the courage to face the soldiers who patrol there every day; or I would be in Bethlehem, where the *shabab* throw stones in the market.

"Not Nahalin. What has Nahalin done? The *shabab* have cut a few of the settlers' trees; they have pulled down fences. But why would a spy care about something so easy? Nahalin is not a serious matter."

My words were having an impact. The young men were looking bemused rather than fierce.

"OK," the one with the T-shirt said. "Drink coffee with us."
He held out a cup of coffee.

"OK," I said, refraining from asking them whether they were
the ones who had stoned me. "OK," I said again. I drained the small
china cup quickly and continued on my way, feeling as if I had won
a battle in my own personal war.

But I was frustrated by illusion. How many layers did I need
to peel away before I could approach the truth? This village that had
seemed almost straightforward when I first saw it seemed more and
more like a tough old onion to me, with layer after layer of obstruc-
tive illusion.

I went to visit Abu Jafer, knowing that his acquaintance gave
me legitimacy as well as clout in the eyes of the suspicious. The
power of Abu Jafer's clan did not make him arrogant. He quietly
played his several roles of shopkeeper, teacher and mediator. At his
shop in the afternoons, he tended to a steady stream of women and
children bearing coins or small bills. If they did not have money, he
entered the debt in a well-thumbed school notebook he kept in a
top drawer.

"I never count how much somebody owes me. I wait until
they come and pay. They will pay if they can. If they can't, why
should I waste my time adding it up?" he said philosophically.

Abu Jafer had me take a seat by the counter and talked as
he weighed rice or fetched tins from the shelves. The latest village
news was that the *mukhtar* had resigned under the pressure of village
opinion, not because he was disliked but because the job was unten-
able. *Mukhtar*s had been quitting all over the West Bank. The job
was impossible to do without angering the villagers. If the Israelis
shut off the water to the village or cut its telephone, the *mukhtar* in
Nahalin was the one who had to go to the offices of the Israeli
military government and beg for a reprieve. He was a factotum for
the Israelis, and the villagers eventually demanded that he quit.

Without the *mukhtar*, though, the villagers had no middleman for dealing with the authorities.

"The peoples' relationship with the military administration is cut," Abu Jafer said. "This is going to cause problems with daily life. No one can talk to the Israelis if the village has a problem. If we need our roads repaired, no one will go to argue our case. Not that they were repairing our roads anyway."

Our conversation was interrupted several times by an order from a customer for a chicken. When chicken meat was needed, Abu Jafer disappeared for a couple of minutes to the pen in the back and, after much squawking, reappeared with a plastic bag containing a cleaned and plucked chicken.

Abu Jafer was as curious about the United States as I was about Nahalin. He mused about how rich Americans were, how educated Americans were and why the American government didn't seem to care about the problems of the Palestinians.

"The Americans," he said, "live in better circumstances than anyone in the history of the world. This is true, right?"

I agreed.

"The Americans believe in their minds that all people in the world have the right to freedom. This is true. So why do they forget about the Palestinians? I think that maybe they don't understand what it is to suffer. They can't imagine what it is like to be occupied. Their lives are easy, so they don't need to think so much. The Palestinians know everything they can about the United States, but the Americans don't know anything about the Palestinians."

I was getting used to living with those of the Shakarnas, led by Abu Jafer's *hamula*, who had accepted me. The neighbors on all sides of my new abode were welcoming. Immediately next door was a family with six daughters. The mother was pregnant and praying for a break in her luck; she needed a son to establish her worth.

Across the road and down a bit was the house of Abu Mazin, the dignified man who refused to shake hands with me except through his pocket lining. This was an unusual family, because it combined clans. Abu Mazin, a Najajra, had married a Shakarna. Imm Mazin was Abu Mazin's opposite, a woman as squarely fat as her husband was wiry and tall. They had produced a large and energetic family. Mazin, the eldest son, was studying in Yugoslavia. Qasim and green-eyed Fou'ad, who were among the brightest students in the village, belonged to the family. Qasim, the oldest son at home, was studying to be an engineer, refusing to stop his studies. He commuted to the town of Ramallah, where professors of Bir Zeit University continued to teach illegally.

The university campus, a group of costly modern buildings on a hillside by the mountain village of Bir Zeit, was off limits. The gates were locked. But the university had not gone to sleep. As with Bethlehem University, classes were held elsewhere. Bir Zeit's tattered administration building in the town of Ramallah became the center of the new campus, whose classrooms were scattered in secret locations. With his textbooks in a sack, Qasim regularly took Abu Sayal's bus into Bethlehem and from there rode by *service* to Ramallah. He was progressing toward his degree, but at what he regarded as a painfully slow speed.

"If the university were open, I would be finished by now. I would have completed a degree. I would be deciding on my professional life. I would be looking for a job or looking for another degree. I would know where I was going. Now I am stumbling down a pathway at a time in my life when I should be running. I should be studying all day. I should be able to go from classroom to classroom," Qasim said.

In the evenings, Qasim traveled to West Jerusalem, where he had a job tending a concession stand on the ground floor of the Israeli government's press building. He did the job enthusiastically, chatting with his customers as he sold potato chips, cola and beer. A movie theater in the same building drew crowds of Israelis. It was an excellent job for him because when business was slow, he sat and studied his engineering textbooks, preparing for his next underground class.

"In a normal country, in a normal time, I might even be an engineer by now and have a good job. I could help my father rather than watch him go off to work," Qasim said.

Abu Mazin owned land in the village, and his crops brought in money, but he supported his family mostly with his earnings from Israel. He worked cleaning the stairwells and gardens of an Israeli apartment complex in Jerusalem, a janitor by day transformed to the head of his household when he returned on the village bus in the late afternoon. With school out, he sometimes took Fou'ad along to aid him with the labor.

Fou'ad was growing bitter. "I think the Israelis are smart enough to know that the only thing they cannot take is our minds. So now they are killing our minds. What can we do?"

Two other sons, Omar and Mohammad, had left school for work. Mohammad had built a house behind his parents' home and insisted on growing a lawn out front, which required a steady sprinkler during the dry season and a stout wire fence to prevent the goats from instantly devouring the tender grass. There was nothing like it in the village. Omar, whose eyes also were an almost transparent green, laughed easily. He and Mohammad were always joking.

The two were sitting on the stairway to Mohammad's house, and Omar looked over at his brother's square of grass.

"You need to buy some spray paint," Omar said.

"Why?"

"For the grass."

"What's wrong with my grass?"

"It's not PLO grass."

"What do you mean it's not PLO grass?"

"It's Hamas grass. It's all green. You need to paint some of it red for Jebha and some of it black for Fatah," Omar continued. "Then if you paint it white, too, you will have the colors of the Palestinian flag. Now it is just green, so it is Hamas."

Rokeya, the eldest daughter in the family was a seamstress, and watched over my efforts at embroidering. With the help of several women, I had managed to complete a foot-long strip of embroidery. The problem was that each had interpreted the pattern in her own way, altering it slightly here and slightly there. Rokeya studied the work and sighed. The strip was filled with errors.

"I tried," I explained, not elaborating on the cause of the problem.

"Would you mind if I took out some of the mistakes?" Rokeya asked, her sense of artistry clearly offended, although she tried in the usual Palestinian fashion to be polite about it. "You are very clever. Many girls make many more mistakes when they begin. Yours is very good."

She sat down on a cushion, stretched out her legs and went to work, tearing out stitches with the point of her needle. She demolished loop after loop of my floral design, then threaded the needle and redid the stitching in less than an hour. Imm Mazin brought tea. Omar left, bored immediately by the embroidery, and a neighbor woman arrived whom I had not met. She and Imm Mazin talked about their rheumatism and the hard financial times brought on by the intifada. Abu Mazin stayed away from the room where the women sat on mats and pillows. He talked to men friends in a more formal outer room. I had seen him walking uphill to the house from where Abu Sayal stopped his bus in the afternoons, and as he walked, he lifted his head. By the time he arrived at the house, he would look not like a sweeper of stairs but like the master of a household blessed with healthy sons.

F I F T E E N

As the weeks went by, the Israeli army did not withdraw from the newly declared Palestinian state. The army removed some of its roadblocks, including the one between Nahalin and Husan, but that was about it. The Palestinian prisoners, who had fomented unrest to earn the world's attention and galvanize their leadership into taking action, remained very much in prison. Nothing changed except in the minds of those people who hoped the declaration of independence would have lasting significance. Farouk remained in detention.

The next time the Najajras actually laid eyes on him was thirty-eight days after his arrest. Ratiba and Fawzi saw him in the chief judge's chamber in a military court at Ramallah. The occasion was a bail hearing his lawyer had requested.

After all the worry, after all the inquiries through the Red Cross and the attempts by his lawyer to find out what was going on, there was no longer any question about what had been happening to Farouk. He had a black eye; the blood from a bruising blow had collected in the eye socket; the cornea of the same eye was red from hemorrhaging; one of his hands bore a slash that had not healed yet; and he needed help getting to his feet.

It was obvious before the first word was uttered that he had been beaten recently, at least once, probably more than once. The whole family knew by then that he was being kept in a special prison section for interrogation, where Shin Bet officials were trying to get information about the intifada and the Palestinians participating in it. But Farouk's family had not known what methods the Shin Bet were using.

It also was not clear what exactly were the charges against Farouk Najajra. He had refused to confess to anything, and his lawyer, Mary Rock, had been able to learn only that he was "suspected of membership in an illegal organization that undermines the security of the area." In other words, he was suspected of working with an organization probably affiliated with the PLO. The charges or allegations against Palestinian prisoners like Farouk did not have to be specified until the Shin Bet was satisfied.

Farouk's lawyer advised him to tell the judge what had happened to him. He did. Notes were taken for the court record, beginning with how five interrogators treated him when they began questioning him at a jail in Hebron, where he was first taken: "In Hebron, they hit me. One of them was tall, blond and gave me a black eye. They tied my hands behind my back and put me on the floor and hit me in the sexual region."

The court notes went on to describe a method that other Palestinian prisoners also complained about, the locking of detainees in a narrow box in which there was hardly room to move. "I was staying all the time in a cupboard," Farouk told the court. He explained that he was also penned in a bathroom: "They tied my hands to the taps in the sink, and when I wanted to use the toilet, they said to me, 'Say thank you.' I said, 'I have nothing to thank you for. I have done nothing.' They also gave me a kick in the throat and in the stomach. They laid me down for two days in the cold. They would leave me on the floor and sit on my back and hit me more and more on my legs. They picked me up by the throat and also hit me freely."

At the Dahiriya prison, where Farouk was taken next, the interrogations continued. He asked the judge to please prevent the continuation of the painful treatment.

A private hearing in the judge's chamber was not the norm in Ramallah military court, but Mary Rock was aggressive enough to obtain it. She lived up to the genes of some of her ancestors. She was descended from a Crusader who originally came to liberate the Holy Land from the people the Christian Europeans believed were heathens. He stayed on and planted his name among the Palestinians. Before the intifada, Mary Rock practiced civil law. But she switched to the more difficult job of defending political prisoners in the military court system out of duty to her fellow Palestinians.

The military judge, after hearing what Farouk had said and after reading a secret report on the charges against him, decided to give the Shin Bet more time to get answers from their prisoner. But he also ordered "medical checks" for Farouk and an investigation into "the claims of the defendant on the subject of violence to his person."

Mary Rock said she was worried about Farouk's state. "I could see the pain in him; all his body was trembling in pain."

Fawzi was terse. "Farouk is not the first, and he will not be the last. That is our situation. We hope it is changing."

As more weeks passed, the daily struggle between the Palestinians and the Israelis continued. On the removed stage of global politics, Arafat was uttering fresh statements about peace and Israel's right to exist. Israeli politicians were fighting with each other about how to respond, and the United States was making overt diplomatic gestures toward the PLO for the first time in history. But in the West Bank, the troubles did not lessen.

One day before the advent of the Christmas season, a Nahalini came marching down one of the village roadways brandishing an olive branch, a stout and newly downed limb rustling with green leaves. He cursed as he swung the branch in wild arcs.

Seeing me coming the other way, he stopped in his tracks, slammed the butt of the branch down like the stock of a giant rifle and started shouting. At first I thought he was a madman. But after I persuaded him to slow his Arabic to my speed of comprehension, I understood what was happening. He was hauling the olive branch back to his house as evidence, splintered proof, of the outrage the Israelis had just committed against his land, against his well-being and his family's well-being for generations to come.

The day before, Israelis—whether it was soldiers or settlers or both, he did not know—had invaded his plot of land on the slope of Daher al-Matarsiya below the new Betar settlement. They had cut down his olive trees, his last remaining grove on the mountainside. He had seen distant figures moving about on his two acres planted in olives. But he did nothing because he knew the Israelis could do what they wanted and an aging man like himself could not stop them. When he went up to the land the next morning, he found devastation. All the olive trees, which he had planted himself more than a decade earlier, had been sawed down, and next to their stumps pine seedlings were nestled in the ground. The pines were unmistakably the work of Israelis. Olives were the sustenance of the villagers and pines the trees that the settlers often cultivated. He had been too upset to count how many trees he had lost.

He showed me his house, whose courtyard already contained a pile of broken olive branches, and I agreed to go with him the next day to the mountain. He told me his name, Abid Rahman Raba Najajra, and explained that he had lived through far worse raids than this one. He was the son of the Nahalin *mukhtar* who was slain with eight others in 1954, when the village was attacked by Israeli commandos, an event that left scars on the memories of the older people in the village.

"I remember it exactly," Abid Rahman told me. "They came in the night and exploded the door of our house. I opened the door. I was fifteen years old when I saw them kill my father."

The morning after I met him in the street, Abid Rahman was waiting to take me to his land, dressed for the occasion in a sport coat and a spotless white *kefiyeh*. His beard was finely trimmed, but his face still was knotted in a perplexed anger. His wife and a grandson came with us as we climbed upward from the gardens by the village spring. We took one of the rough paths that snaked through the boulders at the base of the mountain and then meandered through rocky fields. Abid Rahman's land was easy to spot from a distance because his fields had been plowed for the winter; the earth was deep brown and clean of weeds. Above and below the hillside was thick with thorns and loose stones.

His olive trees, whose trunks were the thickness of a fist, had all been staked up and fenced with wire to protect their bark from the gnawing of the wild gazelles that proliferate in the Judean Mountains. Each tree was neatly sawed, all the way through, although some stood at stilted angles, held by the mesh of the wire. The new pine seedlings were protected by packed circles of earth to catch the rain that was coming ever more frequently with the end of autumn.

Abid Rahman's wife stared at the seedlings. "We can't make oil from these," she said.

Abid Rahman ignored the pines and counted his dead olives, striding from stump to stump.

"Eighty-eight," he announced. "Eighty-eight."

I recorded the number in my notebook and took some photographs, which seemed to end the ceremony of loss. The villager had no plans to raise a fight or go to court. He was accustomed to losing trees and losing in court. Further up on Daher al-Matar-siya, nearer the ridgeline and Betar, Israelis had destroyed about two hundred of his olives a few years back when they bulldozed a road into the settlement site. Years earlier on Abu al-Koroun, the army had taken twenty-five acres of his land and three hundred trees.

The Israelis announced no reason for cutting this latest grove of olive trees, but a look at the larger landscape provided a good guess. The Betar settlement had been growing as steadily as seed planted in fertile earth. The construction crane moved methodically every day, adding stone blocks to the new buildings.

We descended from Abid Rahman's land by a second path, which skirted another field, whose earth was soft and furrowed from a recent plowing by a peasant and his donkey. At intervals along the furrows, more pine seedlings thrust up their needled shoots. As we were picking our way back down through the boulders at the base of Daher al-Matarsiya, two boys with their faces wrapped like those of the older *mulethamin* came running past us at full speed, making an assault on the ridgeline. One was holding aloft a stick from which a rudely stitched Palestinian flag was streaming. Saying nothing to us, they charged upward on their mission, presumably to plant their flag as close by the construction site as possible, to declare at least an iota of resistance to Betar. I guessed from their size that neither was more than twelve years old.

We continued down, circumventing a jumble of massive boulders that were called the Matbakh, the Kitchen, because it was here that Arab soldiers rested and ate during the 1948 war. After the Arab Legion overran the pioneering Kfar Etzion kibbutz south of Nahalin, its soldiers continued on toward Jerusalem. Sporadic raids, including the one in which Abid Rahman's father was killed, followed the war. The men of Nahalin organized an armed watch guard for the village. Near the Kitchen was a natural stone trench looking out toward Jerusalem, which the Nahalinis used as a watch post, not always with complete effectiveness. Later, in the 1967 war, the Israelis had reversed the tide of victory, sweeping from West Jerusalem back across the breadth of the Jordanian-held West Bank to the Jordan River.

Also coming down from the lower slopes of the mountains that day were villagers leading donkeys laden with the pruned branches from the olives trees they were harvesting. The villagers would use the branches for fuel and fodder during the coming *shitta*, the almost constantly rainy spell of winter.

The pine seedlings planted so strategically on the slope below Betar did not survive. Under cover of night, Nahalin's *shabab* went to work. I climbed back up to the Kitchen with some of the older *shabab*, finding the pathways by the light of a moon that also enabled them to find the baby pines. Nine teenagers, most of them of secondary-school age and most of them known to me from my visits to different village homes, were in the group. They did not wrap their heads with *kefiyehs* because they planned to work stealthily, so as not to arouse the soldiers guarding the settlement above. As the Israelis had destroyed their symbol, they went about destroying the Israelis' symbol. I sat among the boulders and watched as the *shabab* brought down armloads of the seedlings, which were easy to uproot. Once they had undone the work of the Israelis, they sprinkled gasoline on the baby pines and lighted an arboreal pyre. They did not want their enemies to find the evidence of their countervandalism. The burning pines had a sweet smell, and the *shabab* warmed their dirt-encrusted fingers over the fire. The light thrown up by the flames cast shadows on their faces, making them look older and more warlike.

Christmas drew near, and the Israeli authorities tried to keep the holiday as normal as they could despite the unrest all around. Jerusalem's city workers were instructed to string multicolored lights along the highway leading to Bethlehem, a sight that looked like Christmas anywhere in the world. The lights spelled out a gigantic MERRY CHRISTMAS at the city's edge and then stopped, abruptly, so that at night the West Bank appeared to drop off into darkness.

The Palestinian Christians of Bethlehem were boycotting Christmas. The *shabab* and the middle-class citizenry—men, women and children—none among them was participating. The standard festivities, which included decorating the town, were canceled. To me, this seemed impossible, contradictory to all my impulses and memories of Christmas celebrated in other countries. Now I was at the heart of the legend, the place where Christmas began, and the holiday was turned on its end. Soldiers, not angels, watched over the town. War, not peace, was at hand.

The Palestinian mayor of Bethlehem, Elias Freij, a man noted for treading a safely conservative political path, did not extend his usual offers to host Israeli dignitaries on Christmas Eve. Christmas invitations did not go out. Freij kept his formerly amiable hand jammed in his pocket. The intifada leadership called a strike and urged the people via leaflets to observe "a day of national mourning." Instead of celebrating their holiday, Palestinian Christians were supposed to pay patriotic visits of condolence to families of those who had died, had been wounded or had been imprisoned during the intifada's first year.

According to statistics published by the United Nations, the Israeli army had fatally shot more than two hundred Palestinians during the year after the beginning of the uprising. More had died from the gunfire of settlers, beatings by the army and inhaling tear gas. Palestinian journalists doubled the figure. At least one young man had died in Bethlehem itself, one in the Deheisheh camp, two in Bethlehem's suburbs and five in the surrounding villages.

In normal times—if the various occupations of the town by

Romans, Byzantines, empire-building Muslims, European Crusaders, Mamlukes, Turks, Jordanians and, finally, Israelis were ever normal—Bethlehem attracted throngs of pilgrims and partygoers come to celebrate Christ's birth with prayers, choruses and revelry.

Bethlehem's Christians were first among the celebrants. But most of the town's other Palestinians, regardless of their faith, came to watch the spectacle at Manger Square on Christmas Eve—the buildings bangled with lights, the hotels jammed with tourists and evangelists, the restaurants overflowing, the local souvenir hawkers making a killing on olive-wood crosses and mother-of-pearl trinkets, the motorcades of visiting dignitaries, the choirs from churches around the world dressed in flowing robes like flocks of earth-bound angels and, grandest of all, the parade of the Roman Catholic patriarch from Jerusalem. Before the intifada, the patriarch was welcomed by a massive reception of the townspeople, his arrival for midnight mass heralded from afar by marching bands. The ecstastic reception of the patriarch was a centuries-old tradition.

Before the 1948 war and the establishment of the Israeli state, Bethlehem was a pastoral town of about ten thousand Palestinian Christians. But the war produced a flood of Muslim refugees from their villages and towns in the broad coastal plains taken by Israelis. Tens of thousands of refugees sought shelter in Bethlehem, settling in the older quarters of town near the square or in camps— Deheisheh at Bethlehem's southern flank and two smaller locations within the city. By the time of the intifada, more than half of Bethlehem's population of thirty thousand was Muslim.

The minarets of five mosques competed with the steeples of twenty churches, the amplified Islamic calls to prayer mixing with the chanting of priests and the ringing of bells. The Christians were wealthier than the Muslims, and many had moved moved from the older neighborhoods around Manger Square to new houses on the adjoining hills that looked down over Shepherd's Field, a greensward where an angel supposedly delivered the news of the holy birth to peasants tending their flocks.

Over the years, Manger Square had become Bethlehem's principal attraction. One of its sides was dominated by the Basilica of the Nativity, a fortress of a church built above the grotto where Mary gave birth to Jesus. One small door, through which visitors stooped to enter, led into the church, whose encircling ramparts were designed to repel invaders over the centuries. It looked like a citadel with bell towers peeking over its weathered stone walls.

The square itself was a valley in the old days, separating the homes of Bethlehem's townspeople and the biblical inn from the caves in which the simpler peasants lived. Some of them built crude rooms above the caves and used the space beneath to stable their animals—the style still used by Nahalinis and other villagers who kept their herds beneath their homes. It was in such a manger that Mary and Joseph found lodging on the eve of Christ's birth.

As the town grew, the valley was filled in. Finally the square was paved for a parking lot able to accommodate the big tour buses that plied the tourist route between the Jersualem hotels and the site of Christ's nativity. The lot also served as a staging area for the Israeli soldiers and police who came in droves to the station that took up a second side of the square. A bushy cedar added a splash of green to the otherwise blank white facade of the police station. Facing the station was the New Tourist Shopping Center, a long building of clean stone fronted by an arched walkway and a gallery of souvenir shops.

The modernized Manger Square was a project that made Mayor Freij proud, being the centerpiece of the tourist trade, which grew to be the town's most lucrative business. It was booming until the intifada dragged the reality of the conflict between Palestinian and Israeli into the middle of Bethlehem, scaring tourists away. The mayor, whose office in the municipal building overlooked the fourth side of the square, estimated unhappily at Christmastime that the uprising had cost his town at least five million dollars in lost trade with tourists.

Beyond the municipal building were the stately Mosque of Omar and then the warren of winding streets and stairways that led to the market where the Nahalinis and others traded. Most tourists did not wander the town's back alleyways but rather were steered to the shops along the square, which cautiously defied the routinized intifada closing hour of noon by leaving a door half-shuttered and a beckoning salesman out front.

When Mayor Freij, caught in the surge of the intifada, declared that the town would eschew decorations, the Israelis took up the burden as best they could. Soldiers from the Israeli Defense Forces decked out the tree by the police station. Having been raised on Hanukkah candles rather than Christmas lights, the soldiers understandably did not perform well. By Christmas Eve, they had managed to fix a large and straggly five-pointed star of green and orange lights in the middle of the tree, leaving the rest of the tree blank. The star made the dark square even less festive.

One of the twists to the scene was the historical fact that the Jews, not the Christians, founded Bethlehem long before Christ's birth. On the main highway, there is the tomb of Rachel, whose life was chronicled in the Book of Genesis. The town was also known to the early Jewish rulers as the birthplace of their great King David. Bethlehem was called the City of David, and now the heirs of David were trying to make the town look festively Christian.

On Christmas Eve, the entire Palestinian population of the town shut its shops and stayed off the streets, obeying the strike call. The Israelis sent soldiers and police in case the holiday sparked trouble. By afternoon, police had barricaded the square and deployed themselves every few yards along the road winding up to it. Army jeeps jammed with soldiers buzzed through the streets. A cold rain fell on the town, as if the heavens were conspiring with the Palestinian leadership to dampen the celebration.

Wanting to witness Christmas, I made my way to the square in the afternoon. No Palestinian would come with me. The Nahalinis were Muslims, and the few Christian acquaintances I had in Bethlehem were determined to stay indoors. When I arrived, the rain had settled down to a constant drizzle that soon soaked the clusters of reporters and pilgrims, largely from Europe and the United States, huddling under umbrellas and listening to taped music blaring from loudspeakers on a pole in the square's parking lot.

The drizzle kept up. Several Palestinians darted across a corner of the square, but when accosted by reporters, they kept going, refusing to talk, not wanting to be noticed. Not a shepherd was to be seen, only well-meaning imported choirs and evangelical Christians preaching to whoever would listen. Also, there were hundreds of Israeli police in rain gear marked with silver reflecting stripes and hundreds of soldiers in army-green ponchos. Contingents of Border Police patrolled the roads, the blue warning lights of their jeeps flashing blearily through the rain.

As the evening wore on, more tourists came, and General Amram Mitzna arrived, standing in for the wise men. He was the wise man, in a sense, of the Bethlehem region, being the chief army commander for the West Bank. He certainly was the strong man of Bethlehem. I had not met him before, and I was drawn to him, fascinated at seeing the man whose job it was to keep the Palestinians quiet. Surrounding him in a loose scrum were five plainclothesmen, one of them dressed inconspicuously except for an radio-telephone bulging under his jacket, with its rubberized antenna sticking up alongside his neck, and another dressed in an ill-fitting white suit, sopping by this time, with a bulky gun partially hidden beneath it. General Mitzna presided over every Palestinian

I knew. He was the highest-ranking officer against whom the *shabab* of the Bethlehem region were fighting. His name was a household word on the West Bank.

He was a tall man with a beard and confident bearing. I was surprised how calm he was as he spoke with several reporters in the rain. He was relaxed even though his troops were impossible to supervise visibly as they emerged and receded from sight in the rain and a rising fog.

"We are ready to go back to a normal life from this unhappiness," he said. "We are not encouraging anyone to come or not to come to Bethlehem. Christmas is mainly a day of thinking about the future. I am optimistic all the time. You have to be optimistic if you want to go on solving the problem."

The general bristled briefly when a radio reporter asked whether he had anything to do with decorating the police-station cedar.

"Some of the the journalists think we are enforcing happiness. We are not doing anything like that. The only thing we have to do is enforce security and let the people come to celebrate if they want to celebrate."

As midnight approached, scant numbers of pilgrims, evangelists and choristers were gathered, waiting for the mass to begin in a church within the basilica. The drizzle never stopped, and with the fog the town of Bethlehem looked black.

There was little ebullience at the midnight mass. The patriarch from Jerusalem, Michel Sabbah, was unsmiling. He was a Palestinian, the first to be appointed to the position, and had to be forced to take part in the procession to the square, with the threat that the Roman Catholics might lose some of their religious rights if he did not. The only person shouting joyously was a young Israeli soldier outside the Church of the Nativity, declaiming "Merry Christmas, Merry Christmas" to all who passed.

Michel Sabbah's Christmas message was short. He read it with a grave face, saying in part:

> The people, the Christian Palestinians in Bethlehem and the Holy Land, have no joy of Christmas in their hearts. Some have had a son or a father killed, others are still in prisons and all face heavy military repression.
>
> On this feast of peace and joy, the Church of Jerusalem addresses an appeal for peace to every man of goodwill. With His Holiness Pope John Paul II we say again that both peoples here must accept their mutual legitimate aspirations and must have trust in the other. They must trust in the goodness of man and free themselves from fear.
>
> On this feast of peace and joy, to the people of the Holy Land still fighting we say, secure borders can be secure only if the hearts are reconciled. Secure borders are not secure by technology or violence or occupied territories. Only reconciled hearts, love and truth make secure borders.

While Michel Sabbah conducted the mass, some *shabab* crept down through the alleyways from the *souq* and threw rocks at the soldiers by the police station. The soldiers gave chase but did not fire.

In the week following Chirstmas, seven more Palestinians were shot and killed in the occupied territories.

S I X T E E N

The Arabic word *shitta* means "winter," and it also means "rain." The two were much the same. By December, the clouds had gathered over the mountains in earnest, stolid layers that blocked the sun for days on end. If it was not raining, it was gray. By January, the whole village was sodden. The rainwater turned the dirt paths to mud and permeated the walls of the houses. The bare stone floors radiated a chill. The villagers kept their coats on inside and cupped their hands around their tea glasses for warmth.

But the earth basked under the extravagance of water. The dun hills of autumn soaked in the rain greedily. The *fellahin* had plowed their terraced fields for the next season's crops, giving the land a furrowed texture. The earth turned a richer brown with each onslaught of rain.

By the time the *shitta* was underway, I had established solid ties with several families in Nahalin. Dozens of children knew my name and would shout it excitedly as I walked along the village roads. They giggled uncontrollably when I shouted back at them in street Arabic, badgering them in return with a litany of friendly questions.

Farouk's family, though, was as miserable as the weather. News filtered out from the prisons, through the Red Cross, through released prisoners or through cousins of cousins who had visited detainees. The word about Farouk was that he had held out for fifty-six days with the Shin Bet. But among the other young men recently arrested from Nahalin were two of his cohorts. After several days, they had broken and implicated Farouk. Few *shabab* lasted longer than a week. Farouk, it was rumored, had been forced to confess when confronted with the testimony of his friends, admitting to throwing stones and, more significantly, belonging to a Jebha "strike force" that implemented attacks on the Israelis. Farouk looked to be facing a long jail sentence.

But the news could be wrong. The best source of information from the prisons had ceased. The Palestinian lawyers who shuttled to and from the prisons had gone on strike to protest what they considered to be a sham of justice. Their complaints ranged from not being allowed to see their clients to the use of torture to extract confessions that would be admitted as binding evidence in court. The prisoners had agreed to the strike because they, too, believed the Israeli system unfair. They agreed with the lawyers' point that attention needed to be called to the injustice that they felt characterized the system. Given the strike, there was only a sliver of hope that Farouk would soon be free.

Deeb, too, was still in the hands of the Israelis, in the Negev Desert at Ansar Three, a detention center consisting entirely of tents and wire fences. And although the nights during the winter season were frigid, since the desert held no warmth, Deeb refused to waver from his hard stance. He wrote in a letter that he did not care whether the Israelis kept him for three months or six months. "They are dogs," he wrote.

Ratiba refused to smile at anything. She had thrown herself into her work, cooking, hefting things around the compound, hauling hay and tending the sheep. I tried to cheer up Sena by bringing her the latest news magazines from Jerusalem and prodding her with

English. I brought more books with me, too. Few Nahalinis owned books of any kind. I did what I could to help with the bored students who had no classes to distract them from the monotony of the *shitta*. I brought fairy tales, American short stories, British novels, books in Arabic or whatever I could find.

I had picked up for Abu Marwan, the idled geography professor, a book in Arabic entitled *The History of Palestine*. When he saw the title, he blanched. He flipped through the book and suggested that I give it to a neighbor of his from whom he could borrow it. He was afraid that even though the book was sold in Jerusalem, it would be banned on the West Bank—more than one thousand books were—and that he would be punished if soldiers happened to raid his house and find it. He said that he read about historical and political matters and then immediately destroyed the books and papers.

"I need to be able to teach, but I cannot afford to take any risks," he said.

Throughout the *shitta,* Nahalin's stone houses, though not as punishing as prison tents, felt as if they were refrigerated. The older villagers, who had survived decades of mean weather and hard labor in the fields, suffered from aches, and I did what I could to relieve their pain. I delivered aspirin and rheumatism medicine to those who suffered.

The old woman with whom I had picked olives, Halima Najajra, regularly complained of rheumatism, and I regularly brought her medicine. She and her husband, Hamid, swept me into their winter quarters, a small and spartanly furnished room.

Halima ordered me to sit on the floor between them and enveloped me in blankets. It was clear that I was going to stay for a while. Halima wriggled free from her own blankets enough to show me how her legs pained her. She hiked up her *thobe* to reveal her swollen knee joints and the broken blood vessels that spotted her legs. Despite the cold, though, she was barefoot. Shoes, even in the winter, were new-fashioned. Thirty years ago in the West Bank villages only the most modern villagers owned them.

Hamid was engulfed in blankets except for his head, on which he wore the white skullcap of a practicing Muslim. His white hair showed underneath.

Halima spoke of her pains, but it was I who complained about the weather. "This rain never stops," I said, huddling in my blankets. "I love the sunlight."

Both of them looked at me blankly, as if I had said something too outlandish to be contemplated. And I had.

Halima creaked to her feet and bent over a kerosene burner, pumping it and then lighting the pressurized gas. The gas made a whooshing blue flame. She went to some shelves by the door and took down the teapot, a sack of sugar and three glasses. She poured water from a cola bottle into the pot and then resettled herself.

Hamid, meantime, stared at the ceiling and decided how to address my naïveté.

"We never say anything bad about the rain. We love it. The fields are happy, and the land is going to live again. Without this rain, we all die. We have a proverb. We say, 'The rain is gold.' And it is thus for all people, Arabs, Christians and Jews."

His speech did not make the rain any less cold, but I never reiterated my complaint.

"Rain is gold," I repeated.

We sipped tea in the darkening room. The gray sunlight of the *shitta* disappeared in the late afternoon as if the steady drizzle had gradually doused it. I was told to stay for supper, although I protested because I presumed that the two of them had little extra. Halima reached up on the shelves and took down a pot of chicken soup. She heated the soup and we ate it together. Once the meal was over, we held our hands out over the flame of the stove, and

Hamid told me what he remembered of the history of the village, which he had stored in his head in detail.

I was collecting every bit of information that I could about Nahalin's past, listening for hours to remembrances and stories. The older people, who had never read anything other than the Koran, memorized what they heard and saw. The *shitta*, trapping people indoors, was the best time to hear about history, about a span of time that began in another era, one in which the *fellahin* did not feel embattled.

I spent the night with Halima and a sister of hers who came to replace Hamid for the night. Hamid went and slept with a cousin so that we women would not lose any dignity. I could not see that it mattered if a man stayed in the room, since we were all bundled in layers of blankets and clothes. None of us changed for the night; we just added sweaters on top of sweaters. I was far warmer there than in my rooms, which seemed lonelier and roomier the colder the weather became. I slept in comfort, almost hibernating between the two women, insulated on both sides by the warmth of their large bodies.

With the dawn, the rain abated and Hamid returned. I did not say what I was thinking, that I was relieved the soaking rain had stopped, if only for a few hours. As we were eating, a tremendous explosion rocked the little room. None of us moved; we all knew it was another dynamite blast at the Betar site. It was a particularly loud one, though.

When I went outside to look, all appeared normal. There was no gaping crater on Daher al-Matarsiya, just the construction crane and the shells of new three-story buildings with what looked to be the beginnings of peaked roofs. Tons of bulldozed earth had been shoved down the mountainside, forming a rough buttress below the settlement. The topsoil was gone, lost in an orangy mix of over-turned dirt and stones.

Elsewhere, the olives and the thorns were a deep, dull green. The pines of Rosh Zurim and the army camp were a brighter green, standing out like sentinels. Beyond the control of anything human, clouds cast moving patches of shade that slipped over the ridges and down the valleys as easily as spirits.

Before the rain began again, I went down to visit Miriam and Abdel Hafith, with whom I had made friends so easily. The sunlight, coming weakly through the windows, carried little warmth with it. I kept a jacket on, and the old Sufis wore blankets like cloaks. We sat on floor mats and drank tea. A spotted cat arrived quietly, not making a rustle in the fallen leaves from the fig tree, and sat down in the open doorway. The thick branches of the tree curved as if they had been frozen in the midst of a weighty dance. The cat knew that Miriam would toss it some scraps, as she had been doing for fifteen years. It watched patiently as Miriam reached into a covered bowl, extracted some chicken bones and threw them onto the doorstep. Performing a much-practiced ritual, the cat took each bone out of sight, ate it and returned for the next.

Abdel Hafith wore a black embroidered skullcap and Miriam a long white scarf under which I could see her cap of coins. This kind of cap, sewn with coins, was once a part of a woman's dowry. It was donned at the time of her marriage and worn for the remainder of her life, hidden under headcloths. Younger women found the tradition burdensome.

Abdel Hafith talked about the old days and the very old days.

"The first people in Palestine were the Canaanites. They lived in villages near where Nahalin is. It was the Canaanites who fought with the Jews, who had come from Egypt after traveling through the Sinai. Prophet David killed the king of the Canaanites, and the Canaanites were broken. David ruled. After that, there were wars and more wars until the Christians ruled. Living here, in this region, there were Christian people before the Muslim people. But Saladin came to change that. He conquered for Islam.

"When I was a boy, we had about one hundred houses in the village, and the people were Muslims. They were farmers and shepherds. They had cows, sheep and goats. On the land, they grew lentils, and chick-peas, tomatoes and hay. When the village had all these animals, everything was here, everything was in the house. No one had to travel to Bethlehem or to Jerusalem.

"There was calm. No one killed anyone. They would only talk about the time a thousand years ago when people killed each other."

I had been listening with interest, but what he said next riveted my attention. He told me the legend of Fatimah, the daughter of the prophet Mohammad. In the minds of those who believed, it was a story that tied Nahalinis to their land through a miracle made manifest.

"The daughter of the prophet once came here. She stopped at Ain Feres because the spring was good then, as it is now. She was with her husband, Ali. At one o'clock in the daytime, it was time to pray, and she prayed. She got down from her horse, and when she did, she left her footprint in the rock."

Miriam nodded.

"It is a white footprint in the middle of a rock in the middle of Daher al-Matarsiya. You can count the five toes," Abdel Hafith said.

"How do you know this footprint was made by Fatimah?" I asked.

"Because every man told his sons about it. I learned it from my father, who learned from his father, who learned it from his father. This is a chain that goes back further than I can say the names."

I asked him whether he had seen the footprint. He said of course he had, but not since he was a younger man. To reach the rock, one had to climb toward the spine of the mountain. I wanted to know exactly where it was.

Abdel Hafith paused. He looked unhappy. "It may be under the dirt they have pushed down from the settlement. No villagers are allowed to go up on the mountain now, so we don't know exactly. The soldiers won't let us go."

Fatimah's footprint. I talked to half a dozen other old villagers, asking them about Nahalin's history and the footprint. They all told me the same story about Fatimah stopping to pray, and they all told me they feared to go near the legendary site now because it was too close to Betar. They were too old to run from the soldiers. Excited by the story, I set out to see the footprint alone, using directions from the villagers as to which paths to take around which boulders. I had sketched a map.

I headed out in a morning rain for a spot a couple of hundred yards below the ridgeline of Daher al-Matarsiya. At the statuesque boulders of the Kitchen, where the *shabab* had burned the pines, I squatted and took out the map. I was supposed to walk about one more kilometer, taking five different forking paths. It had looked easy when I was drawing the map, inspired by the agreement among villagers as to exactly where Fatimah had tarried.

Hunched beside a wet boulder, I examined the map and found it confusing. One path was supposed to lead uphill from where I was, but I saw two. I had not thought about the goats whose trails crisscrossed every bit of land. Any Palestinian knew the difference between a goat path and a human path, but I was not a Palestinian. I took what looked to be the more traveled path. From this path, I was to fork left and take a path that paralleled the ridge. At what looked to be the correct fork, there was no parallel path.

One led up, another down. I took the one that climbed toward the settlement because the villagers had told me the footprint rested in a rock near the avalanches of bulldozed earth. I took another fork and another, guessing and then guessing wildly, aiming at what I thought might be the right heap of earth. The path I was on petered out. I clambered over boulders until I reached the edge of the earth buttress below the settlement. No soldiers would see me there, unless they walked to the edge of their cleared area and looked sharply down.

But where was the footprint? I climbed around the boulders, scrutinized them for indentations that, with imagination, would look like toes—five toes, three toes, any number of toes. There was nothing that looked anything like a footprint melded into the rock. I gave up. The footprint might be there, however, and it might be buried beneath the heaped dirt displaced by Betar. The legend of Fatimah's footprint, whether or not there in truth existed a strangely imprinted rock on the slopes of the mountain, was irrelevant to the fact of the new Betar. Nahalin itself was irrelevant, except that the village laid traditional claims to the land on which the settlement was rising.

As they were building Betar, the Israelis were also reconstructing history. The name for the settlement came from a Jewish stronghold that had stood on the site of what became Battir village.

As with Nahalin, Arabs had populated Battir as far back as local knowledge went. Long before the time of Mohammad and Islam, though, it was known as Betar, a flourishing Jewish town under Roman rule in the second century after Christ's death. Its name stuck in history as the place where Simon bar Kokhba and his companions in arms made their final stand in a revolt against the Romans. During the ensuing centuries, Betar was settled by an Arab population, and the pronunciation of its name was changed slightly, to Battir.

The name of bar Kokhba's Betar was excavated from the past and moved southward over a couple of mountain ridges to the new settlement above Nahalin. The second Betar was founded on the belief that Israelis had the right to settle the West Bank. The irony that the Israelis now were the occupiers, playing the role of the Romans in the eyes of the Palestinians, went unseen when the settlement was named. In these mountains, illusion and truth had mixed in the making of history.

I retreated down to Ain Feres and walked back to Nahalin on the dirt road connecting the village to the spring. According to stories told by the oldest generation of Nahalinis, this same route was trod by warriors of ancient times. A history existed in the minds of the old people, beginning with the time when the caves were inhabited and the spring was a place where wayfarers camped. Shards of pottery found near the village dated to the Bronze Age, a thousand years before God promised the land of Canaan to the Israelites, three thousand years before Jesus Christ walked the land, and thirty-six hundred years before Mohammad preached his doctrine.

On the knoll above Ain Feres, the ruins of the monastery consisted of giant blocks of stone that formed a rectangle. The interior once housed monks but for centuries had been planted by the *fellahin*, the ruined walls protecting the crops from mountain animals. Perhaps a millennium ago, the farmers and shepherds had moved into simple houses built of stone mortared with mud and roofed with sod. The population of the village itself was Muslim from early on. The oldest graves in the village cemeteries, which edged the main roadway, were Islamic and the bodies in them were laid to rest with their faces turned in the direction of Mecca.

The oldest houses in the village were clustered near the central crossroads. When they fell down, other houses were built on the same sites and eventually abandoned as villagers used cement to erect sturdier dwellings.

At the turn of the century, several hundred people lived in Nahalin, a mix like today of Shakarnas and Najajras. Times were less complicated then, and most village squabbles were resolved speedily by means of *sulhas*. The *sulha* system still existed during the season of the intifada, but nothing was ever simple again once politics were added to the daily round of events. The old people talked nostalgically of the Ottoman times before the First World War, when three thousand sheep and seven hundred cows grazed on Nahalin's mountains, when one hundred camels carried stone and limestone down from the mountains for new homes.

Jews came through Nahalin from time to time, itinerant cobblers or stonemasons who lived in larger cities—like Itzhak of Hebron—and had no desire to settle among the villagers. Until the first quarter of this century, the land of Nahalin extended in every direction and measured three thousand acres. The early Zionist Jews who came to Palestine with the mission of building their homeland had not yet bothered with the land in Nahalin's environs.

After the First World War, the village lost about one third of its land swiftly and irrevocably as the result of a quarrel between two families. According to some accounts, a murder was committed. To settle the dispute and prevent revenge, recompense had to be made. The family at fault moved from the village, and its land was sold to outsiders. This same land was sold again later to Jewish settlers, who founded a religious kibbutz to the south of the village. The Kfar Etzion kibbutz was a solitary outpost in Arab territory until it grew three offshoots. The four farm settlements became known as the Gush Etzion bloc.

The village did not come close to the large events of history until after the Arab-Israeli War of 1948. The Green Line of armistice dividing Arab-held land from the borders of the new Jewish state ran a couple of miles northwest of Nahalin. Palestinian refugees poured eastward into the mountains. Many passed through Nahalin.

But Nahalin's proximity to the Green Line brought trouble. The Palestinians, furious about Israel's hard-fought success, continued to make guerrilla raids across the new border. Villages like Nahalin were the staging grounds for these raids and recipients of the retaliatory attacks that were becoming a trademark of Israeli military strategy.

In 1952, Israeli raiders attacked a house at the edge of the village and killed two men, brothers, in their home. Two years later, the Israelis made another, much bloodier attack on Nahalin, the same attack in which the *mukhtar* was killed. I had first heard about this from Abid Rahman, the son of the *mukhtar* and the man who had had his olive trees cut down below Betar. The attack was mounted by a special unit formed to deal with the continual harassment of the Israelis by the Palestinians. The commander of Unit 101 was the young Ariel Sharon. In March 1954, Arabs ambushed an Israeli bus in the Negev, killing eleven passengers. A week later, Nahalinis were blamed for the killing of an Israeli guard in a settlement southwest of Jerusalem. The fury of Unit 101 was unleashed in a night raid against Nahalin.

The Nahalinis expected an Israeli attack, and they stood guard at the flanks of the village with old rifles and scanty ammunition. Abu Marwan, the geography professor, remembered that time from his boyhood: "The men from Nahalin patrolled the boundaries of the village every night. They did what they could, but they only had old rifles. They had to buy their own ammunition, so they were loathe to fire in practice. I don't think they were very skilled."

Outwitting the villagers, the Israeli soldiers came from the east and thereby avoided the sentries. They came for blood, attacking houses on the village's eastern flank with grenades, automatic weapons and gasoline bombs. A Unit 101 commando, Meir Har-Zion, described the raid in his memoirs, after pointing out that the soldiers were seeking revenge for the murder of Israelis: "Each group was equipped with a flashlight to distinguish between men and women. The first house. Explosives tear the door open. An Arab appears at the torn gate. I blow him away with a shot."

The raid was over by four in the morning, with the Israelis claiming nine dead Arabs, including one woman, and fourteen wounded. Six of the dead were Nahalinis, and the other three were Jordanian soldiers rushing to aid the villagers.

The Nahalinis remembered the night with horror and told me details about the Israelis slashing the throats of their victims. Six houses were bombed and the old mosque was sacked. The *mukhtar* put up a desperate battle before he was gunned down while trying to shoot at the advancing Israelis. With dawn, the bodies were carried to the center of the village, and a collective mourning began.

"It made a scar in the minds of a whole generation of the village," Abu Marwan said. "It was a horror."

Afterward Nahalin dropped from notice into its customary obscurity. A Jordanian army barracks on the site of the Kfar Etzion kibbutz, which had been leveled in the 1948 war, was the only foreign mark in the mountains around the village. And so it remained until the next big war between Arab and Jew. Nahalin had little to do with the 1967 war, which passed over and around it.

Under the Jordanian occupation, the Nahalinis were largely unarmed. The newly formed Palestine Liberation Organization had urged the Jordanians to supply the villages near Israel's border with weapons, but little came of the plea. Jordan did not encourage competition from the Palestinian organization, whose goal was to establish an independent nation.

"Maybe if someone in the village went to register for membership in the PLO, the same day the Jordanians would catch him.

Jordan wanted Palestinians to join with it, not their own organization," Abu Marwan recalled.

"I was one of the ones who wanted arms and training. I was a youth. I went with others to another village, and there we waited; twenty-nine of us waited and nothing came. Finally the Jordanians sent a single training soldier. He had only an ancient weapon with five bullets.

"I remember the war in 1967. It began on Monday. I was sitting on the cemetery wall with some friends. We were all quite young. Three Israeli soldiers came and surrounded us and said, 'Hands up.' We expected they would shoot us. One of us was wearing khaki, and the soldiers demanded to know whether we belonged to Fatah. We were just sitting on the wall under a tree, and it was impossible that any one of us was a member. We told them that, and they ordered us into our houses. That was about all that happened in Nahalin during that war."

Outmaneuvered and outfought, the Jordanian soldiers who had been garrisoned in the West Bank since 1948 beat a hasty retreat to the other side of the Jordan River. The truce that ended the Six-Day War left both the West Bank and Gaza in the hands of the Israelis.

Kfar Etzion, the destroyed kibbutz, was the first settlement reestablished on the Israeli-held West Bank. By the time of the intifada, it supported more than five hundred people engaged in tending orchards, breeding turkeys and working in a metal factory.

Rosh Zurim, the kibbutz visible from Nahalin, had more than two hundred Israelis living there. They raised cows and worked in two factories, one that produced electrical equipment for vehicles and another, devices to purify water.

Near Rosh Zurim and just out of sight of the village, Alon Shvut served as a religious community and regional center for settlements. At least 250 families were living in the community, along with four hundred yeshiva students. It had a regional medical clinic, post office, bank, grocery, library, synagogue, regional elementary school and a number of factories. It also boasted a halakic center for the study and interpretation of religious law.

In 1975, Elazar, a small communal settlement of religious Israelis, appeared on the mountain above Nahalin. About three dozen families lived there, sending their children to their own kindergarten and running their own medical clinic. They also had a tapestry workshop, an agricultural laboratory and a restaurant and souvenir shop. The restaurant advertised with a bright rainbow-colored sign on the Hebron road shortly after the junction at Kilo Sabatash, but it had not seen much trade since the intifada.

The settlement of Neve Daniel, next to Elazar, was founded in 1982. It also was a close-knit religious settlement. It was named for the Nebi Daniel army convoy, whose fighters fell nearby in the attempt to bring reinforcements to besieged Kfar Etzion in 1948. Twenty families founded the settlement on land purchased in the years before the Second World War. The Neve Daniel settlers were planning to construct almost two hundred houses.

These five settlements, plus the army camp on Abu al-Koroun, hedged Nahalin on three sides. Only the northern edge of the village remained open when the intifada broke out. The village had almost no doings with the settlers and kibbutzniks. Their clinics, factories and synagogues could have been far away, except for the fact that every villager knew that the land the Israelis had built upon was once Nahalin's. Whether it was bought, traded to settle a dispute or confiscated did not alter the common feeling that the village was ever more embattled.

The final piece of lost land, Betar, turned the horseshoe of settlements into a circle. Since 1967, the Israelis had succeeded in imprinting a new demography on the landscape.

* * *

By early winter, the Israelis were making more arrests in Nahalin. A brother of Hanan was taken one night. Captain Maurice came to the door shortly before midnight and knocked softly. He was polite, asking for both of her brothers. The young men were not home, but the Israeli told the hastily woken family that they had to report to the army station in Bethlehem. The two, knowing that their alternative was hiding in the mountains, turned themselves in. The Israelis kept one and let the other go. That made nine arrests since the shabab's first battle with the army.

I did not see Maurice. That night I was again sleeping away from my rooms, seeking warmth and company. I was staying with relatives of Hanan who lived a short way down the hill. This family had a large compound containing both an old house with a domed ceiling and a new one that sat like a box on the southern slope of the village. In the old house, the family elder, Farid Najajra, sat by a charcoal brazier that warmed the single room well and attracted the other members of the family. The walls and ceilings were blackened by decades of soot. The place was made of thick stone and had only one small window, wonderfully designed to retain the heat and keep out the winter rains.

The old man was smart, his logic sinewy, and he drew me into an argument about the superpowers. He was adamant in his thesis that both the United States and the Soviet Union, rather than Israel or the Arab states, were the real problem for the Palestinians, as each superpower pursued its own strategic interests in the Middle East rather than any humane course. I debated with him for a while, then stopped and instead listened to the wind sharpening itself on the corners of the house.

I was cold that night because I slept with the women in the new house, which had large glass windows and one small electric heater. Five of us fell asleep on beds that lined the walls of the room, not to the sound of the wind but to the typical sound of a television set in the corner. I was content, though, for they had piled six blankets on me after I got into bed.

In the morning, a plentiful breakfast was laid out in the old house, right next to where the old man was sleeping on a straw mat wrapped in his blankets. Eight of us sat next to him on the mat around a tray of cheese, fried eggs, and fresh *taboun* to be dipped in olive oil and thyme. We passed around the wheel of bread, handing it over the old man, who kept snoring. Two of the women had babies with them who were crying. Someone else had turned on a radio. Still the man slept, while his old wife walked down to Ain Fares and came back carrying winter onions picked in the shadow of Betar's construction crane.

SEVENTEEN

Winter did not break. It snowed one afternoon in the mountains, followed by a solid week of rain cut with sleet. The villagers did not suffer the chill as I did. They were hardened to it. At night, I wore two layers of long underwear. The girls and women delighted in watching me adjust my cumbersome attire as I prepared to sleep.

The villagers knew that the earth was rejuvenating itself. The wells were filling, and the aquifers that fed the springs were swelling. Spring would come. The rain was bringing the first scant green to the countryside.

Every several days, I would walk up the rubbly side paths to Ratiba's house to go over an English lesson with Sena and find out news, if there was any, about Farouk. One day I found the compound buzzing. The good news was that the Israelis were reopening the schools as long as there were no difficulties. If the students once again attending school did not cause trouble, the Israelis could believe the intifada was calming. The students were torn between their rebelliousness and their desire to learn. Sena was almost happy. She had piled her texts and exercise books along a windowsill, ready to go. She only wished that Farouk was also able to return to school.

The other news was that Farouk indeed had confessed. Mary

Rock had seen him again in Dahiriya around Christmastime, just before the lawyers' strike, and confirmed that the Israelis had laid serious charges against him. But he was out of interrogation and being transferred to a relatively comfortable detention center. Betunia, a prison of tents on a smaller scale than the one in the Negev, held *shabab* who were awaiting trial at the military court in nearby Ramallah. It had no dread questioning section, and the inmates were allowed outdoors, a big change after the cells of Dahiriya or Hebron. Even though it was winter, the prisoners could walk outside their tents and breathe unfettered air.

No one knew how long Farouk would be in prison. The schedule for trials was overburdened and irregular. It could be weeks; it could be months; it could even stretch into a year. Mary Rock and the other lawyers had continued their strike into a second month, with the agreement of the Palestinian prisoners, who had been polled unofficially through one or another of the illicit channels of sneaking information out of prison.

Betunia was fairly easy for a prisoner's family to visit. The Najajras were going there and invited me along. Although I was convinced the Israelis would stop me, I went anyway. I assumed the prison guards would notice me in a minute, although I had stripped myself of anything that might identify me as a journalist.

I squeezed into Fawzi's Peugeot early on a morning, making the fifth passenger. Ratiba was coming, of course, dressed in her best *thobe*, which was heavily embroidered in green, and a matching green sweater. She carried a tightly packed plastic bag, containing underwear, socks and *miramiya*, a leafy herb with which villagers spiced their tea. Also in the car was Raatib, one of Ratiba's brothers, a fat man with a gruff manner. Compensating for Raatib's bulk was little Shawki, whom Ratiba had allowed to stay away from school for the day. Refusing to miss her classes, Sena did not come along. On the way to Ramallah, no one in the car spoke much.

From Nahalin, we drove first to Jerusalem, skirting the ramparts of the old city and then heading through new blocks of Israeli apartments until we crossed again into the West Bank. Betunia was on a secondary road that followed the roll of the hills northward. The sky was steely.

The roadside by the detention center looked as though people had been drawn to the place for some lugubrious ceremony. Fawzi parked behind two shabby buses that the Red Cross employed to ferry families to prisons. The cars of wealthier visitors were parked in a shallow ditch along the road. It was hard to see anything of the detention camp because of the hundreds of people gathered in front of it, all kinds of Palestinians, from *fellahin* to smartly dressed women from the city. Most of the village women were in their good *thobes*. Many of the men were in their good white *kefiyeh*s anchored with glossy black headbands, dressed to see their sons and cousins, their brothers and friends.

Betunia lies on a plain between two slouching hills. With winter, the plain had turned into a field of mud pocked with icy pools. Fences and rolled barbed wire marked the perimeters of the prison, which were visible beyond the crowd.

We joined the confusion. I stuck to Ratiba and Shawki, holding both their hands, not for their sake but for mine, since they knew more than I about how to behave in the environs of an Israeli prison. The crowd was not pliant. People pressed in various directions, depending upon what they thought to be the location of the gate, the opening in the maze of fences. A few visitors slipped and fell as they pressed forward on the muddy ground. Others helped them up. This went on for hours. Nothing happened. No one appeared from inside Betunia to tell us what to do.

Finally a loudspeaker rasped. In Arabic, a man's voice read off a dozen names, none Farouk's. People who recognized the names surged toward the fences and a barbed-wire corral, where the first check of the visitors began. Fawzi pushed his way over to us and explained that the loudspeaker voice belonged to a representative of the prisoners. With a Palestinian organizing the roll call, the visitors were amenable to the commands. An Israeli voice would stir the crowd like a bitter wind.

At twenty-minute intervals, new batches of names were announced. Each time the crowd split and shifted, and the fortunate ones among us scrunched their shoulders and pushed forward. The process seemed fruitless. The size of the crowd did not diminish. We stood and waited and worried.

Ratiba wrapped my winter scarf over my hair in a vain effort to make me look less out of place. I had not tried to look Palestinian because I could not.

A fat woman who was crammed next to us gave up standing, kicked a few stones out from underfoot and settled on the ground. Finally we heard the name in a chain of others—Mohammad Farouk Bader Najajra. I gripped more tightly Ratiba's and Shawki's hands and wedged forward. The men joined us.

Soldiers closed in behind, herding a group of about one hundred into the three-sided corral. We milled about, not knowing what to do until the soldiers barked orders: women to the left, men to the right. I let go of Shawki and held onto Ratiba as we were funneled into a tent by women soldiers. The green of their uniforms matched the tent. I did what the other women were doing, which was to stand in rough lines waiting to be frisked. A woman patted down Ratiba and then looked at me.

"Who is she?" the woman soldier asked in halting Arabic.

I said nothing.

"*Karayeb,*" Ratiba said, pointing to me and then herself. "Relatives."

Harried by the mass of relatives pressing through the tent that day, the only one of the week on which families were allowed to visit, the soldier looked at me for a long fraction of a second. That was it. She frisked me to make certain I was not concealing any weapons and checked me with a metal detector. It beeped at my bracelet, which I took off and showed to the soldier. It beeped at my watch, which I also took off. I said nothing, knowing that any word might get me into trouble. I passed the check. The soldier took Ratiba's precious bag of gifts for Farouk and motioned us out the other side of the tent. We were in another barbed-wired enclosure with twenty other women. If the Israelis had known I was a journalist, they would have forbidden my entry.

The Israelis censored almost all information that came out of the prisons, or they tried to. Letters going in were censored. Letters going out were censored. But it was impossible to stop information from getting out in the minds of freed *shabab*. Messages could also be smuggled out. A common trick was to write a message on paper, roll it into a tight cylinder, wrap it with the cellophane from a cigarette back, seal it with a match to make it waterproof and then have it swallowed by a departing prisoner. Once outside, the former prisoner with the message in his guts forced out the pellet with a homemade laxative of olive oil and milk, cleaned it off and delivered it.

The prisoners cooperated with each other inside Betunia. The first thing a newcomer did was choose a political faction to stay with. The Israelis allowed the Palestinians to choose their quarters, rather than face possible fighting within the tents. When Farouk arrived at Betunia, he went to a tent with Jebha prisoners suspended like him somewhere between their arrest and their trial.

Soldiers with rifles stood on the far side of the rolled wire, between us and the camp, where tents were boxed off by fences within fences on a field of blank earth, the vegetation trodden away long ago. More Palestinian women hustled into the enclosure until the group numbered about fifty. The soldiers with the rifles shouted at other soldiers nearer the camp who shouted back. Down a fenced chute, another group of Palestinians appeared, walking quickly and looking dazed. Some of the women were crying. That was the group ahead of us.

Once they had cleared the chute, we were hurried into it. The men from whom we had been separated at the first enclosure streamed in with us. We all rushed along a slippery pathway that opened onto a final enclosure, whose longest side was blocked by a sturdy chain link fence about twelve feet high. Soldiers watched. About two yards away was a second chain link fence. In between were more coils of barbed wire.

The prisoners filed out from the tents escorted by more armed soldiers. They walked at a steady pace, docile and evenly spaced. We were hanging onto our side of the fencing with our hands. It was an advantage to have Raatib with us. His bulk was enough to shelter Shawki, me and Ratiba from the crush of pushing visitors.

We saw Farouk. He stopped opposite us, raising his arms to grip the chain link. He was dressed in several layers of clothes, which made him look clumsy. His face had a yellow cast to it, the sallow color of someone who has been ill. But signs that he had been beaten were gone, and during the visit he maintained a smile.

Everyone was shouting, gripping the chain link and trying to get closer. It was difficult to hear.

Farouk yelled to his family. Then he yelled to me, saying he had heard about the stones being thrown at me and that he was sorry.

"Kull ishi tamam," I said. "Everything is OK."

In the din, that message was the most frequent as both the prisoners and their visitors tried to reassure each other. Not much else could be communicated. Ratiba did little shouting. She clung to the fence and stared at Farouk.

When the time was up, the guards prodded the prisoners, and they went easily. We waved. Farouk waved. Ratiba started to weep. She waved until Farouk had disappeared behind a row of tents.

Once we had been shunted back through the various enclosures and regained Ratiba's bag, I walked with Ratiba and told her that Betunia was known to be one of the better detention camps. She answered that there were no good prisons. Meanwhile Fawzi had gone to a food stand by the roadside and bought us each a falafel sandwich. We chewed on our sandwiches on the return trip, not talking. There was nothing much left to say. The happiness at seeing Farouk was torn in half by the misery of watching him file back into the camp.

Two days later the crisis came. I was driving to Nahalin from Jerusalem, not paying sharp attention to the scene. I was becoming accustomed to the soldiers with their guns manning the roadblock at Bethlehem and to the army jeeps protected by steel-mesh windshields and bulletproof sides that were fitted with small portholes for guns. I had absorbed a sense that troubles soaked the land as thoroughly as the rain. I hardly noticed the fear that shuttered the shops on the Bethlehem road, the graffiti that clashed furiously with themselves, the shattered hunks of the demolished houses at El Khader, the guarded faces of the Palestinians, the ancient land and the modern settlements, the upthrust arms of the children with their first two fingers parted in the classic victory sign.

When I passed the intersection with the road to Battir, I hardly saw the beat-up Peugeot sedan stalled and empty on the shoulder of the road. It looked as if the car's driver had pulled over carelessly or suddenly. It was parked the wrong way around.

As I came down the Valley of the Cow and past an entrance road to Betar, I noticed the ashes of a burned tire and some broken

glass marking the *shabab*'s latest ineffective assault against the settlement. I made the turn into the village and came upon a Nahalin-
sized traffic jam caused by several men ladling hot tar onto the
roadway. The villagers had decided to repair their own road because
the military government had not. Over the past year, the narrow
road had been getting steadily worse, so that it was not possible to
drive down from Husan without hitting potholes or swerving onto
the dirt shoulder. Although it had been repaved by the Israelis with
smooth new asphalt as far as the settlement's entrance, the rest had
been left to the weather. As I was inching along, a man who I did
not recognize called out my name in a clear voice and said he wanted
to talk to me. He was well dressed in a tweedy sport jacket, black
scarf, jeans and running shoes. He had been helping with the road-
work.

"Helen," he said, "I have to tell you this. They have taken
Fawzi."

Not wanting to believe it, I waited for him to explain what
had happened. The man told me that Fawzi had been taken by the
army on his way to work. The Husan villagers had seen Israeli
soldiers stop his car, talk to him, order him onto the road, handcuff
him and take him away.

The man then introduced himself as Mohammad Musalam,
a brother-in-law of Fawzi and the only lawyer in Nahalin. He continued, saying he did not know where Fawzi was but that it was
crucial to locate him. I knew this was true and I knew the over-
whelmed Red Cross might not be much help.

Fawzi had been driving to Jerusalem, to the Swedish organization where he supervised the care of handicapped children. Without Fawzi, what would they do?

And what would everybody else do who depended on him?
Adding together his mother, his two children, the children of his
brother Sa'ed, his sisters and his first cousins without work, some

fifteen people counted on him. And what would happen to his animals? In the past year, he had taught himself veterinary medicine in order to care for the chickens and the Romanian sheep. Besides the thousand chickens, he had almost three dozen sheep. Fawzi diagnosed and innoculated them. Who was going to clip the chickens' beaks so that they would not peck one another to death? The last time I had visited the compound, I helped Shawki and Ratiba catch sheep that needed calcium innoculations. We grabbed and held them so that Fawzi could stick the needle into their rear legs. Who was going to take care of everything? Who was going to head the family? Who was going to make the thoughtful decisions?

I was going to miss him, too. Fawzi was the one Nahalini who had trusted me without reservation from the start. Fawzi had no delusions about who I was.

Mohammad Musalam calculated that Fawzi had been taken immediately to one of two places, the Moscobia or the Basaa. The problem was that he was not about to go barging into either. No Palestinian would want to. They were both formidable bastions. The Moscobia, the former Russian pilgrims' compound in the heart of Jerusalem, had been converted into a prison. Behind its grand walls, which were topped with barbed wire, Palestinians were jailed by the score. The Shin Bet conducted interrogations there. Equally daunting was the Basaa, a former British fort converted into the headquarters for the Bethlehem region's army and Shin Bet. This was where Captain Maurice worked. The building, an L-shaped outer structure that protected invisible inner courtyards, was fortified with cement-filled barrels, fences and more barbed wire. Its aspect was menacing, its workings secret.

The Basaa was on the main Bethlehem road and fairly close, so I started there. I drove to the barricaded fort I had gone past scores of times assuming I would never have reason to stop there. Occasionally I would see a couple of peasant women standing out-

side the guarded gate, waiting in supplication, I supposed, for information about their sons.

I pulled up between a fence and the row of barrels and
walked around to a side driveway where I had seen an open gate.
Some soldiers were lounging there on the roof of a guardhouse.
They waved at me to halt, and I waved back at them with my blue
American passport, my three-billion-dollar passport. It was a passport with wallop, since the American government was giving Israel
more than that amount every year.

I explained who I was and that I had noticed something
strange in Husan. I was hedging about what I knew. I said I had
noticed a car abandoned on the side of the road and thought it
might belong to an acquaintance. I told them I was bothered because
it looked as if someone had dragged him from his car, maybe someone from Husan, what with the clan disputes that went on in the
Palestinian villages, or maybe he had had an accident or maybe even
the army had taken him for some reason. Among the soldiers were
men in blue jeans and sneakers, the obvious plainclothes of the Shin
Bet.

I kept asking questions in English and walking further into
the compound. The plainclothesmen simply ignored me, but some
of the soldiers were surly. One ordered me to leave and go ask at
the hospital if I was so concerned about the health of this Palestinian. Another told me to ask at the police station at Manger
Square, that the Basaa was not the place for inquiries of any kind.
I refused to listen. Then one soldier asked me the age of the man
I wanted. When I said he was thirty-one and a Nahalini, the soldier
replied that no one that old was being kept at the Basaa, only
teenagers or younger men.

As he was talking, though, a short man in loose white pants
and shirt, wearing the skullcap of a religious Jew, appeared at the
door to one of the buildings. He overheard the conversation.

"Just wait there. I will look," he said and went around a corner.

The soldiers in the vicinity stared at me uneasily, but they made no move to eject me. The man in white reappeared after several minutes.

"He is here," he said.

"He's here?" I exclaimed. "How is he?"

"He is clean, and he has a good bed and good food," the man in white said.

"I am going to see him," I said, trying to keep my luck rolling.

"But he is arrested. You cannot see him. In any case, this is not my business."

I was puzzled.

"I am the cook," he said by way of explanation. "I don't know anything more than what I have said."

I backed off my arguments and asked him what his culinary specialty was, doing anything to keep him talking. He said knishes were his forte and invited me to come back to the Basaa for a taste. I demurred and started pushing him again about seeing Fawzi. He said that was impossible because such a breach of routine would have to be authorized. No commanders were present because it was Friday afternoon, approaching the eve of the Sabbath. I would have to talk with one of them on Sunday morning if I wanted to pursue the matter. He gave me the name of Captain Kamal. As with Captain Maurice, Captain Kamal had taken an alias as a working name. *Kamal* in Arabic means "perfect."

I left with a feeling of foreboding. Fawzi was in serious trouble. By then I was fairly certain that Fawzi was suspected of being a local PLO leader with the Jebha faction. Back in Nahalin, I told Mohammad Musalam that Fawzi was in the Basaa. I did not go up to tell Ratiba. I would let Mohammad do that for me. I did not want to see anyone from Fawzi's family. I was too upset myself.

A couple of weeks later the news came. Fawzi was imprisoned in Ansar Three, which meant he was not being interrogated but that he might be gone for a while. His lawyers, Mary Rock and Mohammad Musalam, had word that he was under administrative detention, the special category of imprisonment for political prisoners. No charges were made public. Fawzi had disappeared into the most complete void. Families never visited the Negev, only lawyers. Fawzi had been assigned to desolation.

I screwed up my courage and went up to the Najajras' compound. Fawzi's wife, Nadia, had moved up there with the two children, wanting company until her husband returned. She had got a list of things that Fawzi wanted. She was clutching a piece of paper on which he had written "soap, pajamas, towels and underclothes." Nadia was crying without pause. The pain of not knowing her husband's fate was replaced by the pain of knowing he was in the desert. Ratiba was not talking at all. It seemed that everything had gone wrong.

The intifada continued without Fawzi, Farouk or the thousands of other political prisoners incarcerated at the time. It was the fourteenth month of the uprising. Neither the rain nor the Israeli Defense Forces had stopped the stones, the leaflets, the strikes or the anger. Nothing short of arresting all of the *shabab* as well as their leaders and keeping them locked up permanently would do that. Almost every day Israeli soldiers fatally shot at least one Palestinian, wounded more and arrested others. The intifada had turned into a season of stones, lasting through the year and varying in intensity like the rains of the winter or the fires of the summer. Some of the leaders of the intifada had been caught, but others took their places. When *shabab* were arrested, others who had served their time were released and resumed their battles. Most important, the boys who had yet to throw their first stone at an Israeli were growing up.

Unless peace was made, they would become the next generation of *shabab*.

After Fawzi's arrest, I arranged a second meeting with the man from Fatah, the one who had assured my safety. I thought he might be able to tell me something about Fawzi's condition. He was bound to have information about what was going on inside the prisons. I could not call him directly, so I left a message with an intermediary. He agreed to meet me if I picked him up in a car from an East Jerusalem street corner.

The lanky figure of the man from Fatah was easy to recognize amid the morning shoppers hurrying to finish their business before the stores closed. On the paving, peasant women squatted with bags of dried grape leaves, figs and raisins that they were selling. The man held himself stiffly and limped slightly as he walked. Once he was in the car, his eyes did not stop moving, and his hands lighted cigarette after cigarette. His eyes were bloodshot from a permanent fatigue. Working two jobs, his normal aboveground job and his helter-skelter underground job, he went with little sleep. I asked him how he dared parade himself in public, and he said the Israelis knew him well, but they thought he was long frozen, out of action.

"They think I just do my job and do not involve myself in making any politics. If I talk to a journalist, this will not bother them."

I remained nervous. How could they not know what he was doing? They had only to follow him.

"They are too busy to follow everybody. When they decide to follow me again, I will go to prison again. I am expecting this, so it cannot bother me."

He told me he would talk about himself if I pledged to keep his identity secret. Agreeing to his rules, I drove up onto the nearby Mount of Olives. It was not raining that day in Jerusalem. We sat on a low wall and looked down at the golden, rounded roof of the

Dome of the Rock, one of Islam's most holy sites. It was from a white rock beneath the dome that the prophet Mohammad, mounted on his horse, made his legendary night ride to heaven. The softening winter light made the dome seem to glow from within. A boy came by looking for tourists and tried to sell us a photograph of the view. Other than that no one bothered us.

"Last night when it was raining, we had to make the main distributions of the *bayanat*. The problem was that our car was old and breaking down. I and three others who came with me were worried, what were we going to do if the car was stopped and the *jaysh* stopped and asked us what we were doing? The rain was so thick we could hardly see the road. Maybe that is why the Israelis did not see us."

He told other stories, all the time watching, as if a platoon of soldiers might emerge on the slopes below. He talked about Abu Jihad, the PLO military commander who was assassinated earlier in the intifada. Abu Jihad had been this man's mentor, educating him and a cadre of other young Palestinians in the politics of revolt and the tactics of guerrilla warfare. Because of Israeli checkpoints, Abu Jihad could not enter the West Bank, but he had means of communicating. He received messages smuggled across the Jordan River bridges and into Arab territory. One method was to slip a message inside the belly of a fish and have it carried over the river.

Several years back, the man from Fatah had needed to pass a note to Abu Jihad in Jordan. He wrote the message, folded it up and put it in the gutted belly of a St. Peter's fish. He gave the flat, bony fish to a woman to take to Jordan by way of the heavily monitored Allenby Bridge. The Israelis checking the woman's possessions found the incriminating message and forced her to reveal who had authored it. He recounted that the Israelis arrested and interrogated him without result. Finally some Shin Bet agents escorted him to the fishmonger's shop in Tiberias on the Sea of

Galilee where he told them he had bought the fish. They wanted to find out whether the fishmonger had sold the fish whole or gutted. The terrified man, stammering, said he could not remember the fish or its purchaser. He did not know what the secret police wanted, but he knew ignorance was his safest bet. He told the Shin Bet that he sold some fish whole and some fish with their bellies cleaned. The fishmonger was safe. The Israelis were unhappy, and they kept their prisoner in detention, putting more pressure on him. They beat him and broke the bones in one of his feet. He would limp thereafter.

As for Fawzi, the man from Fatah told me that the Israelis had taken him to the Negev camp, where Deeb already was incarcerated. He assured me Fawzi would be all right and that his term might be shortened to five months.

The Ansar Three detention camp was much larger and more strictly guarded than Betunia. Fences hemmed the Ansar prisoners' tents into a series of compartments unrelieved by anything of beauty. The prisoners were divided into isolating sections. The whole area was paved, and beyond the prison fences there was nothing but empty desert. The cots inside the tents were crowded together in two rows with a pinched corridor between them. Soldiers on guard with guns made the tents more claustrophobic. In the wasteland of the desert, the winter lashed the inmates with cold. In the summer, the tents absorbed the heat concentrated by the asphalt, and giant desert flies bred in fetid latrine trenches. Sonic booms from the Israeli jet fighters based in the Negev punctuated each day.

Ansar was the chief detention center for educated Palestinians, those accused not of mere stone throwing but of more elaborate plans to overturn the Israelis. Ansar's prisoners included those who led the popular committees that organized villages and city neighborhoods, those who led the strike committees that organized the *shabab* and those who had devoted themselves to a vision of the

Palestinian state. Ansar was the university for the intifada, just as prisons like Betunia were its high schools. The Ansar prisoners held classes in Marxism, economics, revolution, history and also biology, chemistry, literature or whatever might be the specialties of the many professors who ended up in administrative detention. One ingenious detainee, a professor of biology at Bethlehem University, devised a model of a DNA helix from cigarette boxes and wire to teach his fellow prisoners the fundamentals of genetics.

"The Negev is not the worst place to be. It is part of the intifada. The Palestinians must endure it," the man from Fatah said. His face was cold, as fixed as his political stance. "We have no choice, and so we cannot care what they do to us. We cannot cry about one person suffering in the desert. He is one of many representatives of Palestine."

When he had said what he wished, I agreed to drive the man from Fatah to an Arab township north of the city. We passed several jeeploads of soldiers, and each time he cursed with a soft hiss, the way a cat reacts to a large dog. I dropped him at the end of several looping, muddy streets deep inside a labyrinthine neighborhood.

"Forget where you took me," he said.

By the time all this had happened, the countryside was showing vernal signs. The Valley of the Cow was ornamented with blooming almond trees, which had started to put out white blossoms shaded with the faintest pink. In the hills, the delicate flowers were showing—poppies with papery crimson leaves and cyclamens with mauve whirligig petals. Grass was sprouting where the earth had been bare. But still the rains were pouring down almost daily, as if winter were trying to wring itself out.

EIGHTEEN

In Nahalin, the apricot trees outside the window of my bedroom had grown heavy with green fruits, hard and tart to the taste. The children in the neighborhood, who numbered in the dozens, liked to pick them off, take a bite and then toss them on the ground or, if they were boys, at a target. The boys were perfecting their aim for the days they would spend herding sheep in the mountains and, more dramatically, for the coming time when stones would be their weapons against Israeli soldiers.

As the *shitta* let up, the fuzz of green on the slopes of the mountain was turning into tender grass under clearing skies. A transparent light, which had been rinsed clean by a hundred rains, touched down upon the valleys and the mountains tentatively, as if this were the first time the sun had shone upon the earth. The spring was as gentle as the times were hard.

The leadership of the intifada was calling regular strikes and exhorting the *shabab* to attack the army and the settlers. Every day Palestinians protested, throwing stones and demonstrating. Every day the Israeli soldiers fired at them. The schools on the West Bank, after a brief reopening, had been shut again. Sena had shrugged and insisted that she had expected nothing else. I was tutoring her again.

One day she came to visit me in my rooms with a handful

of her fellow students. I seated them as best I could. One sat on my single chair and four in a row on my bed. Once I had them seated, I scurried into the other room, where I had my kerosene stove set up on the floor in a corner.

My guests, however, did not stay put. They followed me into the other room to provide advice as I clumsily pumped and lighted my stove. They could operate a kerosene stove as easily as an American would switch on an electric oven. Lighted, the stove made a great deal of noise, chugging and flaming.

The next trick was to produce Arabic coffee. When I persuaded them to reseat themselves in the other room and delivered a tray of coffee poured into miniature cups, they were polite.

"Good," said Sena.

"What do you mean, 'good,' " I queried.

"Well, not bad."

"What you mean is that my coffee could be better."

"Maybe," she said.

"What should I do?"

"Maybe next time you should put in a little more sugar. Next time, I could make it for you," she finally suggested.

The subject changed to schools. The others listened as Sena explained to me how the last day had gone in the girls' secondary school in the village of El Khader.

"We had to walk home in the morning. After what had happened, we knew our school was going to be closed."

I asked her what the trouble had been that had caused the Israeli authorities to halt classes again after only a few weeks of school.

"The same thing as always. We had problems with the army."

The others nodded in assent, but they were shy and said nothing.

"We were in our first class. It was mathematics class. I was being careful. I took only one notebook to school so that if anything happened, I would not lose all my lessons. I was copying the mathematics work into the back of my notebook because the front was for other subjects. The lesson was calculating the areas of geometric figures. For example, trapezoids and pentagons. We had been studying about five minutes and the *jaysh* came, two jeeps came and stopped at the gate. One of the students from inside the school threw a stone, and it landed on the road. The soldiers called out at us. They called us names. They called us donkeys and they called us prostitutes. We could not keep studying. We all left the classes and went out on the road. The soldiers drove their jeeps at us so that we would get off the road. We jumped off the road but we jumped on again immediately. Some of us took stones and threw them at the soldiers. After that, they fired tear gas. We all ran down the road and into the hills. We had to walk home. Then we heard the announcement that both secondary schools, for the girls and the boys, were going to be closed again."

The emptied boys' school in El Khader was being used by a squad of soldiers as a temporary base of operations.

"Did you throw stones?" I asked.

"Why not?" she answered. "If we can't study, what else is there to do?"

The fact that the schools were closed once more was dismaying. I had come to understand how the Nahalinis felt about education. It was not an abstract nicety; it was survival. It was the only thing that no occupier had been able to take from them, no matter how harsh the occupation or how high the taxes. Education meant the chance to get a paying job and a steady wage, to survive in a world without a state.

My morning was not destined to be placid. As soon as my visitors left, Inam came down with her boys. The three could not be controlled simultaneously. While one was dragging shoes out from under the bed, the second was trying to pull the hands off my bedside clock and the youngest was crying because he had wet his pants. Inam, dealing with the chaos calmly, invited me upstairs to talk while she went about her housework.

Young as she was, Inam had accumulated plenty of problems. She was short of money, sometimes having so little food in the house that she and her sons subsisted on powdered hummus, which she mixed with water to make a paste that was eaten with bread. She longed for new clothes for her sons and herself. The bit of luxury she could afford was in the garden next to the house, where she had planted mint and flowers. She told me wistfully that she had toured Jerusalem once in her life, when she was yet a schoolgirl.

Our conversation moved on to women and fashion. Inam wanted to know how American women dealt with unwanted hair on their legs. She thought it funny when I explained that they often shaved. She explained to me that Palestinian village women rid themselves of culturally unsightly hair with a method not so different from leg waxing. For the purpose of learning about it, I accepted her offer to demonstrate on my legs.

One afternoon Inam sent her boys away to a neighbor's house and locked the front door. I had brought my kerosene stove upstairs, as Inam had ordered, because its flame gave a higher heat than her double-burner stove that ran from a tank of gas.

I sat in the middle of the kitchen floor and lighted the stove, pumping up a good flame.

As Inam went about selecting a a frying pan, an explosion from the settlement rocked the house. Neither of us paid more than passing attention. The blasting had almost become another village noise.

Inam kept working, mixing a tea glass of sugar with a tea glass of water, adding a dash of lemon salt "to make it nice." She dumped the mixture into the frying pan and heated it until it had the consistency of taffy. Then she peeled the burning-hot mixture off the bottom of the pan and flipped it onto the tile of the floor.

I pulled the skirt of my long dress up to my knees. Inam molded the sugar mixture into a ball, tossed it back and forth from hand to hand like a hot potato, smacked it onto my leg and quickly fingered it out flat. Then, as you would yank off a Band-Aid, she yanked off the "wax," and with it came the hairs off my shin. She divided the sugary wax ball and handed me half the lump, which had cooled. To reheat the stuff, we held it over the blue flame of the stove. Again Inam tossed her ball on her fingertips and smacked it onto my leg. I had no choice but to do the same. It was just hot enough that it did not quite burn my skin.

The procedure was painful and lengthy. We had been at it for almost an hour when we heard knocking on the door. Hassan's younger brother, Taysir, and two male cousins had dropped by to visit. Inam peeked out the door and, terribly embarrassed, rushed back into the kitchen, warned me that men were at the door, closed the door to the kitchen, hurried back to the front door and told the visitors to come back later. Clearly this was not something men were supposed to witness or even know much about. We finished hastily.

With the spring weather, I stopped seeking out warmer houses in which to sleep and settled into my pair of rooms. Even though I was living in the village, the suspicions about my motives never quite died. One rumor illustrated how desperate some Nahalinis were to understand why in the world I had come to live with them. I had rented rooms in the village, the story went, because I wanted to live like a miser and this was the cheapest rent around.

All in all, though, the village seemed resigned to me. There were far more obvious threats. The Border Police had been visiting Nahalin, driving through slowly as if to taunt the villagers. And each time a jeep loaded with Border Police came through, the *shabab* grew more angry. These were not soldiers of the regular Israeli army. These were soldiers who made their careers fighting the Palestinians. The *shabab* tried to ambush the patrols by lying in wait in the olive groves. But the Nahalinis were unable to touch the patrolling Border Police. They threw stones, but the jeeps drove on, leaving the village tangled in knots of tension. Border Police were stepping up their patrols all over the West Bank with the idea that they could perhaps do a more efficient job of suppressing the intifada than the army. The result in Nahalin was that everyone was more unsettled, including Hassan and Inam.

Every time the jeeps came through when he was home, Hassan dispatched Inam to Abu Jafer's store for a supply of cigarettes in case trouble erupted and resulted in a curfew or worse. Rumors would speed from house to house. When she got back with the cigarettes, Inam would stay by the front windows and watch. Hassan would chain-smoke and stay out of sight, lest the soldiers be looking to arrest someone. Hassan was not suspected of any political crimes, but he was, like all Palestinians, constantly afraid of running afoul of the authorities. By the time spring was unfolding, the Border Police were driving through the village almost once a week.

In the meantime, Inam had been sent a note warning her that she must not leave the house without covering her luxuriant hair. The note came from Hamas. The Islamic organization's membership was growing in tandem with a general frustration. The Israelis were not going away. The opposite was true. They were settling the West Bank piece by piece, settlement by settlement; their army and their police were roving everywhere, keeping their mobile pressure on the Palestinians. Hamas offered an alternative. Its leaders preached a return to the religious values of the past, stringent codes that dated to the time of Islam's zenith, a time when Arabic culture was in ascendancy from the Middle East across North Africa and into southern Europe. Under the most stringent tenets of Islamic culture, women were supposed to serve their men and their families and guard their modesty against the world by covering their features and their figures. Inam grumbled but complied. I bought a larger scarf under which I could hide every hair on my head. I was more than willing to be amenable. I doubted, however, that this would be sufficient. Hamas was a new force.

The next day I tied my hair up in a gray scarf, put on my longest dress and went shopping. I stopped at Abid's store to buy oranges that had been shipped up from the warm valley around Jericho and found him deep in discussion with three old women, his mother and her two sisters. One of them was popping pinches of snuff between her bottom lip and teeth. Another peered through milky-blue cataracts and shrugged the brittle bones of her shoulders when she made a point.

The talk was about the most serious matter a villager would ever have to confront personally. Abid's wife had been unable to bear him children. The older women were urging him to take a second, fertile wife. Otherwise, so their argument went, he would never have a son. Without a son, he would be unable to live out his life properly. Without a family growing up around his knees, he would stand like a single tree, unprotected by the grove from the winds of time, unshielded from death by new bodies to carry his blood into the future. Abid repeatedly shook his head. His wife, whom he loved, would be devastated if he took a second spouse, as is legal under Islamic law. The old women kept trying to corner him, to force him to believe that heirs were more important than the feelings of his wife. Shaking his head and weighing out oranges, Abid was stubborn in the face of the trio representing tradition. He, too, wanted children, but he refused to hurt his wife.

Typical of village matters, the discussion was not private. Topics that would be whispered about behind closed doors elsewhere were publicly scrutinized in Nahalin. In the back of the shop, unperturbed by the debates up front, the usual foursome huddled over a backgammon board, passing the hours of the intifada to the sound of clacking dice.

My entrance into the shop gradually distracted the women from Abid. I had my embroidery with me, and they made room for me to sit among them. They passed my strip of stitching back and forth, pointing out the several mistakes embedded in the pattern and then exhorting me to hurry up and finish it.

One evening not long afterward, Inam came running excitedly around the house and clanged her fists on my door.

"Quickly, come quickly, Helen. The *shabab* are coming for you."

I was shocked. What did she mean? But she did not explain, running instead back to the front of the house. I grabbed my scarf and followed her to the side of the road.

"You don't need the scarf," she said.

Coming around the curve from the village below were about thirty hooded figures wearing the usual tennis shoes of *shabab* ready for action.

"It's Jebha," Inam whispered.

The marchers stopped at a loop in the roadway above the house. One raised a bullhorn to his mouth. I could only watch and lean toward Inam for whatever support I could get. Hassan was not home, and Inam had left the boys inside.

The bullhorn boomed out a sentence.

"This is where Helen lives."

The voice behind the bullhorn paused. I caught my breath.

"And Helen is good."

With that, the marchers succinctly turned on their heels and started back down the hill, stopping at intervals to repeat the contention about my integrity. Nahalin seemed to be getting organized.

Inam and I went inside to drink tea and wait for Hassan to return from visiting his father in the lower part of the village. When he did get back, he had heard the news. He explained that the *shabab* of both Jebha and Fatah had had a meeting about me that had precipitated the public announcement. He said the word was out that I had a friend in the leadership. That combined with the power of his family and Inam's clan was enough to convince the PLO factions that my presence was good and, perhaps, even a boon.

He predicted that the following night the Fatah faction would repeat the bullhorn performance, and it did. That left only Hamas, separate from the PLO factions, to declare its feelings.

After Hassan and Inam went to sleep, I stayed up, savoring an interlude of solitary time. I sat outside my door on a piece of cinder block, refusing to worry about the scorpions Hassan said lived in the wall below the house, and looked out over the village and its scattered lights. I heard an occasional shout or snatches of music from a radio. A dog barked. The wind was cool and playful. A man was relaxing on a nearby balcony; maybe, like me, he was just looking, mesmerized by the feel of the ancient valley, its geologic strength and its darkened peace, a quiet that could shatter at any moment, making it all the more potent.

After moving into Nahalin, I spent long hours visiting and listening. The task was easier than it had been. My Arabic was serviceable, and I had made friends on both sides of the clan lines. I split my time between Najajras and Shakarnas, trying my best not to irritate anybody.

As I walked past Imm Mazin's house, Rokeya or one of her brothers would call out to me and invite me to come talk. Omar, lively and sharp-witted, would shout at me to come have a drink.

"No," I shouted back from the roadway. "*Mish atshane.* Not thirsty."

"Don't you ever learn," he shouted back from the front porch of the family house. "*Mish mish atshane.* Not not thirsty." In other words, hospitality was mandatory. The exchange had become a joke between us.

The younger brother, Fou'ad, liked to practice his English by conversing with me. He told me about his fear that he was forgetting facts that he would never be able to relearn if the West Bank schools reopened for a sustained period, something longer than several weeks.

"Once you have learned something—how to read English, for example—I think you forget it if you don't practice it. You don't forget all of it, but you forget the most difficult words. You remember the ordinary words, but you forget the extraordinary ones. I forgot the word *extraordinary,* and I went back to my books to find it again. I try to think about my lessons, I look through my books, but I know I am losing my education. Education without practice is like dirt without a terrace, it gets washed down the mountain."

Qasim, the older brother was worried, too, about Palestinian youths slipping backward educationally.

"I watch the graffiti on the walls. I think that the spelling is getting worse. Either the older *shabab* are forgetting how to spell, or the younger *shabab* are writing on the walls. Either way, it doesn't look good when you come into a village and see on the walls that words have mistakes. What is happening to us?"

Another of Imm Mazin's sons, Ibrahim, engaged me in a debate as to whether the intifada was more like a flower or fire. I argued that the flower produces something in the end, whereas fire just destroys. The intifada, if it brought freedom, would be more like a flower. He argued it was more like fire, enveloping and overwhelming.

"You feel it more," he said.

The leaders of the intifada had declared that no one on the West Bank was to celebrate; the rebellion was serious, and the people had to sacrifice their public enjoyment. Parties ended. Weddings took place but without the festivities required by tradition. In the village, a wedding was an event of the largest proportion possible. It was a celebration of marriage, but it also was a celebration for the entirety of both families. In decades past, villagers boasted of hosting thousands of wedding guests for feasts accompanied by music and dancing that went on for days. In a village where women passed their days laboring in the fields or at home and the men also worked on the land or at menial jobs in Israel, a routine broken only by holidays, in a village where no nightlife existed even before the intifada, except for the endless rounds of visits to relatives and friends, in a village where the social drinking consisted of tea and coffee—in such a village, weddings were big. And the bigger the wedding, the more prestige fell to the families. But intifada weddings were not much fun. The only part of the celebration that was not curtailed was the food.

A wedding put an end to the dilemma of Nura, whose heart had brought trouble. She was married in the early spring to a young man to whom she had not declared her love. It was a proper marriage, arranged and agreed upon by Hilmi and the other elders of the families. There was to be no more village gossip about her.

The wedding was set for a Saturday, the Jewish Sabbath, the day of rest for Israelis and also a day off for the Israelis' Palestinian workers. If the villagers worked for Israelis, they had to follow the Israeli schedule. Because of this, many of the men of Nahalin were home on Saturdays.

The morning of the wedding I went down to Hilmi's house for the first time in weeks. Rula and the younger girls were all outfitted in their best dresses and crammed into the bedroom with women visitors come to see the bride before the groom came to fetch her. In the center of the room, propped in a chair as stiffly as a doll, was Nura in a white dress, elegant and starchy. In lieu of an expression, her face was decorated with makeup. Over the makeup, a layer of whitish powder was applied and, on both cheeks, large circles of rouge. Her lips and eyes did not smile. Her hands gripped a white beaded purse on her lap. When I congratulated her, she hardly replied.

Her relatives filed into the bedroom and formally bade her good-bye—although they would, of course, be seeing her all the time in the village. The groom, a slight young man who hid his emotions behind a mask of gravity, arrived with his relatives. They led Nura away to a car, which chauffeured the pair to the groom's family's house. The somber-looking pair seated themselves on two elevated chairs. Some balloons were strung along the wall behind them. The wedding guests crowded into the room and talked among themselves, mostly ignoring the newly married couple. A feast of sheep meat drew people to a second room, where they ate around large platters. The wedding never budded into a party.

One evening when I was upstairs keeping Inam company, Taysir came by to visit again. A studious teenager who always seemed to be in the process of formulating a question about something, Taysir wanted to know more about this foreigner living beneath his older brother's house. He was puzzled not by my desire to write about a village but by the way I had managed such a drastic change in life style. He obviously had absorbed too much from the American television programs shown on the Jordanian channel.

"How is life for you here in this house?" he asked. We were

sitting in a plain room with a tiled floor, a sofa, two chairs and a wooden table supporting a black-and-white television set.

"Fine," I said.

"But how do you live without your culture? How do you live without parties? Are you bored? Don't you want to have champagne and cognac?"

"The life in Nahalin is not boring for me at all," I told him. "The reason is that I am learning; I am seeing. How many Americans have the chance to watch the intifada happening? I am watching history. How can that be boring?"

I was indeed bored at times. I missed having a beer. I grew tired from speaking Arabic. But, in truth, there was nowhere else I wanted to be.

Hassan got back late that night, exhausted from his work on a temporary plastering job. He had earned the equivalent of seventeen dollars for eight hours and to that he had added seven dollars for staying on for two hours of overtime.

That night well after midnight I was sound asleep in my narrow bed when I was awakened by a brilliant pain on my right forearm. A sixth sense told me that I had been stung by a scorpion. I switched on the lightbulb hanging from the ceiling, and cradling my arm, I hunted the scorpion down. I was frightened that I would find it but more frightened that I might not and be bitten again. I found it in the sheets. I picked up a paperback I had by the bed, a book about the difficulties of living in an African village, and aimed. With each second, the pain in may arm became worse. I smashed the book onto the bed but did not kill the scorpion, which leapt to the wall. I dragged the bed away from the wall and aimed again, concentrating until I was calm. I aimed again, and it fell to the floor, a brownish gray bug about three inches long with a curved stinging tail. I smashed it again and again until it was hardly recognizable. Then I wrapped it in a plastic bag, knotted the bag, put the bag inside another bag and knotted that one. In my fear, I had to make more than one-hundred-percent certain that even if it did miraculously rise from the dead, it would not escape.

Then I stood in the middle of the room and considered the odds of there being a second scorpion around.

"Do scorpions travel in pairs?" I asked myself.

I decided that the beasts probably are loners. Then I wondered how bad was the poison. My forearm swelled up, but the pain did not spread much above the elbow. I decided I would live, that I would not have to sound the alarm and wake weary Hassan. I poured myself a glass of orangeade and seated myself gingerly on the edge of the bed. I stared at my arm. I had another orangeade and near dawn lay down to sleep, wishing for the bottle of cognac I had so glibly done without in my evening conversation.

N I N E T E E N

Fawzi was in the Negev when Farouk was brought to trial. It was early April, almost six months after his arrest. The last clouds were dissipating under a warming sun, and the almond trees were dropping their blossoms in the Valley of the Cow. The stone apartment blocks of Betar had quintupled in number, row upon row of raw, unfinished buildings standing in winter's leftover mud on the flattened ridge of Daher al-Matarsiya.

In the confession he had signed, Farouk admitted in a Hebrew he did not speak to throwing stones, building roadblocks, tearing down an Israeli fence and, most significantly, belonging to a Jebha strike force. According to the charges against him, Farouk recruited other young Nahalinis to join the force of *shabab*.

More than a year into the intifada, Nahalin's *shabab* had not wounded a single person. They had succeeded only in vandalizing trees. Nevertheless, Farouk—and every other Palestinian charged with throwing a stone or writing a graffito on a wall or performing some other act against the Israeli occupation—was classified as a "security" prisoner and, therefore, a threat to the Israeli state.

The Palestinian lawyers had ended their strike, with little result except that they were appearing again in court for the first

time since December. Farouk's trial was scheduled for the usual
military court in Ramallah. The day was set, but the time was not,
so the families of prisoners converged early in the morning at the
military base where the court was located. It was nothing more than
a room with a couple of attendant offices tucked into a fortified side
of the base. Like others on the West Bank, the fort was originally
built by the British and passed on to the Jordanians and then the
Israelis.

By ten in the morning, the families of the prisoners were still
waiting behind a fence at the main gate. A soldier on guard was
barking orders at those who strayed up the driveway toward the
gate. He was wiry and squat with a green beret tipped on his head.
He shouted in tough street Arabic.

"Get back. Go. Go away. Not here. You cannot stay. There.
Go there."

He opened and closed the white-painted metal gate for a
stream of jeeps and trucks. Inside the fence were dirt lots for vehicles, barracks and a main building with two holding cells for the
detainees collected from various prisons.

The waiting Palestinians were herded to a subsidiary gate and
admitted one by one. The men were separated out and escorted into
a concrete cubicle where soldiers frisked them. An open window
allowed me to watch. The younger of the men automatically turned
and stood with their backs to the soldiers, their arms up and the
palms of their hands on a wall. They had been searched before, on
the street or in prison. The older men were puzzled. Some stood
limply with their arms at their sides until a soldier ordered them to
hold their arms straight out. Some did not understand until a soldier
mimicked the gesture he wanted, flapping his arms up like a great
bird. Another guard stood by the doorway to the cubicle, holding
an assault rifle in case any of the Palestinians tried anything. The

women went to another room to be searched. I had not seen the Najajras among the Palestinians, but I assumed they were waiting down the line.

I proceeded to the courtroom. It was a narrow chamber jammed with narrow benches, which already were almost filled with relatives of the prisoners. Lighted with fluorescent tubes, it had no windows onto the outside world. Behind the judge's raised bench were two emblems, one for the military court and one for the army. Flanking the bench were two Israeli flags. Three or four soldiers stood at the back of the room, armed with Uzis and with rifles equipped with tear-gas canisters. The soldiers were relaxed. This was procedure, guarding prisoners and their families. They were accustomed to it. I had become accustomed, too, to seeing soldiers with guns, but the fact that they were in a courtroom seemed outlandish to me. Courts were for calm, neutral reflection on the crimes and the woes of humanity. Guns jarred with that notion.

I spotted Farouk. He was one of seven prisoners seated in a railed pen at the side of the room, only a couple of feet away from their families. For many, it was the closest they had been for a while. Impulsively I squeezed between the benches, made my way over to the railing and shook hands with Farouk. I asked him how he was.

"Good," he answered, but he did not look good. The luster was gone from his eyes. He looked like what he was—a teenager who had got tangled in the intifada, then was interrogated and beaten by experts and was facing a future that was going to be determined by the Israeli military judge who had just entered the room. Everyone rose, but the hum of conversation did not stop.

I asked Farouk how Betunia was.

"Not good and not bad," he answered.

I found a space to sit on the edge of one of the benches. Behind me were Ratiba, Sena and Sa'ed, who was acting as head of the family in Fawzi's stead. I shook hands with them silently.

*   *   *

We had been in the same room a few months before, the difference being that then Farouk was absent. It was back in the winter, while he was in the hands of Shin Bet interrogators who were persisting in their efforts to get him to break. The Najajras had kept craning their necks in the hopes of seeing him. The cases of the first eight prisoners were all postponed, which meant the young men were sent back to detention camps to wait. Since they were security prisoners, bail was not granted. Ratiba held a bag of clothes that she hugged between her knees, waiting for a chance to pass it to her son. Each time he failed to appear, she resumed her pose, her head bent down and the fingers of a stubbed hand propping a cheek. At times, she leaned her face into both her hands, so that her head almost disappeared under her best, pale yellow scarf.

When the court recessed at midday, the Najajras were conducted by Mary Rock into the chief judge's chamber. The judge, an anemic and balding man who was known as being a moderate within the military justice system, was sitting at a table with a man from the Shin Bet. The judge was dressed in a a drab green sweater with three stars on each shoulder. He, like the other judges, was appointed by the military government of the West Bank. Along one wall of his office were shelves of law books. Hanging on another wall was a photograph of an armored personnel carrier.

The Shin Bet man looked his part: he was wearing blue jeans, a jean jacket and sneakers. He was a big man who leaned back in his chair nonchalantly, his thick silvering hair cut short. He was self-assured. His purpose at the table was to ask for an extension of Farouk's detention. Mary Rock exuded the same sense of purpose, only her intent was the opposite, to lessen Farouk's detention. She was from a family of determined characters who had fought to keep their land and home in West Jerusalem in 1948, lost it and retreated only as far as Bethlehem. She was elegantly dressed, a big-framed woman with strong features that bore up well under her heavy black eye makeup. She was smoking as incessantly as the Shin Bet man. A soldier entered the room, and before anybody else could move, Ratiba got up to give him her seat, since none was empty. After some shuffling, she sat down on the edge of Sena's chair.

A debate began over the evidence against Farouk. Mary Rock argued vociferously that Farouk had been in interrogation for more than a month and a half and by any standard of humanitarianism should be released from the rounds of questioning. She also demanded to know the results of the medical examination the judge had ordered earlier. There were no results; there had been no examination. The judge repeated his order to the Shin Bet man, his voice irritated, on the verge of anger. His forehead furrowed and he crossed his arms. The Shin Bet man nodded nonchalantly.

Mary Rock demanded to know the accusations against Farouk. She wanted a written charge sheet. The judge told her that the interrogation was at too delicate a point. This set her off into a speech.

"The first problem is that my client is not here. The court scheduled his appearance and that has been ignored. No one will give me an answer as to why. The medical examination also has been ignored. He already has been under questioning much longer than is normal. I can only conclude that these actions are designed to break his mind and his body."

The judge listened and then ruled that Farouk remain with the Shin Bet. The discussion ended and the Nahalinis returned to Nahalin.

Now, after confessing, Farouk was in court for his trial, or at least for a settlement of his case. The prosecutor was in place, dressed in military khaki and armed with a pile of pale green folders. Palestinian lawyers crowded into the leftover space near the front of the courtroom. The murmur of voices was punctuated by the sounds of jeeps gunning their engines and officers barking orders. Inside the courtroom, the walkie-talkies carried by the various soldiers buzzed and squawked. Up front, squeezed in next to the lawyers, were two more soldiers. They sat on chairs and held M-16s. Another soldier entered the chamber and leaned against a wall, a rifle slung by a strap from his shoulder and four pairs of handcuffs tucked into his belt.

I turned and took a quick look at Sena. Her eyes were black. The expressions on the faces of the other Palestinians in the court-room were stolid. Many of them were the faces of *fellahin* from the villages, weathered faces under formal scarves and white *kefiyeh*s.

Once the court session was underway, the cases were dis-pensed with quickly. All of them were those of *shabab*, young men in their teens or twenties. When the judge called a case, the accused pressed forward in front of the others to the corner of the railing nearest the bench. His lawyer stood simultaneously. The prosecutor read the charges, a court translator sitting in a chair with a broken armrest in front of the judge repeated the charges in Arabic and the lawyer made a few arguments for the accused and then agreed to a compromise. No full-scale trials were held that day. The Koran and the Bible resting by the judge's bench stayed untouched, unneeded for the swearing of oaths. Full trials were usually not held in military court because the Palestinians had learned that their chances of winning were slim. The judge was a military appointee, the Shin Bet's information was considered reliable and confessions were taken as evidence even though they were made behind the Shin Bet's closed doors.

Palestinians had a proverb that they liked to apply to their situation before an Israeli military judge: *"Iza al sultan aduwuk, la min tishki hamak?* If the sultan is your enemy, to whom can you complain about your plight?"

The three cases before Farouk's took ten minutes. At the

same time, those on the benches talked to the prisoners behind the railing, taking advantage of the opportunity. The woman sitting next to me was from the Deheisheh camp and, while holding an infant on her lap, carried on a conversation with her husband. Occasionally a soldier ordered them to be quiet. The men behind the railing were all accused of supporting the Palestinian cause in some manner. Despite what they faced in court, they had a comradely air about them, joking with each other a little. They all wore sport clothes, casual jackets and sneakers.

While this was going on, Mary Rock entered, threw a black advocate's gown around her shoulders and went to the railing to consult with Farouk. She had told me earlier that she wanted to bring his case to trial, since she had rare evidence in the form of the judge's demand for a medical examination, suggesting that the prisoner had been abused. She wanted to call Shin Bet men as witnesses in an effort to prove that Farouk had signed a confession only after almost two months of interrogation.

Farouk, though, had had enough. He also knew that the odds were against him and that if he did win, the trial could take years. He had a couple of pressured minutes to decide what to do before his case came up. He considered and told Mary Rock that he would rather not fight the charges, that he would rather be free as soon as possible. She estimated that without a legal fight she could bargain an eight-month sentence from the prosecutor. Farouk told her that would be all right; he would have to endure less than three months more in detention and he would not have to face the Shin Bet again. Mary Rock polled the family, and they agreed that plea bargaining was preferable to a possibly interminable trial.

The judge read Farouk's name. Farouk pushed his way to the front and held onto the corner of the railing nearest the bench. He gripped the balustrade with both hands. The judge stared straight ahead. Mary Rock shouted across the courtroom at the prosecutor.

He shouted back and nodded. She had pleaded guilty for him and he had been given three more months.

Minutes later we were all outside in the corridor that in one direction led to the outside and in the other, to the prisoners' holding cells. Soldiers were crowding around. Before Farouk was taken away the soldiers allowed Sa'ed to hug his younger brother. Sena hugged him. And then Ratiba grabbed him and kissed him over and over. Smaller than her son, she was enveloped in his arms. The soldiers had to pry her loose. She was sobbing. As he was taken away, I put my arm around her shoulders, which felt frailer than I had imagined. We walked slowly down to the main road, where a bus passed us with its windows painted opaque white. I had seen a glimpse of handcuffed prisoners through the front window.

Inconsolable, Ratiba progressed from wailing about Farouk to wailing about Fawzi. Once in the car, which Sa'ed drove, her misery quieted to a soft crying, which she kept up the entire trip back to the village—down through Jerusalem, past the crenellated walls of the old city and southward across the Green Line toward Bethlehem.

Back in Nahalin life was more miserable than ever without Fawzi to take care of things. Sena told me the chickens were in trouble. The family was hard-pressed to come up with money for feed, and the chickens were not laying as well as before.

T W E N T Y

Ramadan arrived again but Nahalin was not the same. With the warm weather, almost no one climbed to the rooftops to sleep because of the common fear of army and Border-Police patrols. The soldiers might come at night, and so the villagers slept together inside their homes. Outside, the lights from Betar joined those of the other settlements, making a rough circle that crowded the night. People rose to eat breakfast before the daylight fasting began. Someone in every house peered out at the final bit of night to see whether it yet held a surprise of soldiers. The Israelis probably would not be spied so easily, but it made the Nahalinis feel more sure of themselves as they faced the morning.

It was April, and the days of Ramadan were slipping by. The apricots were ripening on the trees by my rooms. It was the sound of these apricots plunking into pails that woke me one morning. Hassan's father and mother were at work. His father looked the part of the patriarch, complete with a white beard that flowed like water and a dignity that etched his face. He wore a long, tailored coat over a white robe. Hassan's mother was dressed for the job, wearing a workaday *thobe*, its embroidery faded and ground into the fabric. She also bore an air of dignity, earned from decades of hard work that had turned her skin to leather. She had borne good children, and they had married and multiplied; she had cooked tens of thousands of meals; she had scrubbed stone floors too many times to count; she had embroidered dozens of *thobes*; and she had harvested the vegetables and fruits of every season.

The old gentleman had tied his donkey to a fence, and the pair of them had started picking, first hanging buckets on the lower boughs of apricot trees. Once I was awake, I hastily fired up my stove and made a pot of tea to take out to them. I helped harvest the yellow apricots until the fruits filled a large straw basket as well as two buckets. I fetched the donkey, leading it to the trees, where I expected the apricots would be loaded. I offered to help hoist the basket onto the donkey's back.

"No, no, no," the old woman said.

She grabbed the basket as if it weighed no more than a load of feathers and balanced it on her head. She took a bucket in each hand and trudged toward home at the bottom of the village. Riding the donkey, the old man followed her.

Some things continued normally in Nahalin but others did not. Instead of teaching, Abu Jafer presided over his groceries and his clan. I stopped by his shop and found him tired, having stayed up late the night before mediating a *sulha*. The dispute was between two men, neighbors, each of whom accused the other of collaborating. They came to Abu Jafer and asked for his wisdom.

"The solution was not so difficult," he said. "I told them that I thought they both were right. They realized that meant they were both collaborators. They did not like that idea. So I asked them next whether they preferred me to say they both were wrong. Then neither was a collaborator, and they could live as honest neighbors. This gave them a way out if they wanted it. Even if one was a collaborator, he could stop informing on his neighbor, and that would end the immediate problem. The bigger problem, that collaborators exist in Nahalin, is not something I can solve. Collaborators have existed here ever since the Jews came to take the land from the Arabs."

After we talked in the shop, we went upstairs, where his wife, Jamila, fed us a tray of Arabic sweetmeats made of a creamy cheese covered with an orange sugar sauce. The sweets set him musing about the Palestinian psychology.

"It does not matter if it is sweet or sour to us," he stated flatly.

"Why do you say that?"

"Because there is no future. All we have ahead is darkness. Hope has escaped us."

Abu Jafer was not usually so gloomy. But the intifada made everyone's spirits droop from time to time. The rebellion could seem as scattered, as ungraspable, yet as omnipresent as the dust blowing from the eastern deserts when the spring winds were high. The intifada also seemed at times as changeable as the mountain wind. One minute it was calm, but the next it was restless, threatening squalls of violence.

We were upstairs in Abu Jafer's guest room when we heard the sound of a loudspeaker from down in the village. It was approaching. I had learned to differentiate the sound of army speakers, which were accompanied by radio static and the sounds of powerful jeep engines, from the sound of "watermelon" speakers, which were attached to trucks that came through the village hawking vegetables or fruits. "*Baaatteeekh. Baaatteekh. Baaatteekh.* Waaatermelons. Waaatermelons. Waaatermelons." The first time I heard the truck coming through the village, I jumped to my feet, not recognizing the drawn-out Arabic syllables, and my companions had laughingly reassured me that it was not soldiers shouting orders but a vendor shouting about summertime fruits. The army also was identifiable by the piercing whistles of the *shabab*—a warning system that worked unless the army came under cover of darkness.

No whistles accompanied this approaching loudspeaker. I leaned out the window and saw to my amazement a march of *mule-thamin*, their heads wrapped in *kefiyeh*s and most of them in khaki uniforms, striding two abreast up the street. One of the masked figures in front had a bullhorn and was yelling, "Tomorrow is a strike. You can sell only vegetables and chickens. Only live things for sale. And bread. Sell bread and live things. Nothing from the shelf."

Three dozen figures had passed in formation, and behind them followed twice as many villagers. Abu Jafer had me stay upstairs while he went down to talk. He returned ten minutes later. The marchers had checked the contents of his shelves to ascertain whether his shop was in keeping with intifada orders—no Israeli products, except those for which there were no alternatives, were to be sold. Abu Jafer's meager assortment of tinned goods had passed. He was pleased, even though they had dared to question an elder of his stature.

"The future is always with the youth," he said. "The youth are everywhere. They are in Nahalin, in Husan, in El Khader, in Battir, in Bethlehem, in Jerusalem."

The soldiers of the Israeli army were capable of overpowering any group of young Palestinians who tried to make trouble. But they could not keep the Palestinians from trying. At the Bethlehem market, *shabab* ambushed patrolling soldiers almost every day, and the soldiers shot back. Danger was becoming part of the status quo. Not far from the market, sporadic battles took place between soldiers stationed at Rachel's Tomb and Palestinians in a small refugee camp on a hillside by the tomb. The *shabab* at the Aida refugee camp made a point of harassing the squad of soldiers guarding the tomb, and the soldiers did the same to the Palestinians. The *shabab* burned tires and struggled to get stones as far as the soldiers. The Israelis replied with tear gas and live ammunition. As the intifada entered its second spring, the skirmishing at Rachel's Tomb had become a constant. The *shabab* hoped to wound the soldiers, and the soldiers amused themselves by sitting on the wall by the tomb and taking potshots at young men moving at the periphery of the camp. Bethlehem had utterly lost its innocence.

In the greening countryside around Bethlehem, the mood between Palestinians and Israelis was bitter. At a time of the year when the mountains were pleasant, when the driving, cold rains had stopped and the dusty heat of the summer had yet to settle, people were not rejoicing.

Construction had continued on the Betar settlement through the winter with little pause for the difficulties of building on the exposed mountain. Dozens and dozens of apartment blocks stood on the ridge, their orange-tiled roofs pointing into the soft blue of the new season's sky. The settlement loomed over Nahalin, the walls of the apartments like those of a hilltop fortress skirted not by a moat but by bulldozed earth that made a forbidding escarpment. The planners of Betar were making no pretense about the neighboring Palestinians; they extended no architectural invitations to the villagers. But psychologically every Nahalini was touched by the anxiety of having an Israeli settlement growing on Daher al-Matarsiya.

New roads to the settlement looped down from the village of Husan to Betar, wide roads that sliced through the humble landscape of peasant fields. The traffic for the settlement—the vehicles carrying the laborers from Hebron, the cement mixers, the soldiers who guarded the settlement, the Israelis who were planning a religious community that would include a synagogue and a building for ritual baths—came along the top of the Valley of the Cow to get to the new-cut roads.

The shepherds no longer went up the ridge to Daher al-

Matarsiya. But the grass was green again between the boulders, the poppies were dropping their first petals and the thorns were opening their purple blooms. The sheep and the goats could, for a brief spell at least, graze until their bellies were full. While the mountains were lush, the loss of the mountaintops was not grave. The limits on the pasturage would be felt later, when the grasses dried.

In many ways, Nahalin was almost as cut off from the larger world as it had been in the era that the oldest villagers remembered. Women now went to the Bethlehem market by bus rather than on foot or camelback. Men went to jobs in Israel rather than just working the land. But the schoolchildren stayed home. At night, no shops were open, no parties were held and no one walked in the pathways too late for fear of encountering soldiers or Captain Maurice. Instead of going to school, the boys repainted the village walls with graffiti. The girls sewed Palestinian flags. The older *shabab* talked of throwing Molotovs at the traffic on the main road between Jerusalem and Hebron. They plotted routes through the mountains so that they could get to the road and then flee. Unlike Husan, through which the settlers passed, Nahalin did not have easy targets. Whether the *shabab* would actually make an attack on the main road was questionable. They had yet to try anything so daring.

The mood in Nahalin was not friendly. Soldiers in their jeeps were the only regular interlopers, and they did not linger. One day a car from the Red Cross, passing through Nahalin to check whether more olive trees had been cut in the area, was stoned by Nahalin's *shabab*. No serious damage was done to the car or the Swiss officer driving it, but the event showed how edgy the villagers were.

Deeb had returned from prison in the Negev desert with another notch on his political belt.

"Nahalin," he said, "has learned to throw stones. Nahalin has progressed. The problem here is that Nahalin has not taken the next step. Nahalin has not learned how to be effective."

Deeb had no job, and since he had just come from prison, the Israelis prohibited him from traveling beyond the West Bank. He had little to do except muse on the state of the village.

"Nahalin is not in the vanguard of the intifada. It has no chance to be there. Nahalin has lain outside the mainstream, and history has not shaped its consciousness. If you analyze Nahalin objectively, you cannot expect it to be a collective force for revolution. Many people in the village have not advanced beyond religion. How can they perceive reality? The answer is they cannot. They are satisfied to dream."

Holding forth to anyone who would listen, Deeb sat for hours in his house near the top of the village. Next door the Najajras were watching Fawzi's farm fall apart. The chickens still were not laying well. Sa'ed had scraped up the money to put them on a special feed, but it didn't appear to be helping. The chickens were producing less than half what they had been. Since the Israelis had taken Fawzi, eleven of the Romanian lambs had died. Sa'ed, try as he might, could not keep the animals healthy or the books balanced. He did not have his older brother's knack for impromptu veterinary medicine. He did not have the same patience. Tiring of responsibility, Sa'ed would lean his back against an olive tree and play his flute for hours. His wife, Ibtisam, made meat pastries to cheer people up. But neither music nor food dispelled the family's difficulty. Ratiba worked harder than ever, which meant every waking minute, and grieved for her missing sons. Shawki bought six shiny fish from a shop in the Bethlehem market and liberated them in the concrete pond Farouk had built for his ducks. Shawki thought Farouk would like the fish. Sena channeled her pain into a burst of energy with which she repainted the inside of the house, to cheer her brothers whenever they returned.

After his day in court, Farouk was transferred to the Negev camp, where Fawzi also was. The weather was heating up. News had come from Fawzi in the form of a letter from the Negev. It was written on a square sheet of paper in tiny letters, both sides filled with ink. Fawzi's words were so compacted that they were hard to decipher.

"There is not enough food for a chicken to eat all day. It is hot, very hot." The letter greeted each member of the family and tried to reassure everyone. "I am staying well despite the hardships here," he wrote.

The Najajras wrote back dutifully, enclosing photographs that I had taken of the family and the animals, all posed so that the situation took on the best possible light. Shawki held up a baby rabbit and a rose for one snapshot. Ratiba stood straight as a stick beside the house for another. Sena sat in front of a flowering bush. Sa'ed bent over a sheep he was shearing.

So it was when the Border Police began to bother Nahalin. One afternoon a jeepload of the soldierlike police parked on a hillock a couple of hundred yards from the edge of the village, near where Sheikh Deeb lived. The police could see the villagers coming and going through the town center. One pulled out a megaphone and began taunting whomever they pleased, particularly the women.

"Hey, you, in the red dress," the words blared over the microphone. "Come over here. Come buy our tomatoes and cucumbers. We want to kiss you."

The villagers were horrified. No one spoke to a woman like that in public. Such words were scandalous. People went indoors, covering their ears, but the squad of police stayed on the hillock, repeating their insults.

The next day they came back to lounge at the same spot. This time, with the broadcast taunts, one of the armed men pulled down his pants and waggled his penis. The insult to the entire village was profound. The third day the Border Police also returned. They shouted at the villagers, "Abu Jihad is dead. And tomorrow so will be Arafat."

Nahalin had had enough. Three elders were dispatched to see the military governor in Bethlehem and ask him to intervene with the soldiers, only to be informed that he was busy with other matters. The village elders came back to Nahalin with the word that they had not been received by the military governor. The *shabab* were boiling with anger.

The Border Police were continuing with their insults.

"You boys of Nahalin, you are sons of dogs."

The *shabab* were grouping near the village center.

"You boys can't fuck your own women. We are here to do it for you."

The insults were shouted in excellent Arabic, the words of Druze soldiers who numbered among the Israeli soldiers in the jeep.

"Are you too weak to come down and fight us?"

That did it. A contingent of *shabab* clutching stones headed out of the village toward the hillock, ready to do anything to defend Nahalin's honor. The Border Police shot a few times, maybe rubber bullets, maybe plastic bullets, maybe live ammunition. No one was hit. The *shabab* backed off, and then the Border Police backed off.

One of the soldiers in the jeep threatened that the village should expect "an accident."

T W E N T Y - O N E

Before the next day's dawn, the soldiers of the Border Police came in force. The dark of the valley night was mixing with the first light as the soldiers came on foot. They came quietly from the flanks of the village, leaving their jeeps parked on the ridges. Suddenly they opened fire, shooting at shapes that moved and shapes that did not.

Two score soldiers were advancing from several directions, from the ravines and valleys, from the north and the south. As the light strengthened, they could make out their targets with more accuracy. The first living thing they shot and killed was a donkey, tethered near a row of shabby houses defining the village's north-west flank and facing the slopes of Abu al-Koroun. A squad of soldiers moved methodically through this side of the village. They shot holes in water tanks. They shot holes in windows. They shot two dogs, one sheep and a cat. They barged into one house and sent a middle-aged man and his wife cowering into a corner while they broke a couple of windows with truncheons. They shot the windows out of a parked car.

When they had beat their way up the slope to the middle of the village, they marched through the open gate into Sheikh Deeb's compound and retreated hastily from the stinging wrath of the old man's alarmed bees. They kicked open the gate to the compound of the Sufis Miriam and Abdel Hafith and shot rounds of ammunition into the fig tree populated by the spirits, the *djin,* with whom the couple communed. The two old people lay flat on their stomachs on their sleeping mats not daring to budge. The soldiers kept going, meeting up with other squads whose progress also was marked by trails of bullet holes. They merged at Nahalin's central crossroads, the wall of the domed mosque on one side and the kindergarten on the other. They stationed themselves at the intersection as well as along the three main roads. Some squads were waiting outside the village in the hills. The soldiers of the Border Police had surrounded the village.

Because the month was Ramadan, many Nahalinis had risen before dawn to eat and drink. The most devout of the village's Muslims had breakfasted and hurried to the mosques for the prayers performed during Ramadan. They were inside the mosques when the soldiers advanced. Some of the less devout villagers were already heading for work. As soon as the *shabab* heard the shooting, they came racing from their homes, confused and clutching slingshots and stones. The gunfire was echoing through the mountains, bullets were ricocheting and they could not tell where the Israeli soldiers were. They knew that this was no ordinary raid. No amplified orders placing the village under curfew had been announced from patrolling jeeps, no tear gas had been fired, no measures had been taken to force the villagers to stay inside while the army went about its business. The *shabab,* with no forethought or organization, ran toward the village center, where the firing sounded heaviest. Some came from Fatah, some from Jebha and some from Hamas. They descended into a chaos.

Worshipers in both mosques, the small one and the larger one a couple of hundred yards away, were scrambling toward safety, fleeing for olive groves, for sheltered pathways and for the protection of the walls of the nearby cemeteries. Children in the streets bolted for home. The *shabab* grouped in the village's higher cemetery overlooking the main roadway near the small mosque. The soldiers kept firing, seemingly at anything.

A pair of soldiers climbed to the second floor of a building next to the kindergarten. The building was unfinished, a skeleton of stone with gaping arched windows. The tallest structure in the village except for the minaret rising from the large mosque, it provided excellent vantage and cover.

The first Palestinian the two Israeli snipers fatally shot was Sobhe Mohammad Shakarna, who had fled from the small mosque onto the top of a row of shop roofs nearby. He was felled by a bullet from above that ripped through his back and out his chest. Another bullet smashed his arm. Sobhe staggered and then toppled onto some grass on the hillside abutting the back of the one-room shops. He lay in clear view of the marksmen. His cousin, Ahmed Shakarna, saw the shooting and ran to his aid. Ahmed was a burly young man, and he tucked the lighter-weight Sobhe under an arm and made for cover. The soldiers blasted Ahmed's elbow, and he dropped his cousin as he raced to get out of the line of fire. Sobhe was alive, but he could not move; he lay bleeding to death on the ground.

Sobhe was twenty-two, one of eleven children from a family like many others in the village that had struggled always to make ends meet. He had quit school after the eleventh grade and earned his keep as a day laborer, digging ditches and hauling stone in Israel. After the intifada reached Nahalin, he joined Hamas. Sobhe went to the mosque every morning during Ramadan, but otherwise he took the rituals of Islam more casually, attending the mosque irregularly. Shortly before the April raid, he had been released from detention, nothing unusual, just the eighteen-day arrest without charges used to pick up anybody whose activities had aroused the suspicions of the Shin Bet or the collaborators. Whether Sobhe had been throwing stones, or trying to throw stones, was impossible to know.

The gunfire did not stop. Soldiers were shooting in the roadways as well. But it was the pair in the building who struck with the most accuracy.

Sobhe was unmarried. He had no children. The second villager fatally wounded was older, twenty-seven, the father of three girls and a boy. Riyadh Mohammad Ali Shakarna, too, was a penurious worker. He, though, was a devout practioner of Islamic ritual, going to the Friday sermons if he was not in Israel working, and praying five times each day. When the shooting started, he was in the mosque. He fell not far from Sobhe, shot through the chest as he stood near a patch of high grass beyond the shops. He lay in the grass and moaned. Women in a nearby house heard him calling out for his children. When one of them stepped from the shadows of the doorway to go to his side, bullets spattered around the entranceway. The woman ducked back inside.

Hearing the gunfire, Mohammad Hassan Mohammad Shakarna also fled from the same small mosque and within twenty yards of its entrance was riddled with bullets. He was twenty-two, and his wife had given birth to their first child, a girl, two months earlier. He had gone to the mosque at four o'clock in the morning, and his family never saw him again. His body lay beside a wall for hours before the melee calmed and villagers came upon the corpse. They counted fourteen bullet holes in his upper body.

The fourth to die was Fou'ad Yusuf Abu Awad Najajra. By the rules with which the Israelis fought the Palestinian *shabab*, Fou'ad was a fair target. He had planted himself with a slingshot atop a flat gravestone in the village's lower cemetery, in direct line with the soldiers sniping from the building. He was doing battle with the soldiers, even though he was almost a boy and he was armed with the most meager of weapons. Bullets blew off a hunk of his skull, and he fell forward, his brains splattering on a rock, his slingshot in his hand.

One of Fou'ad's brothers, light-eyed Omar, was in the higher cemetery. He saw Fou'ad shot and lunged down the slope, wanting to reach the crumpled body, unthinking and yelling, "*Yaa Allah. Ooh God.*" Before he reached the open roadway, where dozens of soldiers as well as the snipers were concentrating their fire, a couple of the other *shabab* jumped on him and wrestled him to the ground.

"I am going to get Fou'ad," he shouted. "*Yaa Allah. Yaa Allah.*"

"You will die," one of the others shouted in his face. "You will die like a rabbit running in front of a hunter. You will die."

The *shabab* dragged Omar behind the shielding wall of the mausoleum and pinned him with their bodies. Gradually he stopped shouting and went limp as if his lifeblood, too, were draining out on the village hillside.

Two Nahalinis were dead and two fatally injured. Another young man had fallen to the ground on a slab of rock near the cemetery, his stomach torn open by bullets and his intestines spilling out. Seeing this, a soldier on the ground tried with his foot to push the intestines back inside the villager's abdomen. This man would somehow live.

Only ten minutes had elapsed since the snipers had started firing. Meanwhile more Border Police were fanning out through the village, shooting in every direction. A few shot rubber-coated steel bullets, but most shot live ammunition, high-velocity bullets meant to maim if not kill.

On a side street near the village center, Kamal Shakarna woke to the sound of the gunfire. On a normal morning, he would have had breakfast and then traveled to East Jerusalem, where he worked in a pharmacy. He was a well-educated man, and his observations were precise. He described what happened to him in almost clinical terms.

"The soldiers came to the village many times before this, but this time was completely different. They came without warning, without cars. We woke feeling that abnormal things were going to happen.

"The daughter of my brother, who lives in the next house here, went outside. Her name is Fatmah. In a minute, she was shot. In the neck. A few more centimeters and she would have died immediately. She is fifteen. She is a girl, not a soldier.

"After they shot her, she was bleeding. I knew we had to evacuate her. Time was important. Abu Nimar is our neighbor. He took his car, and we put Fatmah in the rear seat, lying down. Abu Nimar drove. I sat next to him. We heard shooting everywhere, but we had to go. Fatmah was bleeding from her neck and a second wound on her shoulder. Abu Nimar drove to the main road and turned left to go to Bethlehem, to go to a hospital. He was driving as fast as he could.

"We went about fifty meters, and then the Border Police shot us. They shot from behind, and the bullets went through the back window and out the front window. They shot us with automatic rifles so that the bullets came in bunches. Fatmah was not hit because she was lying down. They hit my ear, my neck and my shoulder. Blood was running down my face. I looked at Abu Nimar, and he also was bleeding. He was hit on the top of the head. The bullets passed through the skin on the top of his head. They did not hit into the bone. You know him. He runs the stone factory. He is an old man. He is sixty years old. I think they could have killed him. For any one of us, a centimeter in the wrong direction would mean death. We were lucky.

"When we reached the end of the village, there were soldiers. They stopped us. We said we were bleeding. One of the soldiers was laughing. I said to him in Hebrew, 'Why are you laughing?' He did not say anything more. He quit laughing, but he stopped us there for five minutes. All this time we were bleeding. Then they let us go."

Abu Marwan, the calm professor of geography, was one of the first to organize first aid for the injured. He had not been to the mosques that morning, but the sound of the guns was all he needed to know. He could not see to the bottom of the village from the porch of his home. He ordered his wife and children to stay inside, and taking alcohol and gauze bandages, he ran out into the street and down toward the noise. He did not get far. Bullets were clanging against water tanks, thudding into walls, bouncing off stones. He saw no way for anyone to get down to where the worst of the shooting was going on. Bullets zinged past his head.

In the meantime, the village women had become the rescuers. As trigger-happy as the soldiers were, they did not shoot as several women, holding their arms aloft in a gesture of defenselessness, left their houses. Slowly the women made their way to the open hillside where Sobhe and Riyadh lay dying. They dragged the two into the shelter of a house. From there, villagers hoisted the semicoherent men into blankets and carried them uphill away from the shooting.

Abu Marwan joined a group of men and boys standing in a cluster near Abu Jafer's store, presuming to be at a safe remove from the bullets. They decided to build their own roadblock, thinking that this would somehow shelter the upper part of the village from the onslaught; they were desperate enough to try anything that might curb the shooting and protect their homes. Boys armed with stones joined the men, who were rolling heavy rocks into the roadway.

One of the boys was Ali Mahmoud Fanoun, thirteen years old and a relative of Abu Marwan. He was standing with the others one minute, and the next he was collapsed on the ground like a puppet cut from its strings. Ali had been shot through the hips. The bullet tore through one kidney, sliced his spinal cord, plowed through his liver and tore through his second kidney. Border Police soldiers were moving up the roadway, but they stopped short of the cluster of men frantically trying to administer to Ali. From another direction, villagers emerged carrying Sobhe and Riyadh.

While this was happening, Abu Nimar was driving to the hospital, his car filled with glass shards and its seats soaking up blood. But they had made it by the soldiers and out of Nahalin. Others were not as fortunate.

With three badly injured people on their hands, some villagers decided to make an escape by the high road to Kilo Sabatash. They had to tear down the stone and earth roadblock that had cut off the back road for months to get their wounded out. Ali was whimpering; the two others, Sobhe and Riyadh, had ceased moaning, but they were still breathing. Abu Marwan loaded two of the wounded into his car. A neighbor took the third. Another carload of men followed with picks and shovels; they were going to break through the army's barricade no matter what. Beyond it they would be able to speed past the fences of Neve Daniel and turn left onto the main highway. The nearest hospital was in Bethlehem, a ten-minute drive from the roadblock.

Abu Marwan and the others barreled up the dirt lane, passing the stone factory and the line of high boulders. They encountered no soldiers; the Israelis had not manned the ridge directly above the village. They drove fast toward the roadblock, thinking escape might be possible. The men had their hands on their shovels. Then they saw the soldier, standing astride the barricade, his feet planted wide, his gun pointing straight at Abu Marwan's windshield, his eyes squinting at the oncoming cars. With the sun rising behind him, the soldier threw a long shadow down the road. The

Palestinians did not pause to find out whether the soldier would shoot or not. It seemed that morning that the Border Police were liable to do anything.

The three drivers threw their cars into reverse and careened back down the road. They turned around at the stone factory and gingerly drove back into the village. The wounded boy and the two dying men were carried into a house and laid on the softest blankets that could be found. Women took clean cloths and staunched the blood.

The shooting went on for an hour, maybe two; no one was keeping track. After six in the morning, an ambulance from Bethlehem's Palestinian-staffed hospital reached the entrance of the village at the Valley of the Cow. The villagers in Husan had heard the shooting and telephoned. The soldiers refused to let the ambulance proceed; they ordered it to wait at the side of the road. The medics and the driver argued to the backdrop of gunfire.

A short while later an official from the Red Cross arrived to find the ambulance as well as a squad of regular army soldiers bunched up in half a dozen jeeps and reluctant to enter Nahalin. It seemed they didn't want to join in the shooting. Appalled by the whole scene, the Swiss official sprang from his Red Cross car and yelled at the soldiers. They gave way, and the Red Cross car moved along the main roadway with the ambulance following. Seeing the ambulance, women ran out from their houses, beseeching the medics to tend to their wounded. The medics took four casualties and turned back for Bethlehem. Sobhe and Riyadh were not picked up in the first load.

More ambulances came and the Border Police let them pass. The regular soldiers advanced cautiously into the village. The Red Cross man had never before seen anything like it. Border Police soldiers, their guns hot, were still firing at will. It seemed to him that they were out of their minds, feverish, disoriented as if they were drugged, drunk on killing. One of their officers passed the Swiss official on the roadway, and they shouted at one another for a minute.

"You have to stop this," the Red Cross man yelled.

"What can I do? What should I do with them? You can see the problem," the Border Police officer yelled back. His soldiers were out of control.

The regular army soldiers, who met up with the Border Police on the roadway between the high and low cemeteries, also were shocked. Some of the Border Police raced up to them, screamed that they were running out of ammunition and demanded a resupply. The regular soldiers refused. One of them saw a Border Police soldier beating a youth, interfered and got in a fistfight. The fight was broken up, but the shooting continued. Some of the most daring *shabab* continued to throw stones at the soldiers, while others fled into the hills alone or carrying comrades who were wounded. The idea was to prevent the Israelis from getting their hands on any of the wounded. By Israeli rules, a wound was the brand of a troublemaker. Presumably if a young man were inside asleep, he would not be wounded. Similarly, if a young man were outside and shot, he was shot for a reason. These rules did not account for stray bullets, of which there were many that morning in Nahalin.

Dozens of villagers were wounded. The exact number would never be known because those who were not taken to the grave or the emergency room avoided the hospitals. They bandaged themselves until they could get to a doctor. The young men helped the injured to caves, where they would be safe, or to Ain Feres and from there through the valleys to Wadi Fukin, a poor village at the end of a road generally not frequented by soldiers. Border Police stationed in the hills near the village shot at them. At some point in the *majzara*—"the massacre," as the villagers all came to call the event—the soldiers posted in the hills shot two shepherds, one in the abdomen and one in the back. Both staggered into the village and were driven to the Bethlehem hospital in cars. Their sheep ran astray. By that time, the regular army soldiers had advanced part way into the village, and they were letting private cars carry away the wounded. The Border Police were almost out of bullets.

Many of the *shabab* had stayed put, grouping in olive groves and incensed beyond fear. They continued to throw stones. Some more were shot and wounded, although not fatally, like Fou'ad, Mohammed, Sobhe and Riyadh. Women ducked into the pathways to collect the wounded. Three soldiers of the Border Police were scraped by flying stones, not enough to hospitalize them but enough so that the Israelis could announce that their side was not entirely free of casualties.

Ambulances kept tearing down the Valley of the Cow, their sirens wailing to warn the military jeeps to make way. The wounded were evacuated by twos and threes and fours. The worst cases were tended singly. At about seven-thirty in the morning, Sobhe and Riyadh were loaded into ambulances. The medics did what they could. Both men were dead by the time the ambulances reached the hospital.

At the top of the village, the people were spared the worst. The soldiers did not get up to the high Sobiha neighborhood, although the terrifying racket did. Inam and Hassan crawled under their bed and held their sons who were bawling with fright. Woken by the first gunshots, Deeb took a studied position at his front door and tried to get a picture of what tactics the *shabab* were using. Ahmed had the courage to make a pot of tea. As the morning passed, Deeb realized that the Nahalinis were in trouble. He saw the village cars speeding toward Kilo Sabatash and returning. Before the morning was out he concluded that the *shabab* had not organized this battle.

The Najajras ran together into the chicken shed, where they

hid in a corner, hoping that the soldiers would not be concerned with poultry that day. Ratiba, Sa'ed, Sena and Shawki crouched for hours on the floor of the shed until the noise stopped below.

Word spread that something terrible was happening in Nahalin. A roving United Nations officer showed up about eight-thirty that morning. Several minutes later another contingent of Border Police came speeding into the village in nine jeeps; they had been sent as reinforcements. They caught the fever, jumping from their jeeps and giving chase to the villagers in the streets, who were mainly women by this time. The Red Cross man and the UN man tried to reason with them, but they kept after the women, chasing them into their homes and threatening them with weapons. From the loudspeakers on their vehicles, they shouted obscenities. Some were singing and dancing in the roadways as if they were ending some debauched party. But after about fifteen minutes of this, the captain of the Border Police ordered all his men out of the village.

The army declared the village closed to all outsiders and imposed a curfew. The few journalists who managed to get to the village were greeted by hails of stones. The *shabab,* curfew or no, army or no, wanted to avenge themselves. It was about this time that some of them came upon Mohammad's body near the wall of the mosque. The death toll had reached four.

Walid Abdullah Safi Najajra took the body in a car and sped toward Husan. Walid was taking the body to the small cemetery in Husan, where three of the morning's dead were already sealed away in crypts. He delivered the corpse. Husanis and Nahalinis quickly conducted the fourth truncated funeral of the morning and sealed another crypt. Driving away from the cemetery, Walid was stopped by Israelis and shot in the head. Witnesses were not in agreement about whether the fatal shot came from the Border Police or an Israeli truck driver passing through the village; by that time, confusion was rampant. Walid was twenty-three when he was shot. He did not die immediately and was taken to a Palestinian hospital in East Jerusalem, where doctors hooked him to tubes and respirators that kept his lungs breathing and his heart beating. But his brain was dead.

The UN man had raced up to Husan and then returned to Nahalin, where he encountered Captain Kamal, the Shin Bet chief in the Bethlehem area. An Uzi submachine gun in his hands, Captain Kamal was stopped outside the village. The *shabab* were in the olive groves pelting the road and aiming for Captain Kamal's gray jeep.

But from around the curve in the road, an army bulldozer materialized and passed the jeep. Its driver began crunching into the nearest wall, which happened to front the house of Abid Shakarna. The former policeman came bursting furiously out the door. He told the driver to go ahead and bulldoze the whole house, he didn't give a damn. The tirade was enough. The bulldozer reversed and disappeared back around the curve.

The UN man started piecing together what had happened. He counted bullet holes. In the wall of one house, he counted twenty-five holes. In one rooftop water tank, he counted fifty. He counted the same number in a single car.

By midmorning, twenty-three Nahalinis were in the hospital: Hussein Hospital on the edge of Bethlehem or Mokassed Hospital in East Jerusalem. At least twenty more—probably forty or fifty more—took themselves to private doctors.

At the Bethlehem hospital that morning, many Nahalinis were crowding the parking lot by the emergency room. Most were too anguished or too angry to talk. Women were weeping, pulling their long, white headscarves over their mouths and clasping their hands over their eyes, as if to shut out reality. Abu Nimar's car, its windows smashed, was parked at a skewed angle by the emergency-room entrance. Abu Nimar was in a hospital bed, and he would live, as would Kamal Shakarna and the girl, Fatmah.

For some reason, a gaily painted bus filled with tourists turned down the hospital street. The tourists gawked at the uproar at the hospital. Some local *shabab,* riled by reports of the *majzara* in Nahalin, stoned the bus. An army patrol appeared and shot wildly at the *shabab,* who had vanished into a valley of olive trees. Palestinian doctors, nurses and orderlies rushed from the hospital, ready to collect more wounded. But the *shabab* were gone, and no one was shot. Instead, the soldiers broke into the house immediately below the hospital and arrested a young man, dragging him away by the back of his collar. The bus disappeared as quickly as the *shabab.* Bethlehem was enraged. Even tourists, who are usually left to tend to their own sightseeing, so seemingly irrelevant in a war zone, were not immune.

At the Jerusalem hospital, where the critically wounded were transferred, Nahalinis crowded the corridors. Many waited outside the intensive care unit, where Walid Najajra was in a coma and young Ali Fanoun was delirious after surgery, during which the doctors had to remove one kidney, repair the second and slice away the irreparably damaged lower part of his liver. The young man whose gut had been ripped open by gunfire, Ibrahim Mohammad Mahmoud Shakarna, was also recovering from surgery. Doctors had cut out a part of his spilled intestines, sewn back the rest and had hopes that he would mend.

The Nahalinis were in a state of numbness. Abu Marwan was sitting with a knot of his relatives. He had little to say after he gave a bare explanation of trying to get through the blockade. He lapsed into silence. Too much had happened.

I was in East Jerusalem the morning of the raid and had missed seeing most of it. A friend telephoned and said that a massacre was going on. When I got to the village, the soldiers were being rounded up. I saw the bloodstains by the shops and held back tears at the spot where Fou'ad had died. I wandered around the lower part of the village. I saw the dead donkey, blood matted in its hair. I saw the blood where the dead men had lain. I saw the broken windows. I also looked up at the mountains and saw the regimented buildings of Betar, the expanding fields of Neve Daniel, the long cow sheds of Rosh Zurim, the army outpost on Abu al-Koroun. Nahalin, tucked below the ridges, was no longer remote.

I went up to the little cemetery in Husan, where a hundred people had gathered. Husan's *shabab* had nailed flags to the poles around the cemetery. Villagers had come from Battir and El Khader. The commanders of the Border Police kept their soldiers out of the other villages once word had spread of the raid and the deaths. About three dozen who had taken part in the raid were collected in a group in a stony field outside Husan above the Valley of the Cow. Officers came and went in jeeps, trying to understand what went wrong with the Nahalin operation. Its purpose had been to arrest a few *shabab* suspected of throwing stones and ineffectual gasoline bombs.

The soldiers sprawled in the field, exhausted from their morning. One sat hunched over with his head in his hands as if he were in a state of mental anguish, unable to rid his mind's eye of nightmare images. The rest seemed tired but nonchalant, as if they had done nothing more than their job. I tried to walk into the field and was chased off by an officer. I went back to the cemetery and stared at the simple, oblong crypts.

Fou'ad was the only dead Nahalini whom I had known well. Fou'ad. How could Fou'ad have had his brains blown out? Bright Fou'ad. Lively Fou'ad. A mere boy, who in the United States would be too young to drive a car. In my notes that day, all I wrote about Fou'ad was "Not Fou'ad."

TWENTY-TWO

No great wailing went up from Nahalin after the Border Police raid. The Palestinians mourned stoically and collectively. After the army lifted the curfew, the village was oddly quiet. The event had made the front pages of major newspapers around the globe, but the villagers withdrew into their homes as if they could do the impossible, shut out the larger world and go back to a time when Nahalin was a long way from anywhere, to a time measured by seasons, not battles.

I paid a visit to Fou'ad's family. Men dressed in *kefiyeh*s and suit jackets lined the main room. Those who could not find room on the chairs stood solemnly against the walls. Abu Mazin, Fou'ad's father, his thin face set in stern angles, was pouring sugarless ceremonial coffee into small white cups from an ornate brass pot, a vessel not used for ordinary occasions.

Abu Mazin poured me a cup of coffee and pointed through a doorway. In a back room, the women of the family and neighborhood had gathered. The embroidery on their good *thobe*s glistened in the light from a window. Only Imm Mazin and her sister wore old dresses. They sat side by side on a mat, their legs stretched out in front of them, their backs upright against a wall, their arms akimbo and their eyes unfocused. I sensed that if they did focus, tears would come flooding out with great racking sobs. They were both hefty women and they absorbed the sorrow in the room.

Not much was said. A girl passed around cola and then orangeade.

"He was a good son," Fou'ad's mother said.

The women in the room nodded.

"He was not my firstborn and he was not my lastborn, but he was good. He was intelligent."

"He was," others in the room echoed.

Silence pervaded the room. Time would tame the grief. The village women knew this and so they sat with Imm Mazin and drank soda. The mourning would go on for days in much the same fashion.

Fou'ad's brothers also were grouped in mutual misery. They were sitting on the steps above Mohammad's garden where the grass was green from the sprinkler. Mohammad went inside and returned with a white cloth twisted and knotted around his head.

"My head aches," he said. "I was the one who went to the hospital to identify Fou'ad. I looked at my brother's face. Half of it was not there. Now when you see me laughing, you can know that I have something else in my thoughts. I always will have something else in my thoughts."

Omar sat on the step above Mohammad. His eyes, the same green color Fou'ad's had been, were clouded.

"Fou'ad did not die in vain. No, he died defending his philosophy. He believed in Palestine. He thought he could defend it with his slingshot. He is a *shahid.* He is a martyr."

Qasim sat on the step above Omar.

"I can't go back there to Israel to work," he said. "My job was good. I could study my books. And all the time I was talking to Israelis. I was not angry. Now if I went back, all I could think was that these were Israelis and Israelis killed my brother. But how can I forget my brother? I won't even go back and get my books."

In the evening, I went back to the women's room. Imm Mazin asked Rokeya to bring an extra pallet. I situated myself for the night between Imm Mazin and her sister. Their bulkiness seemed a bulwark against further tragedy. Rokeya and six other women also slept in the room. The warmth of the slumbering bodies proved that the family was still alive. It was only in the middle of the night that I woke to hear a muffled sobbing coming from Imm Mazin's blankets.

At the houses of the other dead, the families also collected. At Sobhe Shakarna's house, people gathered around his mother, who sat in a corner, her hands clasping the chair so that her knuckles were white. Her son had been the first to die. Before that April morning, the village had no martyrs to the intifada. Sobhe's photograph was passed around the room. It was safe now to praise him for his convictions. As a member of Hamas, he had believed that a return to pure Islam would liberate the Palestinian people. Of the five dead, Fou'ad was the single member of Jebha. The other three were with Fatah.

Riyadh Shakarna, the next to be killed, left a family. He was a typical Nahalini; he owned a modest amount of land on which he grew grapes and olives. To make a living, he worked in Israel, laboring or tending the gardens that beautifed many sections of Jerusalem. His house was down at the bottom of the village, near the school. The walls of its three rooms were raw, unpainted plaster. When I went to see his family a few days after the raid, the visitors' room was crowded. The visitors discussed how Riyadh had died as devoutly as he had lived, calling for his family and for Allah. Riyadh's wife was unmistakable among the other women. Her face was pale. The long fingers of one graceful hand hid part of her face. Riyadh's mother entered the room, tears running down the wrinkles of her face like water in a lacing of miniscule streambeds. She was leading the four newly fatherless children. The children were too young to understand the enormity of their father's death.

The house of the dead Mohammad Shakarna was nearer the center of the village and was more prosperous. Mohammad's widow, mother of the two-month-old girl, was too shocked to speak. Before the intifada began, Mohammad had been studying in a small college in Ramallah. But he completed only three months before the uprising interrupted his studies. He married after that. He had barely begun his adult life.

At Mokassed Hospital, Walid Najajra lay unconscious in a hospital bed, his face puffed with red splotches. The respirator kept chugging, tubes ensnared his body and needles bristled from his arms. In the next cubicle, Ali Fanoun was gradually turning yellow. His lone kidney was struggling. His relatives hovered over his bed, not knowing when to tell him that he was going to be paralyzed for life from his waist down. The boy did not complain. He watched the comings and goings with big eyes made bigger by the thinness of his face.

Outside the door of the intensive care unit, one of the *shabab* was on guard, waiting for Walid to become a corpse. Seven days after the raid the doctors declared him dead and unhooked him. Alerted in advance, Walid's relatives whisked his body away so that the Israelis could not touch it. Walid was buried beside the others in Husan, bringing the number of dead Nahalinis to five. By that time in the intifada, at least four hundred and twenty Palestinians and seventeen Israelis had died.

In the aftermath of the raid, the village had no reprieve from publicity and militant sympathy. Foreign correspondents, who first had to search for the tiny dot of Nahalin on their maps, came in droves with translators and camera crews. Even many Palestinians could not have located the village before the raid. But now Nahalin was famous, the site of the single most bloody incident since the start of the uprising. It had become a symbol of the intifada.

Along with the journalists came groups of human-rights advocates, decrying what had happened. Israeli lawyers, the few who sympathized with Palestinians, took affidavits and counted the wounded. They saw arms, necks, backs and a few legs hit by bullets. They concluded that the soldiers were shooting to kill.

Nahalin's elders, representatives from each of the village's six *hamulas*, took position in the yard in front of the preparatory school. They formed a long receiving line. The schoolyard was decked out with wreathes of flowers for the dead, as well as Palestinian flags and banners. The broad side of the big mausoleum in the cemetery was painted with the Palestinian colors. The Islamic green flags of the Hamas movement also flew.

One of the banners was a bold declaration in English, for the benefit of foreign visitors: "We are not fear of missing our friends. We promiss to continue the way of the intifada." It was signed with a painted flag and and the letters *PLO.*

For days, groups of Palestinians came carrying condolences and venting anger. They came from all the neighboring villages, from the Deheisheh refugee camp, from Bethlehem, from Hebron and from Jerusalem.

The army tried to block off Nahalin. On the road that came over the shoulder of Abu al-Koroun by the army base, the soldiers had rebuilt the blockade and posted sentries. The army also blocked the road from Husan with a heap of boulders bulldozed into place. The Israeli authorities did not want outsiders inflaming the village. But the first convoy of sympathizers from Battir reopened the way. At the roadblock, Battiris piled out of buses and cars and set to work.

"*Yalla.* Let's go," they shouted. "*Yalla.*"

They pulled, shoved and heaved at the boulders, which weighed tons. Dust rose into the air as the Palestinians rolled the boulders aside one by one until they had made a way through.

Almost immediately the army stationed soldiers at the spot, determined to force isolation upon Nahalin. It didn't work; people walked to the village. One contingent of Israelis came by foot from Kilo Sabatash. They were members of the Peace Now movement, motivated by the belief that settling the West Bank was injuring both Arab and Jew. They wanted an end to war and were willing to give up the West Bank and take the risk of living next to a Palestinian state. They made compassionate speeches, and afterward Abu Sayal offered to drive them up the road toward Husan.

The soldiers on guard stopped the bus. The Israelis climbed down and trudged in a group up the hill to Husan. A few glared back over their shoulders at the soldiers.

"Stupid Israelis like those are going to kill us all," one said, loud enough to be heard.

"You should be turned into a pillar of salt like the wife of Lot," one of the soldiers shouted back.

For all of their sympathy, the speechmakers could not explain why the village had been attacked. During the year before the fatal morning, nothing had happened to single out Nahalin. The *shabab* had tried to threaten the Israelis by putting rocks in the roads, burning tires, destroying fences, celebrating November 15 as independence day, hoisting flags, circumventing roadblocks, aiming stones at the jeeps of soldiers, and harassing the nearby settlers by cutting down their fruit trees. It did not add up. Even if some of the *shabab* had been talking about gasoline bombs, Nahalin did not merit the raid. Only ten of Nahalin's young men had been arrested. Other villages were far more dangerous. Perhaps Nahalin was simply in the way of Israeli progress on the West Bank. Or perhaps the

Israelis did believe what they said about Nahalin's ferocity in the pronouncements made while the bloodstains of the village's dead and wounded were still fresh on the stones.

The whole scene was eerily reminiscent of the raid a quarter of a century earlier, when the Israelis had attacked defenseless houses on the edge of the village, killing the *mukhtar* and whomever else they could. Nahalin seemed destined to be an unwilling battlefield in the unending war for the land.

The Israelis arrested Deeb on the assumption that he must have been involved. They led him away in handcuffs, but they held him for just one day. Deeb had not masterminded the trouble. After he was released, he stayed close to home, sitting long hours on his front steps, pushing his glasses into place on his nose and gazing over the sprouting garden he had planted as a step toward independence from Israel's markets. In the clay soil of his front yard, only the bravest vegetables survived, and their leaves were ragged.

"People shut their eyes to reality," he mused, "until it fires a gun at them."

The army itself did not know what had gone awry with its plan to raid Nahalin, arrest any suspected troublemakers and thus teach the village a lesson in obedience. General Mitzna, the commander on the West Bank, ordered an investigation. The frowning general threw in a preliminary justification for the violence. He said that the Nahalinis had put up "an exceptionally violent resistance" to the entrance of the Border Police into the village. He also said that Nahalin was known as a nest of "religious extremists."

Even with the general's explanations, it did not add up. No witness saw a stone thrown before the first shots were fired. The concept that Nahalin was brimming with religious radicals seemed to come out of nowhere. The members of Hamas in the village were a minority, while the Sufis lived in a world of metaphysics.

While the Israelis were looking for explanations, others made their criticisms public. The United Nations agency working with Palestinian refugees pointed out that in the week of the Nahalin raid, a total of thirteen Palestinians had been shot dead by Israeli forces, including five boys aged between ten and fifteen. The agency called for a halt to the use of lethal firepower against civilians young and old.

Amnesty International said that it was "gravely concerned that senior Israeli authorities appear to have been condoning if not encouraging the excessive use of force by soldiers and Border Police, knowing it would result in the death or injury of Palestinians."

From its Geneva headquarters, the Red Cross issued a rare statement. "The International Committee of the Red Cross vigorously protests against this latest tragic incident, during which troops opened fire without discrimination and without restraint. For several months, the ICRC has been extremely concerned about the increasingly frequent use of firearms and by acts of physical violence against defenseless civilians. In addition, the evacuation of the injured has been hampered, as well as the work of medical staffs and hospitals in the occupied territories."

American consular officials reacted angrily, too. In a report that went all the way to the desk of American Secretary of State James Baker, they condemned the raid as unjustified.

A month after Fou'ad and the others died, the Israelis concluded that the shooting had been "excessive and contradicted standard operating procedures" and that the whole operation had been planned poorly.

The punishments were not severe. The army's lieutenant colonel in charge of the Bethlehem area, who was not at the village that day, was transferred from his post. Demoralized by what had happened, he voluntarily left the army and returned to his kibbutz.

The man above him in the military hierarchy, the colonel command-ing the southern region of the West Bank was summoned to General Mitzna's office and "reprimanded."

A second investigation of the Border Police resulted in little more. One of the officers was removed from the Border Police in the occupied territories and reassigned to a seaport police unit in Israel. He was also fined. The officer who was in command in the village itself that morning was transferred into Israel and then resigned voluntarily. Several soldiers were taken from duty in the occupied territories and transferred to service within Israel proper, where they would not go on any further raids against Palestinian villagers.

The Nahalinis were not mollified. "This case they made of it was like trying to cover the sun with their hand," Abu Marwan said as we sat in the front room of his home. While he was talking, we heard a commotion. It was the newly founded Nahalin unit of the Jaysh Shabiya, the Popular Army that the intifada's leaders had been organizing to boost the spirit of revolt. About twenty-five young men in matching khaki uniforms, their heads wrapped in khaki sacks with eyeholes cut in them, came stamping up the road, shouting, "By our blood and our souls, our martyrs will be re-deemed."

An Israeli military helicopter arrived at the same time. The pilot flew low and circled a couple of hundred yards over the Pales-tinians. The soldiers of the people's army took slingshots from under their shirts and aimed up at the sky. A few of their stones bounced off the belly of the big helicopter. The helicopter flew off undam-aged, up over Abu al-Koroun, where the sunlight on the mountain glinted off an Israeli telescope mounted among the pines and trained on the village.

Even though Nahalin had not initiated the catastrophic Bor-der Police raid, the Israelis began punishing it in new ways. As the delegations of sympathetic visitors petered out, the numbers of army units patrolling the village increased.

Abu Jafer's mother, who had sat before the raid in Abid's vegetable store and planned her trip to Mecca, was miserable. When she had plotted her journey to Saudi Arabia for the holy hajj, her wrinkled face lifted in a thousand hopeful patterns. But when she learned that the military government was not giving permits to Nahalinis to travel across the Allenby Bridge into Jordan for the first step of the pilgrimage, her wrinkles sagged. She looked gray. No explanation was handed down as to why Nahalinis were being denied this permission.

Abu Mukhles, the former *mukhtar*, refused to try to intervene with the military government.

"If he goes to Bethlehem, he is afraid the Israelis will beat him because he resigned," commented one of the men playing backgammon once more at the back of the store.

"The Nahalinis will beat him, too," the second player said. "If he goes to Bethlehem now, the village will call him a collaborator. The Israelis won't have to do the work."

"The problem," concluded Abid, "is that we are Nahalinis. First they shoot us, and then they blame us, and then they punish us."

In Israel, Nahalinis suddenly were undesirable. Laborers had trouble getting work when the contractors discovered where they were from. At the common assembly ground at Jerusalem's no-man's-land, Nahalinis were shunned. Israelis seemed to believe that Nahalin had deserved the bloodletting. The logic was simple and twisted: only a bad village would have brought down such woe upon itself.

One Nahalini had an old dented car that he drove to Jerusalem each day, carrying other laborers with him. He was poor, and the extra shekels he made from fares helped him scrape by. He had a big problem: he was not being allowed to renew the mandatory annual permit for his car. He became so desperate that he went to the most powerful collaborator he knew, a Palestinian who lived in Hebron and was known far and wide for being able to fix almost any difficulty with the Israeli bureaucracy for a steep price.

"I traveled all the way to Hebron," he said, sitting on his bed that also served as a couch. "Then I couldn't believe it. This big collaborator was gone. The Israelis put him in prison. I don't know why. His family didn't know why. Now I have no chance of saving my car."

The Israeli bureaucracy had crossed its arms when it came to Nahalin. It was hard to get the most basic things done, as Omar found out when his wife gave birth to their first baby. The family members were still in mourning for Fou'ad, but they relented to rejoice over the new boy. There was no question as to what his name was going to be. He became Fou'ad. Omar went to Bethlehem to get a birth certificate and was refused. It would have to wait. The baby did not officially exist.

Qasim was singled out from among passengers in a group taxi and prohibited from continuing to his class in Ramallah. His *hawiya* revealed that he was from Nahalin, and that was enough for the soldiers. He hitchhiked back to the village.

At the same time, the military government was drawing up drastic plans that would stymie the growth of Nahalin and change the villagers' way of life forever. Saying that the village must evolve in an orderly manner, Israeli officials devised a plan prohibiting Nahalinis from building on land they owned outside the perimeter of the village. New houses for sons and daughters would have to be constructed somewhere within the village, a rule that would eventually strangle Nahalin. The villagers needed to expand on the land they still owned; otherwise they would not be able to keep their families together. Their age-old system of brother living beside brother and cousin helping cousin would be shattered.

Betar, though, was growing faster daily. The bulldozers were cutting closer and closer to the village. The lowest cut was about three hundred yards above the nearest village house. The settlement's sewage-treatment tanks were to be installed there, below the site and just above the winding Valley of Father Hair, where I had first walked with the *shabab* after the battle of the Valley of the Cow.

At the top of the village, the Najajras still waited. Farouk had another month of his sentence to serve in the Negev prison and Fawzi more than that. The farm was failing. Several of the thoroughbred sheep and four hundred chickens had died. In the hopes of her brothers' return, Sena had planted a welcoming bed of flowers by the steps to the visitors' porch, and Ratiba watered it every morning. An occasional letter came from one of them. The news was never pleasant. The most recent had complained, "There are guns all around our heads."

One morning, the Najajras set off for the Jerusalem Red Cross to dispatch letters to the Negev, but they never got past the archway at El Khader village. The unused portal was covered with graffiti, but the emblem of Saint George, too high to reach, was untouched. The saint pursued a lonely struggle with his own dragon.

The Najajras in the car had no inkling that the news of a mass arrest of 250 Hamas members in the Gaza Strip would bear directly on them. The Israelis had to clear out space in the Negev prison, so they released dozens of other political prisoners, and one of them was standing beside the archway, bearded and gaunt, yelling and waving at the Najajras' car.

Then Sena yelled. "Farouk."

Sa'ed screeched the car to a halt, oblivious to the fact that he had stopped in the middle of the road, and an army squad at the crossroads was watching with consternation. He and the others scrambled out of the car, and all at once hugged Farouk. Farouk, who had not known the names of those wounded in the Border Police raid, was overjoyed that his immediate family had survived. They returned to Nahalin, where a new calf was waiting in the pen under the olive tree and new clothes were folded in a closet. As if she would never let Farouk out of sight again, Ratiba fluttered around her son, bringing him platter after platter of food. His bruises had healed, but he was tired and his voice subdued. He had shaved, revealing hundreds of bumps from a fungal infection pocking his face, a contagion from the prisons.

Relatives and then young men from all over the village gathered on Ratiba's porch. Farouk had become a village celebrity for standing up to the *mukhabarat* for almost sixty days. The villagers listened to him without interrupting. Sena and Shawki sat proudly next to him.

Farouk talked about how he had been released, bused to a village north of the Negev. The villagers there embraced him and the other freed prisoners. "The people all came out of their houses carrying lambs on their shoulders so that they could cook the meat for us. They gave us a feast and gave us beds until the next morning, when we could travel home."

He talked about what the Negev was like. When the prisoners became too frustrated by the misery of the place, they rioted. "Our section had one big demonstration. We gathered at the fence and shouted, 'We must die for the life of Palestine.' We tore up the planking of the tent platforms and attacked the guards. But they had the guns, so they fired canisters at us, tear gas and rubber bullets. Then you have nowhere to run. You try not to get hit, but you cannot escape the tear gas. You breathe it until you feel as if you are dying, and then slowly you can breathe again, until they fire another canister. We threw our cups and plates at them. The only thing we wouldn't throw was our food, because it was too valuable."

Farouk rambled from thought to thought, but his audience was rapt. He talked about the beatings during the interrogations in the present tense, as if the pain had yet to become a thing of the past. "I am handcuffed, and I have a sack over my head. I am very thirsty. I knock at the door. A soldier asks me what I want. I say I want to drink. He says, 'Shut up; you must die here.'

"Then, I am on the floor. They make me kneel on my hands and knees. One of them sits on my back and begins to to read a newspaper in Hebrew. I am a chair. The others beat me, and then they burn me with a cigarette. Still I am like a chair. Then it is back to the cell like a cupboard, then back again to the *mukhabarat*. This time I am blindfolded. They put nails into the seat of the chair, and they order me to sit. I sit. I jump up from the nails and they laugh. Then I refused to do what they said.

"It doesn't stop. I am twenty days in the cupboard. I keep my mind by imagining a Palestinian person who is strong. I cannot think of my mother and my family, or I know I will cry. I think of the heroes of Palestine. I begin to count. I count from one until a million."

He went on to finish the story of how he confessed when faced by his fellow *shabab* who had told the interrogators everything Farouk had done.

"The *mukhabarat* beat me until I become like dead. They had to move my hand to put the pen onto the paper giving my confession."

The court-ordered medical examination was finally conducted, but it might as well have been skipped. "They took me to a medic after I confessed, and I told him my whole body was sick," Farouk said. "He gave me aspirin."

In the prisons, Farouk had learned. He had read, thought

and listened to the revolutionary ideas of the others. "We would have classes. We learned about Marx and Lenin, and we learned about the use of airplanes in warfare and how to take freedom. We learned about revolution in Algeria, Yugoslavia, Vietnam and Cuba.

"No one is paying attention to the Palestinians' cause; the world is not paying attention. I can't understand how from ancient times, we have come to be modern but without any rights. How can there be people like Palestinians who are treated like servants? A Palestinian must be angry all his life."

Farouk put his hand over his heart in his familiar gesture of earnestness. "All the time a Palestinian is in prison, whether it is called prison or not. The West Bank is a big prison. If we travel to the next village, to Husan, then there are soldiers. This is a prison because we can't go freely. And when I look to the future, I see the universities are closed. I want to study but there is no way out. So this is our life."

When the visitors eventually left, Farouk went out to look at the animals. He scratched the jumpy calf behind its ears until it calmed. He admired Shawki's fish and stared at his rabbits, which had multiplied severalfold. "The old rabbits know me. The new ones don't recognize me; they run away," he said.

As always, he clicked his tongue and whistled at the sheep, making them turn their heads and look at him as if trying to remember something.

By the time Farouk was free, spring was well along. The wheat and barley, which were planted when the rains stopped, were ripe. The stalks were heavy with seed in the narrow fields that ran in tawny passages through the mountains. The grapes were in full green leaf again, and the villagers sat in the shade of their arbors. A patina of dust lay on the streets, the walls, the trees, on everything except the floors of the village houses, which the women washed down every day. The huge Palestinian flag painted after the raid on the wall of the mausoleum was dulled by the layer of dust.

Although Nahalin had slid into a wounded silence, the West Bank was abuzz with the latest news. A Palestinian from the Gaza Strip had driven an Israeli bus over a cliff, killing sixteen passengers and wounding more. The act was another landmark in the intifada, another bloodletting in the struggle for the land. The Israelis were on edge. The soldiers patrolling the occupied territories were even edgier.

Inam and I were in her kitchen one morning boiling the leftover meat of a goat into a soup when whistles signaled that the army was coming. I took my camera and hurried down the deserted switchbacks of the high roadway, hitching my dress up with my belt and pulling off my nunlike head scarf so that I wouldn't look like a villager. I didn't want the Israelis mistaking me for a Palestinian. A squad of soldiers was heading for the lower village, and an ambulance from Bethlehem, its sides emblazoned with orange Arabic lettering, was following as if trouble were a certainty.

Within minutes, gunshots fractured the strained quiet that had arrived with the army, and the ambulance came swerving and speeding back to the main roadway and out toward Bethlehem. A village man had been shot in the upper leg, his femur shattered and an artery pierced. He would live but no one knew it then. The soldiers came pounding back toward the village center, putting distance between themselves and a crowd of Nahalinis who were spilling angrily out of their houses. They had been watching and had seen the soldiers shoot the man after arguing with him.

"The Israelis are shooting us," a woman screamed. "The Israelis are beating us. *Shou bidna nsawi?* What can we do? What can we do?"

Caught up in the flow of adrenaline and the surging people,

I was swept down to the place where splashes of blood were soaking into the dust of the roadway in a small neighborhood where Hamas militants congregated. I wanted a photograph, not of the blood, but of the angry disbelief on the faces of the villagers looking at it. People were crowding around me, and I felt something prickling on the back of my shirt. I was far too distracted to react.

Farouk and two of Fou'ad's brothers suddenly appeared at my side. They forced me to retreat from the crowd and then they told me that youths from Hamas had been throwing lighted matches into my hair. I reached back, and a hunk of burned hair came away. I had been lucky; Hamas made the PLO factions look gentle.

Since the raid Hamas had been growing faster in Nahalin. The pain of the intifada had made Hamas attractive to many young Palestinians; if the *shabab* alone could not succeed, perhaps it was time to enlist God. I had bridged the gap between the clans, but I could only stare into the chasm that divided me from Hamas. The Islamic fundamentalists would not accept a single Western woman. Hamas did not like me, and I could not change the reasons for their distaste. The fundamentalists, whom the Israelis had originally encouraged and now feared, were gaining an uncompromising power.

Having knotted my gray scarf around my head and taken pains to tuck in every stray strand of hair, I reached the top of the village without further trouble. In the evening, I continued up to Ratiba's compound and found out that Fawzi, too, had come home. The family and well-wishers were outside the house on two woven straw mats, sitting and lounging on a variety of pillows and blankets that turned the compound into a palatial room, its ceiling the infinitely high night sky spangled with stars, its walls the bluish black distances where the mountains rose and fell.

Fawzi was sitting with the others. Ratiba was talking and laughing, almost skipping in and out of the house to see to the boiling of the tea and the cooking of a meal large enough to serve any guest who came. Nadia slaved over the kerosene cooker in the kitchen, elated that her husband was back. Every member of the family was beaming except Fawzi. He avoided talking about the Negev, speaking instead of his worries about the health of his chickens and his sheep. His words were terse, his tone of voice hard and flat. The laughter, the lightness in his spirit that struck me when I first met him had been dimmed.

"There were always guns. There was always tear gas. There were always jets, every day except on Saturday, the noise of the jets practicing, always. There were too many prisoners. There was no place to put your feet. Thirty were in one tent. Everyone was in a different mood. If one wanted to sleep, another wanted to sing. They kept the mail for a month before you could have it."

Fawzi had been accused of several things. The Israelis had information that he had helped build the detour around the army roadblock across the high road to Kilo Sabatash.

"Of course, I did that," he said. "Nahalin needs this road. What happens if there is an emergency, and we need to get to a hospital, and there is a problem with the Husan road? Someone could die."

He had also been accused of tearing down fencing, of leading one of the village committees organizing the intifada and, most importantly, of being a Jebha leader. He never admitted to these accusations. But for whatever Fawzi had contributed to the Palestinian dream, he had paid.

As I left to go down the hill to my house, Ratiba walked with me to the edge of the compound. "Be careful. Walk slowly. The path has stones. Be careful in the dark," she warned me, as if I were part of the family.

A few days later, Abu Jafer said that he wanted to come to talk to Inam, Hassan and me in the evening. He would come to the well top by the house. I made tea and spiced it with mint from Inam's garden. Hassan and Inam and I sat on the well top waiting. Inam had her youngest son in her arms and was rocking him to sleep with an intifada lullaby.

Abu Jafer came and after a polite amount of time said that Inam and Hassan had asked him to talk to me for them. He was performing a *sulha,* speaking for them about a problem they had. I dropped my embroidery and hugged my knees.

"First I must say that nobody who knows you has any problem with you. But there is a problem of your staying and living in the village. It has returned through a back way. The elders have been coming to me, the old people whom I must respect, have been coming to me and saying that having a foreign woman living alone beneath the house of my sister is bringing ill repute to the family, to the *hamula.*"

I was without words. I stared at my knees.

"I cannot argue against the wishes of the elders. Our custom is to respect our elders. I am very sorry. I cannot save you from the talk; some are saying you are a spy; some are saying you have bad morals, or why would you live alone. I know you are good, but this is not my decision."

I blew up at this new accusation. The elders of both clans knew my conduct was modest; it sounded to me as if this accusation were coming from Hamas. I told Abu Jafer he knew that no man had ever come to my rooms, but he was not the person I needed to convince.

"You don't need to argue with me," he said. "What you need to do is understand that no matter how good you are, you cannot change the differences between your culture and our culture. No matter how many bridges you build, there will always be a space. You will always be strange."

Abu Jafer's words were true, and they were carefully selected. He avoided blaming Hamas outright.

"In this village," he continued, "eighty of one hundred people love you. But there is one group that does not. It would be the best thing for Inam and Hassan if you moved from the house. You can visit, but it is better if you stop living here."

"When should I leave?"

"Tomorrow," he said.

Hassan and Inam added nothing.

"I am sorry," he said. "We are sorry."

I reached out and held Inam's hand. I had heard the word, and I knew there was no way around it. I packed up that night. As I walked from my one room to my other room, I let a little wisdom seep into my head. Nahalin was as tough as I had feared, but not in the ways I had predicted. Not at all. I had not guessed that Hamas would cause me trouble. I had not known a small village in the mountains could be so obstinate. But I also realized the stubbornness of the Nahalinis would keep them alive in the shadow of the settlements on the ridges.

In the early morning, the village women were up, taking platters of fresh, light-purple eggplants to the Bethlehem market. Some also carried tomatoes and the first white grapes of the season. I got on the bus with my small suitcase. Abu Sayal refused my shekel. I stared at the front of the bus, at the windshield on which were pasted the decorative palm trees. In a corner near the driver's seat was the bus's old straw broom, the old wooden money box and the plastic trash can. Everything was in order. The village idiot climbed aboard, all smiles with the morning. Basam kissed Abu Sayal's hands until one of the women quietly shooed him away. Another woman, having no idea that I was moving out, called me over to her seat. I sat with her and handed over my embroidery. She started cross-stitching and counting, mumbling to herself about the pattern as if nothing had changed.

E P I L O G U E

A year after the fatal raid on Nahalin, Israeli settlers began moving into the first completed apartment blocks on the Betar site. The Israeli government was providing generous subsidies to defray the costs of buying the apartments, and this encouraged the religious settlers who wanted to move their families out of cramped quarters in Jerusalem. Betar was cheap, and it had plenty of space. A network of wide and smoothly paved roads replaced the old goat paths that had led along the once spiny ridge of Daher al-Matarsiya. The blocks of apartments obscured the line of the ridge.

From up there, you could see the water tower next to the Alon Shvut settlement well beyond Nahalin. The village looked quaint, even anachronistic, from the perspective of Betar. The minaret on the newer mosque seemed to blend into the limestone houses at the center of the village.

In the aftermath of the raid, the Israelis had said that the Border Police soldiers who participated in shooting the Nahalinis were going to be subjected to a criminal investigation. Several of the soldiers had been reprimanded or dismissed, but the more serious investigation seemed never to be completed. Nahalin faded from the news, but the village could not regain its former obscurity. People did not forget what had happened on that Ramadan morning; the raid had become an event in the larger chronicle of the intifada.

Ignoring the invisible encroachment of history and the visible encroachment of Betar, the Nahalinis continued to try to survive. Some of their problems were the same as before and some were new.

Abu Jafer struggled with the plan that the military government had devised for the land still recognized as belonging to Nahalin. His darkest suspicions were realized when he and some elders of the village traveled to the office near Ramallah where the Israeli military authorities had mapped their vision of Nahalin's future. The boundary outside of which the villagers would not be allowed to build had been marked on a large map made from an aerial photograph of Nahalin and its encompassing ravines, slopes, vineyards, olive groves and vegetable fields. The line was cinched so tightly around the existing houses that Abu Jafer despaired.

"There is no place for our sons to build. If this plan is followed, we will have to have twenty people in every house. Nahalin will become like Deheisheh," he said and then explained his calculations. "In 1972, the population of the village was about fifteen hundred people and the school had about two hundred pupils. The population today is about four thousand and the school has about five hundred pupils. Now imagine after ten years. I imagine in the year two thousand, we will be as many as seven thousand. Now, that many on the same land will be like living in a refugee camp."

Abu Jafer was doing everything he could to stop the plan, consulting lawyers and enlisting the ears of a couple of sympathetic officers in the American consulate in East Jerusalem, which dealt with Palestinian affairs. It was not clear that anyone could prevent the Israeli military government from implementing the plan for

Nahalin and similar ones it was drawing up for other West Bank villages.

Meanwhile, Sena Najajra was making a lonely effort to continue her education. The time was approaching when she should have graduated from secondary school and taken her examination for entrance into a university. Her problem had not changed. The schools were closed and had been, except for a few interludes. Determined to prepare herself for the examination, she sat inside day after day, poring over her textbooks, her eyes dark with concentration. Sena did pass the exam but was stymied once more because Bethlehem University, where Fawzi wanted her to study, remained closed.

Fawzi, subdued after his return from the Negev, immersed himself in his work, funneling his energy into both his job with the handicapped and his farm. He set about doubling the size of the chicken project. When he returned to the village from Jerusalem, he labored until dusk wiring up new cages for the poultry. Farouk helped him when he wasn't in Bethlehem taking a course in veterinary medicine from a Catholic relief agency.

After he finished the course, Farouk made the rounds of the village with a bag of medicines, caring for the Nahalinis' sheep, goats and donkeys. One day he happened upon the cure for the rash that had plagued him since he had contracted it in prison. He applied a veterinary cream for treating fungal infections and the blotches on his face cleared up. He was very busy until he left for the Soviet Union, where he had a scholarship to pursue higher studies. He had hoped to learn more medicine, but he wrote in letters to his family that the Soviets thought him better suited for law. He wrote, too, about how terribly beautiful and terribly cold the snow was. Ratiba worried about the snow. Although she had never seen snow, she imagined how Farouk must feel forging through stuff as cold as ice from a refrigerator.

Other young men in Nahalin were having a hard time. The military authorities had issued special green-colored *hawiya*s to a number of the *shabab* whom they considered particularly undesirable or dangerous. The bearer of a green *hawiya* was not allowed to leave the West Bank, a debilitating restriction for men who would have liked to find work in Jerusalem. Deeb was one of those with the restrictive *hawiya*s, but he refused to despair. Inspired by watching Farouk's calf grow up into a cow, Deeb scraped together his money and bought his own cow. Every morning he trudged around the village with pails of milk, selling it at enough of a profit to keep himself and his siblings alive.

The saddest young man in the village was Ali Fanoun, the relative of Abu Marwan who was crippled by a soldier's high-velocity bullet. Ali's father was the headmaster of the boys' school in the village. His family lived on the main road on the second floor of a house. After Ali was released from the hospital, a wan paraplegic, his brothers would hoist him and his wheelchair in the air to carry him up and down the stairs.

One day the Fanoun family invited me to have tea in their guest room, which was furnished with typical floor mats. Shoes, which members of the family had removed to keep the mats clean, were piled at the doorway. Ali's father reclined on a mat and sipped the tea that his wife had served with efficiency. Ali was not in the room, but two of his able sons listened to the father explain his feelings to me. He talked vehemently and chain-smoked cigarettes from a pack with the brand name of "Good Luck."

"The problem of Palestine will not be solved with stones. It will be with thinking, with give and take between the two sides. It will be solved with understanding. This is what I teach my sons."

The headmaster leaned toward me and stared intensely, as if to make certain that I absorbed what he was saying.

One of the older sons said that he had tried stones and been arrested by the Israelis for attempting to ambush settlers on Daher al-Matarsiya. For this he received imprisonment and then a green *hawiya.*

The other son spoke up. "We want peace. We don't want to throw stones. I am twenty-three years old now. I want to be in the university. I want to study. You must write that. We want peace. We want to be able to do things like normal people."

Ali noiselessly appeared in the doorway, sitting in a gray metal wheelchair. He was silent, as if thinking some faraway thought. The skin on his face was yellow. Before anyone could move, Ali grabbed the wheels of his chair and shoved as hard as he could to get over the unintentional barricade of shoes his family had left at the door. Everybody jumped up to try to help him, and the conversation ended.

Life was not destined to get easier for the Nahalinis. Peace remained as remote an idea as ever. During the upheaval and terror of the Gulf War, the Palestinians paid en masse for believing Saddam Hussein wanted to liberate them as much as the Americans wanted to liberate Kuwait. They cheered when Iraq's missiles hit Israel, many feeling they had scored vicariously. The Israelis locked them into their villages, their camps and their neighborhoods under the most severe of curfews. After the Gulf War ended, the Palestinians and the Israelis continued with their own battles, each side angrier than before.

GLOSSARY OF ARABIC TERMS

Allahu akbar God is great; a war cry
bayanat leaflets written by the intifada leadership
biladi my country
dabke Palestinian dance
dibes grape syrup
djin spirit
Fatah PLO faction headed by Yasir Arafat
fellahin peasants
Hamas faction of Islamic fundamentalists
hamula subclan
Haris al-Hadood Israel's border police
hawiya identification card
idrab strike
intifada uprising; rebellion
jaysh army
Jaysh Shabiya Popular Army
Jebha PLO faction headed by Dr. George Habash
karayeb relatives
kefiyeh man's headcloth
lahem meat
majzara massacre

miramiya a sweet herb

mukhabarat Israeli intelligence police

mukhtar village headman

mulethamin wrapped ones; masked people

nahl bee

narjes sweet-smelling flower

nebi prophet

nuqta military observation post

sehafi journalist

service Palestinian group taxi

shabab youths; the young Palestinians making up the army of the
     intifada

shahid martyr

shitta winter; rain

souq market

sulha meeting to reconcile disputes

taboun village bread

thobe woman's long dress

Abu al-Koroun Father of the Horns; mountain near Nahalin

Ain Feres Spring of the Warrior; spring below Nahalin

Ansar Three prison for Palestinians in the Negev Desert

Basaa Israel's military headquarters at Bethlehem

Battir village near Nahalin

Betunia prison for Palestinians in the West Bank

Daher al-Matarsiya the Backside of Matarsiya; mountain near Naha-
     lin

Dahiriya prison for Palestinians near Hebron

Deheisheh refugee camp near Bethlehem

El Khader village near Nahalin

Green Line armistice line separating the West Bank and Israel

Husan village neighboring Nahalin

Kilo Sabatash Kilometer Seventeen; turnoff on the road to Nahalin
Moscobia prison for Palestinians, in Jerusalem
Ramallah Palestinian town north of Jerusalem
Surif village near Nahalin
Wadi Fukin village near Nahalin
Wadi al-Baqara Valley of the Cow; valley at Nahalin

Note: Transliterating Arabic words into English is difficult and inexact. Some sounds in Arabic do not exist in English, some are difficult for non-Arabic speakers to pronounce and others are difficult to reproduce using a non-Arabic alphabet. I have tried to make the transliterated Arabic words both as accurate and as readable as possible. I have taken liberties with many of the plurals by anglicizing them for the reader who does not speak Arabic.